T0135609

25

BISS MONOGRAPHS

MONOGRAPHS OF THE
BREMEN INSTITUTE
OF SAFE SYSTEMS

R. Drechsler, M. Gogolla, H.-J. Kreowski,
B. Krieg-Brückner, J. Peleska (Series Editors)

MAINTAINING FAMILIES OF RIGOROUS REQUIREMENTS FOR EMBEDDED SOFTWARE SYSTEMS

Jan Bredereke

Vom Fachbereich Mathematik und Informatik
der Universität Bremen
angenommene Habilitationsschrift

Gutachter: Prof. Dr. Jan Peleska, Univ. Bremen
                Prof. Dr. Holger Schlingloff, HU Berlin
                Prof. Dr. Anne E. Haxthausen, DTU

Kolloquium: 16. September 2005

Bibliografische Information der Deutschen Nationalbibliothek

Die Deutsche Nationalbibliothek verzeichnet diese Publikation in der Deutschen
Nationalbibliografie; detaillierte bibliografische Daten sind im Internet über
http://dnb.d-nb.de abrufbar.

ISBN 978-3-8325-1521-8
ISSN 1435-8611

Logos Verlag Berlin
Comeniushof, Gubener Str. 47
D-10243 Berlin
Tel.: +49 030 42 85 10 90
Fax: +49 030 42 85 10 92
Web: http://www.logos-verlag.de

Contact Address for BISS Monographs

Arbeitsgruppe Betriebssysteme, Verteilte Systeme
Bremer Institut für Sichere Systeme
Universität Bremen   fax: (+49) 421-218-3054
Postfach 330 440   jp@informatik.uni-bremen.de
D-28334 Bremen   http://www.informatik.uni-bremen.de/agbs

Abstract

Rigorous requirements for embedded software systems must and can be maintained over the system's life time. Rigorous requirements are necessary to ensure the dependability of the software system. Embedded software systems are often expected to be dependable. Maintenance is inevitable because of frequent requirements changes after and even before delivery. Maintenance is possible by explicitly considering the entire family of requirements and by structuring it suitably. We demonstrate this for telephone switching systems. They are an example of particularly long-lived embedded software systems.

The book is structured into two parts. The first part introduces to families of rigorous software requirements, and how to organize them into requirements modules. A family of requirements must be organized rather differently than the requirements for a single system. We first take a step back to the foundations. We start with the information hiding principle in particular and develop our notion of requirements module from it. We then step forward again and add this concept to a current approach. Our notion of requirements module allows us to understand some current problems better, and also to propose solutions.

The second part looks at one of the requirements modules in more detail, which is the user interface requirements module. We look at how the requirements for the user interface can be encapsulated. We also make a link back to one kind of the current maintenance problems, which are the "feature interaction" problems. We view these problems from the perspective of human-computer interaction. This gives us interesting new means for reducing them.

Editor's Preface

This book is about *families of requirements*, that is, collections of specifications concerning different variants of the same or of similar products. This topic is currently of considerable interest in the fields of software engineering and formal methods: the preservation of behavioural correctness and non-functional capabilities (dependability, usability etc.) in presence of product modifications plays a central rôle in nearly all areas of information technology. Needless to say that the management of families of requirements is of particular importance in the world of embedded systems: in this area, the negative effects of flawed product variants range from severe customer dissatisfaction – think of new versions of operating systems and application software for mobile telephones – to safety hazards – think of avionic or automotive controllers and computers managing railway interlocking or medical systems. In spite of their mission or safety criticality these embedded applications frequently require even more variety and more complex configuration capabilities than what is usually expected from standard software: this is mainly due to the fact that for embedded systems hardware and software variants have to be considered in a simultaneous way.

Jan Bredereke's work is structured into two main parts, each addressing one of the sub-topics of this field which are currently considered to be the most challenging ones: in Part I, the notion of *features* and *feature interaction* is introduced. The latter term denotes the impact or effect of changes purposefully designed for a behavioural or non-function aspect of a product on other aspects which typically should remain unchanged or change consistently with the modified or added features. Based on an extension of the widely spread specification language Z, the author introduces a formalism for the concise description of requirements modules and interfaces, as well as for the construction of features from requirements.

In Part II of this book, the author specialises on human-machine interaction and elaborates on the problem of *mode confusions*, where erroneous assumptions of users about the internal state of the controlling hardware and software lead to faulty – and often safety-critical – actions and reactions at the man-machine interface.

The comprehensive description of the topic and the accompanying examples and case studies have resulted in a book which serves as an ideal introduction into the field of families of requirements, in particular feature interaction and mode confusion. Moreover, readers will also get a good impression about current research activities in the field.

Bremen, March 13th, 2007   Jan Peleska

Contents Overview

Contents in Detail

Chapter 1

Introduction

Rigorous requirements for embedded software systems must and can be maintained over the system's life time. Rigorous requirements are necessary to ensure the dependability of the software system. Embedded software systems are often expected to be dependable. Maintenance is inevitable because of frequent requirements changes after and even before delivery. Maintenance is possible by explicitly considering the entire family of requirements and by structuring it suitably. We demonstrate this for telephone switching systems. They are an example of particularly long-lived embedded software systems.

This introductory chapter is structured as follows. We start with an overview on requirements engineering in general, and we show where the work in this book fits in (Sect. 1.1). This establishes the context. We then point out some current requirements structuring problems (Sect. 1.2). Solutions for these will be the topic of the remainder of this book. The next section presents an overview of the contents of the book (Sect. 1.3). The final section identifies the contributions by other people to this book (Sect. 1.4).

1.1 Requirements Engineering – an Overview

We start with an overview on requirements engineering in general, and we show where the work in this book fits in. This establishes the context for this book.

The Question – How Can We Do Requirements Engineering? How can we analyze the intended application to determine the requirements that must be satisfied? How should we record those requirements in a precise, well-organized and easily-used document?

Requirements Engineering is the understanding, describing and managing of what users desire, need and can afford in a system-to-be-developed. The goal of requirements engineering is a complete, correct, and unambiguous understanding of the users' requirements. The product is a precise description of the requirements in a well-organized document that can be read and reviewed by both users and software developers.

Short Answer – Partially Solved. In practice, this goal is rarely achieved. In most projects, a significant number of software development errors can be traced to incomplete or misunderstood requirements. Worse, requirements errors are often not detected until later phases of the software project, when it is much more difficult and expensive to make significant changes. There is also evidence that requirements errors are more likely to be safety-critical than design or implementation errors.

Long Answer. The above short answer is dissatisfying because it doesn't convey the different aspects of the question. The answer depends on

- the task to be performed (e. g., elicitation, documentation, validation)

- the application domain (e. g., reactive system, information system, scientific applications)

- the degree of familiarity (i. e., innovative vs. routine applications)

- the degree of perfection desired (e. g., 100% perfection or "good enough to keep the customer satisfied")

Rather than provide a complete answer, we choose to answer the question on the basis of the different requirements engineering tasks. With respect to the other aspects of the problem, our answers are domain-independent, they apply to innovative applications rather than routine applications, and they apply to the development of high-quality software. If we had considered a different slice of the problem, we would have arrived at different answers.

1.1.1   Substructure of the Problem

We divide requirements engineering into five tasks:

Elicitation – extracting from the users an understanding of what they desire and need in a software system, and what they can afford.

Description/Representation - recording the user's requirements in a precise, well-organized and easily-used document.

Validation – evaluating the requirements document with respect to the users' understanding of their requirements. This sub-task also involves checking that the requirements document is internally consistent, complete, and unambiguous.

Management – monitoring and controlling the process of developing and evaluating the requirements document to ease its maintenance and to track the accountability of faults.

Cost/Value Estimation – analyzing the costs and benefits of both the product and the requirements engineering activities. This sub-task also includes estimating the feasibility of the product from the requirements.

Table 1.1: Structure of the topics of requirements engineering.

- Elicitation
    - Gathering Information (interviews, questionnaires, joint meetings, ...)
    - Requirements analysis methods (SA, OOA, scenarios, ...)
    - Prototyping
    - Consensus building and view integration

- Description/representation
    - Natural language description
    - Semiformal modelling of functional requirements
    - Formal modelling of functional requirements
    - Documentation of non-functional requirements
    - Documentation of expected changes

- Validation
    - Reviews (all kinds: inspection, walkthrough, ...)
    - Prototyping (direct validation by using prototype / testing the prototype)
    - Simulation of requirements models
    - Automated checking (consistency, model checking)
    - Proof

- Management
    - Baselining requirements and simple change management
    - Evolution of requirements
    - Pre-tracing (information source(s) $\leftrightarrow$ requirement)
    - Post-tracing (requirement $\leftrightarrow$ design decision(s) & implementation)
    - Requirements phase planning (cost, resources, ...)

- Cost/value estimation
    - Estimating requirements costs
    - Determining costs and benefits of RE activities
    - Determining costs and benefits of a system (from the requirements)
    - Estimating feasibility of a system

For each task, we determine a selection of techniques that have been proposed as solutions to that task (see Table 1.1). This list should neither be considered complete, nor should it be interpreted as our opinion of the best techniques; it is simply a sampling of the solution space of the task.

Also, we do not consider any specific techniques for any task (e. g., UML collaboration diagrams). Instead, we consider how well classes of techniques solve a particular task. Answers for specific techniques would be more interesting and more useful than answers for classes of techniques, but would have greatly lengthened this chapter.

1.1.2   Ranking of the Different Aspects

The tables in this section provide an evaluation of how well classes of techniques
solve the problems posed by performing the task.

Problem: Elicitation

Solution	Effective-ness	Afford-ability	Teach-ability	Used in practice
Gathering information (interviews, questionnaires, joint meetings, ...)	medium	high	high	ad hoc: high sound: low
Requirements analysis methods and languages (SA, OOA, ...)	medium	medium	high?[a]	low
Prototyping	high	low	medium	ad hoc: high sound: low
Consensus building & view integration	medium	low	medium?	low

[a]Analysis as such is hard to teach, but some concrete language and method is easy

Problem: Description

Solution	Effective-ness	Afford-ability	Teach-ability	Used in practice
Natural language description	medium?	high	medium	high
Semi-formal modelling of functional requirements	medium–high	high	high	medium?
Formal modelling of functional requirements	medium	low[a]	medium	low
Documentation of non-functional requirements[b]	high	low	low–medium?	low
Documentation of expected changes	high	high	medium	low

[a]Affordability is high in specific situations when checking important or safety-critical properties

[b]Rankings are for those techniques we know (however, we do not know enough)

Problem: Validation

Solution	Effective-ness	Afford-ability	Teach-ability	Used in practice
Reviews (all kinds)	high	high	high	high
Prototyping	high	medium	medium	medium
Simulation	high, if feasible	low–medium	medium	low
Automated checking (consistency, model check)	high, if feasible	medium	high	low
Proof	high, if feasible	low (except safety-critical systems)	low	low

Problem: Management

Solution	Effective-ness	Afford-ability	Teach-ability	Used in practice
Baselining requirements, simple change management	high	high	high	medium
Evolution of requirements	high	medium–high	low–medium?	low
Pre-tracing (info sources ↔ rqmt)	medium	medium?	medium	very low
Post-tracing (rqmt ↔ design&impl)	medium–high	low–medium?	low–medium?	very low
Requirements phase planning	high	high	high?	medium

Problem: Cost/Value Estimation

Solution	Effective-ness	Afford-ability	Teach-ability	Used in practice
Estimating requirements cost[a]	medium	medium	medium	low
Determining cost/benefit of RE activities[b]	low	low	low	low
Estimating costs/benefits of a system (from the requirements)[c]	medium	medium	low	low
Estimating feasibility	medium	low	low	medium

[a] Experience-based techniques dominate in practice
[b] Only ad hoc techniques motivated by fear of not doing them
[c] Requires marketing techniques as well as technical ones

1.1.3   Where This Book Fits In

The above overview shows where the work in this book fits in. *Rigorous* requirements are necessary for embedded and in particular for dependable software systems. Three of the above five tasks are particularly relevant for rigorous requirements: *description*, *validation*, and *management*.

For the description of safety-critical requirements, two techniques are the most interesting: the *formal modelling of functional requirements* is effective, even though it is expensive. The *documentation of expected changes* is even very effective and very affordable, despite it is little used. Both techniques are applied in this book.

For the validation, *automated checking* and also *simulation* help a lot, if they can be done. A prerequisite is the formal modelling. In this book, we use automated checking.

Two management techniques are especially relevant for maintaining requirements: *baselining requirements*, including simple change management, and the *evolution of requirements*. Baselining of informal requirements is very effective, and it is used in practice to some degree. This book now develops this technique for formal requirements, too. Planning the evolution of requirements is also very effective, but little used in practice. This book also applies this for formal requirements.

1.2   Requirements Structuring Problems

We point out some current requirements structuring problems in telephone switching, which is an example of particularly long-lived embedded software systems. Solutions for these will be the topic of the remainder of this book. In this section, we identify four problems which make the requirements hard to change consistently. These problems are that such systems have monolithic requirements or at most a single layer of extension, that new services depend implicitly on new concepts, that the concerns of the users' interface are spread out, and that naive feature orientation does not scale.

1.2.1   Monolithic Requirements or Single Layer of Extension

Existing PSTNs (Public Switched Telephone Networks) are hard to modify, because at the upper, application oriented layers, one monolithic service provides lots of separate functionalities. For example, an ISDN user basically uses only one application service, ISDN-DSS1 [ITU93a]. Any extension to the ISDN protocol potentially affects all parts of it and thus is difficult. The IN (Intelligent Network) [ITU01] is an attempt to solve this problem, by defining an extension interface for POTS (Plain Old Telephone Service).

Unfortunately the IN does not allow services (= features) to be created on top of other services. Services must be independent of each other. This is because all new services must be built on the POIs (Points of Invocation) and PORs (Points of Return) of the Basic Call Process.

Table 1.2: Some new concepts in telephone switching.

conditional call setup blocking
dialled number translation
multi-party call/session
service session without communication session
distinction user – terminal device
distinction user – subscriber
mobility of users and of terminals
multiple service providers, billing separately

Independent services have the advantage that they can be developed independently. But if two services, in some sense, overlap, undesirable interactions may occur. For example, CF (Call Forwarding) allows calls to one telephone to be forwarded to another. OCS (Originating Call Screening) allows particular numbers to be blocked; for example parents can restrict the phone access of their children. When both services are available, an unexpected service interaction can happen; a youth might circumvent OCS by programming the desired number as the call forwarding target, and then calling his own number. The call will be forwarded to the target and will defeat the screening if OCS is processed before and independently of CF.

The interaction problem cannot be solved by simply reversing the order of processing. The user might have blocked all long-distance calls using OCS. Later, he attempts to forward all his calls to a friend which he will visit and who lives in a neighbour town. When CF is processed before and independently of OCS, all incoming calls will be blocked instead of forwarded.

The notion of a called user is extended and thus changed by CF; all services that rely on this notion must be defined on top of CF in order to solve the interaction problem. They must use the extended notion of a called user.

1.2.2 New Services Depend Implicitly on New Concepts

Undesired service interactions can happen, because fundamentally new concepts often are introduced only implicitly. Table 1.2 lists some new concepts. It is difficult to understand a new concept fully while it is used by only one service. This makes it hard to express the concept explicitly. Also, a new concept may need a new layer in the architecture, which cannot be added explicitly to a non-layered architecture such as the IN.

One such new, implicit concept is the n-party session. It is a generalisation of the "call", which always has two end points. It is necessary for such services as Consultation Call, Conference Call, Call Forwarding, and Universal Personal Telecommunications. The latter allows its users to register with any terminal device and then have all their calls and services available there. This new concept is not explicit in the terminology or architecture of current switching requirements. In the IN, the Call Forwarding service is expressed by two conventional calls glued together in the middle. The above interactions between OCS and CF occur because the CF service changes the semantics of a call implicitly, which invalidates assumptions of the OCS service about a call.

Another such new, implicit concept is terminal mobility. More than 50% of the terminal devices are now mobile in some countries. The requirements architecture of any current telephone switching network does not allow to add mobility easily. This is so even though mobility doesn't change the set of requirements much from a strictly user-oriented point of view. The user-oriented view has one big node which represents the network, with many terminal devices attached. Mobility means that there is no piece of wire anymore. Any current requirements architecture represents the network by a set of interconnected nodes. Each represents a switch. Terminal devices can be associated to one such switch only. A description of terminal mobility therefore needs complex hand-over procedures between nodes. The description of the switching network as a set of interconnected nodes had good reasons. But it now prevents us from describing terminal mobility requirements "naturally" from the user-oriented point of view. It prevents us from encapsulating mobility in the design architecture into a separate description of how mobile terminal devices and base stations inter-work.

1.2.3 Concerns of the Users' Interface Are Spread Out

The requirements documents are difficult to maintain if the requirements for one concern are spread out far through the documents; the users' interface is such a concern. There is no systematic coordination among the services of the IN about the use of the physical signals at a terminal device. A terminal device often has only few syntactic signals available: twelve buttons, a hook switch, and a few signal tones. Many services are available currently. Together they require a large number of signals, many more than are available physically on most terminal devices. Physical signals must be reused in different modes of operation. But the definitions of several services implicitly assume exclusive access to the user's terminal device. When this assumption is violated, undesired service interactions can, and frequently do, occur.

The service interaction between a calling card service and a voice mail service is an example. We describe it in Section 1.2.4 below. Both services assume exclusive access to the "#" button.

This service interaction can be resolved by adding another physical signal. In the calling card service to which the author once subscribed, the "#" button must be pressed at least two seconds to take effect. Unfortunately, the existing terminal devices do not allow additional physical signals in a number sufficient for all services.

1.2.4 Naive Feature Orientation Does Not Scale

A feature-oriented description of a telephone switching system is attractive but also can promote undesired feature interactions. We introduce to the current feature-oriented view and to feature interaction problems.

A feature oriented description of a software system separates a base system from a set of optional features. Each feature extends the base system by an increment of functionality. Feature orientation emphasizes the individual features and makes them explicit. The description of one feature does not consider other extensions of the base system. Any interactions between features are described implicitly by the feature composition operator used.

The idea of "features" is used widely in telephone switching. Many people in this area like to think in terms of a base system which can be enhanced by numerous optional features. Examples for features are as simple as a short code for re-dialling the last number dialled, and as complex as personal communication services, where the user can redirect all calls together with all of his/her other features to a different phone. A feature can also be non-functional such as an increased number of calls that a switch can handle at the same time. The naive feature orientation allows to make *any* change by just adding a new feature.

Feature orientation is attractive. It meets the needs of marketing. Marketing must advertise what distinguishes a new version from its predecessors. Marketing must offer different functionality to different customers, in particular at different prices. Successful marketing also demands a short time to market. This requires that the system can be changed easily. It can be achieved by just adding a new feature. The large body of existing descriptions never needs to be changed.

But naive feature orientation runs into problems with large software systems, such as telephone switching systems.

Naive Feature Orientation

With *naive* feature orientation, a feature extends a base system by an *arbitrary* increment of functionality. The increment is typically chosen to satisfy some new user needs. This selection of user needs happens from a marketing perspective. In particular, the selection is neither particularly aligned to the internal structure of the software system nor to the organization of the system's documented requirements.

Many feature addition operators have been used in practice or proposed on theoretical grounds [AmLo03, CaMa00, KiBo98, DBL97, ChOh95, BoVe94]. They typically share the property that they add code in different places of the base system as needed. They are therefore operators of a syntactic nature.

A canonical example is the structure of the Intelligent Network (IN) [ITU01, GRKK93, DuVi92]. The IN is the telephone switching industry's currently implemented response to the demand for new features. This example demonstrates the naive feature orientation nicely. This remains true even if the IN might be replaced by emerging architectures eventually, such as Voice over IP (VoIP).

The IN specifies the existence of a Basic Call Process (BCP) and defines sets of features. Examples of IN features are listed in Fig. 1.1. When a feature is triggered, processing of the BCP is suspended at a Point of Initiation (POI), see Fig. 1.2. The feature consists of Service-Independent Building Blocks (SIBs), chained together by Global Service Logic. Processing returns to the BCP at a Point of Return (POR). The Basic Call Process consists of two automata-like descriptions, one for the originating side of a call, and one for the terminating side of a call, see Fig. 1.3. In these, a feature can be triggered at a so-called Detection Point, and processing can resume

Abbreviated dialling	Customized ringing
Attendant	Destinating user prompter
Authentication	Follow-me diversion
Authorization code	Mass calling
Automatic call back	Meet-me conference
Call distribution	Multi-way calling
Call forwarding	Off net access
Call forwarding on busy/don't answer	Off net calling
Call gapping	One number
Call hold with announcement	Origin dependent routing
Call limiter	Originating call screening
Call logging	Originating user prompter
Call queueing	Personal numbering
Call transfer	Premium charging
Call waiting	Private numbering plan
Closed user group	Reverse charging
Consultation calling	Split charging
Customer profile management	Terminating call screening
Customized recorded announcement	Time dependent routing

Figure 1.1: The features in the Intelligent Network (version CS 1).

at more or less any other Detection Point. This allows a feature to modify basic call processing arbitrarily.

Jain [dKTG00, JAMS00] has an enhanced IN-like architecture. It is a standard developed currently. Jain offers a portable network interface to application services. This interface can be added on top of any kind of network (PSTN, wireless, Internet). It is written in the Java language. Its call model allows multi-party, multi-media calls. Jain's Java Call Control (JCC) has a call state machine similar to that of the IN, and also uses a similar trigger mechanism. JCC does not handle feature interactions. These must be managed at the application level, or by provisioning and management functions.

There has been considerable research effort on feature composition operators. In particular, in the FIREworks project [GiRy00, GiRy01] (Feature Interactions in Requirements Engineering), various feature operators were proposed and investigated. These operators successfully reflect the practice of arbitrary changes to the base system. The theoretical background is the superimposition idea by Katz [Kat93]: one specifies a base system and textual increments, which are composed by a precisely defined (syntactic) composition operator.

A feature is inherently *non-monotonous* [Vel95]. Most features really change the behaviour of the base system. That is, a feature not only adds to the behaviour of the base system, or only restricts the behaviour of the base system. For example, in telephony a call forwarding feature both restricts and adds to the behaviour. It prevents calls to the original destination, and it newly makes calls to the forwarded-to destination. Therefore, a refinement relation is not suitable to describe adding a

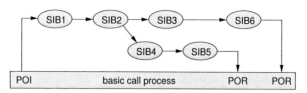

Figure 1.2: feature-oriented extension in the Intelligent Network (from [ITU92, p. 3]).

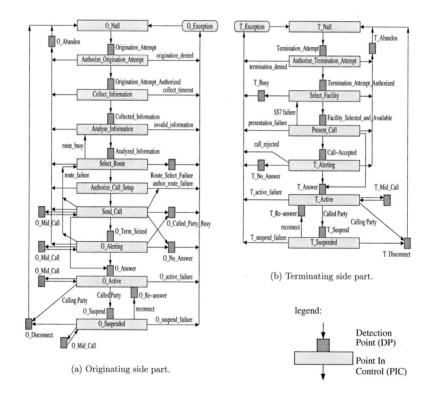

Figure 1.3: The Basic Call State Model of the Intelligent Network (version CS 2, after [ITU97a]).

feature.

Interaction Problems with Features

It turns out that severe feature interaction problems appear if one applies a naive feature oriented approach to a large software system, such as a telephone switching system. It is relatively easy to create a new feature on its own and make it work. But it becomes extremely difficult to make all the potential combinations of the optional features work as the users and providers expect. The telecom industry complains that features often interact in an undesired way [AmLo03, CaMa00, KiBo98, DBL97, ChOh95, BoVe94]. There are already hundreds of telephony features. The combinations cannot be checked anymore because of their sheer number. Undesired interactions annoy the telephone users, and the users are not willing to accept many of them. The users expect reliability from a telephone system much more than from other software-intensive systems such as desktop PCs.

Some typical examples of telephony feature interactions are the following. Chapter 9 has some more.

Calling Card & Voice Mail

We had once a calling card from Bell Canada. It allowed us to make a call from any phone and have the call billed to the account of our home's phone. We had to enter an authentication code before the destination number to protect us against abuse in case of theft. For ease of use, we could make a second call immediately after the first one without any authorization, if we pressed the "#" button instead of hanging up.

We also had a voice mail service from Meridian at work. A caller could leave a voice message when we couldn't answer the phone. We could check for messages later, even remotely. For a remote check, we had to call an access number, dial our mailbox number and then a passcode. At the end of both the mailbox number and the passcode, we had to press the "#" button.

The interpretations of the "#" button were in conflict between these two features. The calling card feature demanded that the call should be terminated. The voice mail feature demanded that the call should be continued, and that the authorization went on with the next step.

This particular feature interaction was resolved by Bell. The calling card feature required that the "#" button was pressed at least two seconds to terminate the call.

Call Waiting & Call Forward on Busy

The call waiting feature allows a caller to get through even when the callee is engaged in another call. The callee hears a signal tone and then has the choice to switch to the new caller by pressing flash hook.

The call forward on busy feature also allows a caller to get through when the callee is busy. The call of the new caller is forwarded to another phone where hopefully somebody else can service the request.

Both features are in conflict when activated simultaneously for the same phone. They are triggered under the same condition. But they specify incompatible actions.

Due to the feature-oriented description, it is not clear which feature should take precedence. A running system will resolve the interaction by giving precedence to one of the features. But the result may surprise the user. There is no way for the system to reconcile the conflict. It must restrict the functionality of one of the features.

Originating Call Screening & Area Number Calling

The originating call screening feature aborts all call attempts to numbers or number prefixes in a list. This is useful if the owner of the phone cannot restrict the access to the phone physically well enough. It can protect the owner of the phone from expensive calls made by others. Typically the owner puts the prefixes of premium rate services and maybe also of long distance calls on the list.

The area number calling feature allows a company to advertise a single telephone number, while calls are actually routed to different destinations, depending on the area the call comes from. For example, a pizza service can have their calls routed to the branch that is nearest to the caller.

These features interact through a requirement on the base system. Call processing must progress always, independently of any incremental features. The switch must provide basic functionality even in case of an infinite loop in the incremental features. An implementation therefore could restrict the number of queries per call to a Service Data Point (SDP). The screening feature must query the SDP for the screening list, and the area number calling feature must query the SDP for the destination number. But the limit on the number of queries could be as low as one. This would prevent any call to a pizza service from a phone with call screening.

This kind of interaction cannot be resolved by increasing the limit on the number of queries. For any useful limit, there is a combination of features with a higher demand of queries.

Call Forwarding & Terminating Call Screening

The call forwarding feature allows to redirect all incoming calls to another phone. The feature can be used as a do-not-disturb feature to delegate answering. It can be also used as a reach-me feature to re-route incoming calls to the current location of the phone owner.

The terminating call screening feature aborts any call attempt from one of the numbers in a specified list. This can protect against harassing calls.

It is not clear what should happen in the following situation: the user at phone C puts phone A on the screening list, the user at phone B forwards all calls to C, and A calls B (Fig. 1.4). If call forwarding is realized by joining two two-party calls together, then phone C will ring. The call at C appears to

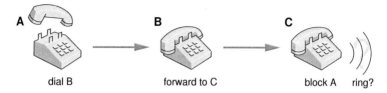

Figure 1.4: Interaction between call forwarding and terminating call screening.

come from B, which is not on the screening list. If we consider the motivation of the user at C, then the call should probably be aborted. It is likely that the user at C wants to be protected from any calls originating at A.

The problem here is to express the requirements in the right way. The most restrictive screening is probably the best one. But if forwarding is specified as two calls "glued" together, then we cannot rely on the notion of call for the specification of screening.

Definition of Feature Interaction

A *feature interaction* occurs when the behaviour of one feature is changed by another feature. This is a commonly accepted informal definition.

Not all feature interactions are undesired. Some features have increased value together with other features. For example, a short code to re-dial the last number dialled saves typing. This is even more helpful when one uses a (long) dialling prefix that selects an alternative, cheaper long-distance carrier. Some features are even intended to improve a system that has specific other features. (Of course, this violates the "pure" feature oriented approach.) For example, a calling number delivery blocking feature interacts with a calling number delivery feature. The latter displays the caller's number at the callee's phone. The former prevents a caller's number to be displayed anywhere for privacy reasons.

More than two features can be involved in one interaction. Most interactions are between two features only. But we are also annoyed personally by an interaction with four features. Figure 1.5 describes all the features and their interaction in length.

Feature Interaction Problems in Other Domains

There can be feature interaction problems in other domains than telephony, too. Kang *et al.* [KLD02] proposed feature-oriented product line software engineering recently. They use it for home integration systems. They argue that feature-orientation is important for successful marketing. Their practical experience shows that undesired features interactions occur for feature-oriented home integration systems, too [KLD02, p. 62]. They find that "analyzing feature interactions for all possible feature combinations [...] is probably too difficult." They sketch roughly how a formal

We experienced an undesired interaction among these four features:

Re-Dial Our phone (a "Siemens euroset 821") has a button that automatically re-dials the last number dialled. Only one number with at most 22 digits is stored due to constrained resources.

Abbreviated Dialling The phone also has a number of buttons that one can program to dial a specific number each. It is possible to dial additional digits afterwards.

No Re-Dial for Abbreviated Dialling The re-dial button re-dials the last number that was entered *manually*. Using an abbreviated dialling button does not overwrite the memory. This holds even when one dials additional digits afterwards.

This feature is exactly a resolution for an undesired feature interaction between the first two features. Nobody wants to overwrite a long sequence with a one-button sequence. The manufacturer had detected that particular interaction and resolved it by adding one more feature.

Alternative Long-Distance Carrier Our German local telephone provider allows us to select an alternative long-distance carrier by dialling a 5-digit (or 6-digit) prefix, e. g., "010xx", before the number proper.

These four features do not work together nicely. We would like to program our favourite long-distance carrier prefixes to some abbreviated dialling buttons. But this defeats the re-dial feature. Any number starting with an abbreviated dialling button is not stored. This holds even when the prefix only has 5 digits and the number proper has 11 digits.

The telephone manufacturer could not foresee this problem. The phone was made in about 1993. The German telephone market was a monopoly then, and the prefixes had not been invented yet for Germany.

The fourth feature invalidates an assumption made by the third feature. It is not true anymore that any number starting with an abbreviated dialling button can be re-dialled manually without effort.

The interaction could be resolved by introducing a lower bound of button presses. For example, they could be saved from five presses on. This should happen regardless of whether abbreviated dialling buttons were involved or not. But such a solution can confuse the user. The number of button presses is rather difficult to keep track of.

Figure 1.5: An undesired interaction among four features.

description using StateCharts could help. The authors do not appear to be aware of the pertinent literature on feature interaction analysis in telephony.

The upcoming Internet telephony will suffer from feature interaction problems, too. Many carriers currently already use Voice Over IP (VoIP) on their backbones. End user equipment for VoIP is available and will proliferate soon. VoIP uses a different architecture, and one might hope that feature interaction problems will vanish together with the old systems. This will not be the case. The feature-oriented view prevails in IP telephony, too. There is even less awareness to interactions here; people are currently busy making the the basic services work. We expect that interaction problems will be even worse in IP telephony. There are many service providers now instead of only one or only a few. There will be no centralized institution anymore that can take care of feature interaction problems.

Causes of Feature Interaction Problems

Cameron *et al.* [CGL+94] have categorized the causes of feature interaction problems in their seminal benchmark paper: violation of feature assumptions, limitations on network support, and intrinsic problems in distributed systems. Some violated feature assumptions are on naming, data availability, the administrative domain, call control, and the signalling protocol. Limitations on network support occur because of limited customer premises equipment signalling capabilities and because of limited functionalities for communications among network components. Some intrinsic problems in distributed systems are resource contention, personalized instantiation, timing and race conditions, distributed support of features, and non-atomic operations.

A rather comprehensive survey of approaches for tackling feature interaction problems was done recently by Calder *et al.* [CKMRM02]. Despite some encouraging advances, important problems still remain unsolved. The rapid change of the telecommunications world even brings many new challenges.

A new view on the causes of feature interaction problems was a main result of the seventh Feature Interaction Workshop [AmLo03]: in order to resolve a conflict at a technical level, we often need to look at the social relations between users to either disambiguate the situation or mediate the conflict.

1.2.5   Needed: A More Modular Requirements Structure

The use of modularization in the information hiding sense is one way of preparing for future changes [Par72]. This means that we identify different concerns and separate them as much as possible. The idea is well known for the design phase, but it can be applied to software requirements, too. In the design phase, one defines an information hiding module for each concern with narrow, precisely documented interfaces between them. Each module hides a "secret", i.e., one implementation decision. Whenever a secret changes, only one module is affected. When we look at telephone switching software *requirements*, we claim that the principle is not applied sufficiently.

The responsibility for the users' interface should be centralised. A few, dedicated requirements documents should describe it. Their maintenance must be coordinated by a single organisational unit. There must be only one such unit within a provider. For some aspects, the unit should be attached even to a standardisation body. In the area of human-computer interfaces (HCI), a centralized user interface is already standard operating procedure. There are good libraries for graphical user interfaces (GUIs). Application requirements are written on the semantic level only ("select file"), never on the syntactic level ("mouse click"). In contrast, the requirements for most telephone services contain users' interface concerns. They are written in such terms as "on-hook" and "flash-hook". Examples are the assignments of the first and the second feature interaction detection contest at FIW'98 [GBGO98] and FIW'00 [KMMR00]. These assignments are accessible, of manageable size, and written by people from industry.

In Chapter 8, we propose such a centralized approach. It encapsulates the syntactic details of the signal-poor current users' interface and provides a sufficient number of semantic signals to other modules. We also sketch an application to the Intelligent Network.

A prerequisite for encapsulating the users' interface is a requirements architecture that supports information hiding modules, such as a layered architecture. In a layered architecture, each layer solves a partial problem and hides its details from the other layers. Computer communication systems today are usually designed in this way. The upper layers of the Internet protocols provide many specialised services, such as HTTP, SMTP, FTP, Telnet, and many more. Changes to one of these services do not affect the others. Nevertheless, some application protocols, which implement their respective service, build on other application services. For example, the HTTP, SMTP, and FTP protocols all build on the Telnet service in order to establish a control connection, but use different ports, and then use their own sets of control commands. In the Internet world new and even more complex services can be constructed on top of the above services, using them as building blocks, without modifying them. An example is a Web browser. The PSTN has a similar structure for the lower communication layers; an example is the architecture of the widely used Signalling System No. 7 [MoSk90]. Compare Fig. 1.6. In contrast, the upper, application oriented part of the PSTN is a single monolithic block. We think that the Internet way of adding services will reduce service interactions, compared to the PSTN and Intelligent Network way.

But first the idea of modularizing the requirements must be accepted more widely; only then the architectural models can be improved. The structure of the assignments for the feature interaction detection contest shows this.

A modular, layered architecture helps to avoid implicit, undocumented assumptions. Layers of information hiding modules are connected by explicit interfaces. Explicit interfaces document the assumptions on modules. Implicit, undocumented assumptions can become invalid by new services. This is one of the main causes of service interaction problems.

An architecture of fully layered services reduces the danger that the same new concept will be introduced by different services. Such a parallel introduction can lead to inconsistency. A layered architecture encourages to define a new concept much earlier. It is cheaper to add another layer than to restructure a monolithic system.

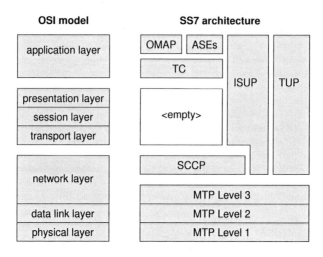

abbreviations used

ASE   application service element
ISUP   ISDN user part
MTP   message transfer part
OMAP   operations, maintenance, and administration part
SCCP   signalling connection control part
TC   transaction capabilities
TUP   telephone user part

Figure 1.6: Architecture of the Signalling System No. 7.

Nevertheless, adding or extending concepts still costs. When we extend the two-ended "call" to a n-party "session", and when we have a dedicated "connection resource" module, then the syntactic definition of its interface will show clearly which other modules use this module and which don't. Unfortunately, at least most of the connection-oriented services must be inspected and many of them must be revised. After this work is done, we can add more services like Call Forwarding, without further work or fear of interactions.

Integrating a new concept needs sufficient confidence in its quality and future success. Changing a software infrastructure of this size is extremely expensive. Nevertheless, integrating some new concepts eventually is inevitable. We think that the session concept now is understood sufficiently well. It therefore should become a first class member of switching requirements. In Section 5.5 below, we will discuss new architectures that go this way.

1.3 Overview of This Book

The remainder of this book aims at making easier the maintenance of families of rigorous requirements for embedded software systems. The book is structured into two parts. The first part introduces to families of rigorous software requirements, and how to organize them into requirements modules. A family of requirements must be organized rather differently than the requirements for a single system. We first take a step back to the foundations. We start with the information hiding principle in particular and develop our notion of requirements module from it. We then step forward again and add this concept to a current approach. Our notion of requirements module allows us to understand some current problems better, and also to propose solutions.

The second part looks at one of the requirements modules in more detail, which is the user interface requirements module. We look at how the requirements for the user interface can be encapsulated. We also make a link back to one kind of the current maintenance problems, which are the "feature interaction" problems. We view these problems from the perspective of human-computer interaction. This gives us interesting new means for reducing them.

Part I: The part on families of requirements first describes the base for and the scope of our work, and then continues by presenting our own solutions. The description of the base and scope introduces to a proven approach to rigorous requirements for a single software system, and it introduces our notion of a family of such requirements. We draw advantage of existing work on families of programs by relating our notion of families of requirements to it. The extensive body of results in object-orientation warrants its own chapter. Thus we have three chapters for the base and scope:

Chapter 2: The requirements for an embedded software system must and can be documented rigorously. The inverted four-variable model is an approach for specifying an embedded software system. Z is a formalization of set theory. We can use it to specify the relations in the inverted four-variable model. We use this approach for all our requirements specifications.

Chapter 3: A family of requirements is a set of requirements specifications for which it pays off to study the common requirements first and then the requirements present in few or individual systems only. Because we are interested in the maintenance of such families, we concentrate on families of requirements where only a subset of the family is specified explicitly in the beginning, and where more members are specified explicitly incrementally over time. Domain Engineering helps to exploit the commonalities of a family. A family of requirements can and should be put under configuration management, analogously to software.

Chapter 4: We summarize the object-oriented principles and mechanisms for organizing a family of programs. Many of these can be used for families of requirements, too.

The part on families of requirements continues with our own solutions. We introduce our notion of requirements module and we support it with concrete mechanisms. We show how we can configure and compose family members from them.

Chapter 5: We show that a family of requirements can be organized into requirements modules to make it easier to maintain; however, existing formal languages do not fully support this. Requirements modules mean encapsulation in the information hiding sense. This approach conforms to the structuring principles for families of object-oriented programs in the literature. Several recent architectures for families of telephone switching systems already separate some inportant concerns into modules and thereby avoid some kinds of undesired feature interactions. But existing formal languages such as the well-known formalisms Z and Object-Z do not fully support hierarchical requirements structuring. We therefore will extend the formalism Z suitably in the next chapter. This extension will also be a necessary base for our feature construct in Chapter 7.

Chapter 6: Several mechanisms and patterns for requirements modules can support the maintenance of requirements modules. Two mechanisms are explicit configuration constraints and explicit interfaces, a pattern is the abstract interface. Explicitly documenting, minimizing and checking the configuration constraints on requirements helps to get consistent configurations; we show how we can document such constraints in the formalism Z. We extend the formalism Z by a hierarchical module structure; via a further extension this is a necessary base for our feature construct in the next chapter. Explicit interfaces between requirements modules help to control dependencies between them; we also add them to our extension of the formalism Z. The pattern of the abstract interface between requirements modules helps to avoid dependencies on those requirements that change. We demonstrate our approach on an example, a family of LAN message services.

Chapter 7: We show how we can configure and compose requirements to complete family members; in this, we must distinguish the notions of a requirements module and of a feature to avoid feature interaction problems. We first show that the underlying concepts are related in software configuration management (SCM) and in requirements configuration management (RCM) for families of requirements; even though the vocabularies are really different. We find that a feature is a set of changes, not a requirements module. We complete our support for families of requirements in the formalism Z by adding a suitable feature construct. We then describe how we can compose the properties in the requirements to a complete system description. We illustrate our approach by presenting some features and family members for our family of LAN message services from Chap. 6 above. Configuring requirements family members needs tool support; some tools already exist, more are planned. We already collected considerable experience with a large case study of a telephone switching system and in an industry project where we had to maintain a set of communication protocol test specifications.

Part II: This part of the book looks in more detail at the user interface module.

Chapter 8: We argue that we can and should encapsulate the requirements for the user interface into a dedicated requirements module. We also propose a suitable design structure. We show how the approach can be applied to a legacy telephone switching architecture and in a new communication system.

Chapter 9: We introduce to mode confusions. A mode confusion occurs when the observed behaviour of a technical system is out of sync with the user's mental model of its behaviour. We present a rigorous way of modelling mode confusions. This leads to a number of design recommendations for avoiding them. Our approach supports the automated detection of remaining mode confusion problems. We apply our approach practically to a wheelchair robot.

Chapter 10: We demonstrate that a considerable number of undesired telephony feature interactions are also shared-control mode confusions. This links the previous chapter into this book. Our aim is to present the new way in which one can view and tackle feature interactions. We can apply the measures from the shared-control area for preventing mode confusions in telephony, too. Additionally, we recommend some specific measures for telephony. Attention to mode confusions helps to design features and sets of features with less undesired surprises.

1.4 Contributions by Other People

Most parts of this book are original work of its author; but some parts result from joint work with other people. Research lives from cooperation and mutual inspiration. It is the author's honour and duty to identify these parts:

1.1 Requirements Engineering – an Overview: A previous (and longer) version of this section appeared as a chapter of a Dagstuhl report [ABB+99]. The chapter of the report is joint work with Joanne Atlee, Wolfram Bartussek, Martin Glinz, Ridha Khedri, Lutz Prechelt, and David Weiss.

7.9 Application: Maintaining a Set of Communication Protocol Test Specifications: This material was part of a conference paper [BrSc02]. The paper was joint work with Holger Schlingloff.

9 User Interface Behaviour Requirements and Mode Confusion Problems: A slightly shorter version of this chapter concurrently appears as a journal article [BrLa05]. The chapter is joint work with Axel Lankenau; except for the comparison of our definition of mode confusion to the literature

(Sect. 9.5), and for the discussion on how the recommendations for avoiding mode confusions are reflected by syntactic properties (Sect. 9.4.2), which is our work only. Also, the following Chapter 10 on mode confusion problems in telephony is our work only.

Additionally, most of three chapters and one section summarize work of others. The summary is by the author of this book, but the research results belong to the respective authors. The chapters are Chap. 2 on rigorous requirements for one embedded software system (except Sect. 2.3 on using the inverted four-variable model for specifying in Z), Chap. 3 on maintaining families (except Sect. 3.1 on an evolution process pattern, and Sect. 3.2.2 on our application to tramway control systems), and Chap. 4 on object-orientation. The section is Sect. 5.1 on information hiding. We provide the references in the respective chapters.

Part I

Organizing a Family of Rigorous Software Requirements

Chapter 2

Rigorous Requirements for One Embedded Software System

The requirements for an embedded software system must and can be documented rigorously. The inverted four-variable model [HeBh00, HABJ05, PaMa95] is an approach for specifying an embedded software system. Z [Z02, Spi95] is a formalization of set theory. We can use it to specify the relations in the inverted four-variable model.

We should record the requirements of an embedded system in a precise, well-organized and easily-used document. In classical engineering, a "blueprint" of the system to build is made first, and then validated. Only after that, the actual system is constructed. In the course of construction, use, and modification, the original documents are always kept up-to-date. The four-variable approach of Parnas and others is engineering in this sense. The approach has been used in many large-scale industry projects. It also is a general-purpose methodology: it leaves a suitable notation to be defined individually for any given project.

In this book, we mainly use the Z notation. It allows for the incremental, constraint-oriented specification style that we will need. It is precisely defined and mature. It is a formal notation with a comparably large community, and it has been used in several large projects in industry. Object-Z [Smi00] is an object-oriented variant of Z, we will discuss the advantages and disadvantages of its object-oriented constructs for our purposes in Sect. 5.6 below.

The inverted four-variable model is a variant of the classical four-variable model. We choose this variant here because it supports the kind of structuring of requirements that we will propose later in this book.

2.1 The Inverted Four-Variable Model

The inverted four-variable model [HeBh00, HABJ05] is an approach for specifying an embedded software system. It allows to specify the required behaviour over a set of variables that describe values of entities in the real world. A first design step separates the software requirements from the requirements on the input and output devices; furthermore, we structure the software requirements in a particular way in order to ease maintenance. The inverted four-variable model is suited best for engineering systems, such as process control, automation, and embedded systems, where the environmental quantities represent physical properties. The approach is a variant of the classical four-variable model by Parnas and others [PaMa95]; it allows particularly well to encapsulate the details of the hardware-software interface. The SCR toolset [HABJ05, HBGL95] provides industrial-strength tool support for the inverted four-variable model.

The four-variable model has been used and is used in a large number of industry and research projects [HABJ05]. It was invented in 1978 in a project to document the requirements for the flight program of the A-7 aircraft [HKPS78, AFHB$^+$92]. Since then, the approach was used by several organizations in industry and government, e. g., Grumman, Bell Laboratories, Ontario Hydro, the U.S. Naval Research Laboratory, and Lockheed, to document the requirements of many practical systems, including a submarine communications system, the shutdown system for the Darlington nuclear power plant, and the flight program for Lockheed's C-130J aircraft (see [HABJ05] for the references).

2.1.1 Requirements for an Embedded System

The inverted four-variable model allows to specify the required behaviour over a set of variables that describe values of entities in the real world. Examples are the position of a robot arm and the temperature in a tank of water. The variables are time-functions; that is, they map points in time to (potentially different) values. For example, the position of the robot arm may change over time.

The requirements are separated into requirements on the system, REQ, and requirements on the environment of the system, NAT. The system needs to fullfill REQ only if its environment ensures NAT.

The variables are separated into a vector of monitored variables $\underline{m}^t$ and a vector of controlled variables $\underline{c}^t$. The value of a monitored variable is determined by the environment, and the value of a controlled variable is determined by the system. Nevertheless, all entities that these variables describe already exist before the system is built.

The environment to be assumed is specified by the relation NAT. NAT describes how the relevant part of the world may behave over time without or despite the system to construct: The relation's domain dom(NAT) exactly contains the instances of $\underline{m}^t$ allowed by the environmental constraints, and the relation's range ran(NAT) exactly contains the instances of $\underline{c}^t$ allowed by the environmental constraints. The property $(\underline{m}^t, \underline{c}^t) \in$ NAT holds if and only if the environmental constraints allow the controlled quantities to take on the values described by $\underline{c}^t$, if the values of the monitored quantities are described by $\underline{m}^t$.

The world, as it may behave with the system present, is described by the intersection NAT∩REQ. The relation REQ may restrict the behaviour of controlled variables only, but not of monitored variables: dom(REQ) exactly contains the instances of $\underline{m}^t$ allowed by the environmental constraints, and ran(REQ) exactly contains the instances of $\underline{c}^t$ allowed by a correct system. The property $(\underline{m}^t, \underline{c}^t) \in$ REQ holds if and only if the system should permit the controlled quantities to take on the values described by $\underline{c}^t$ when the values of the monitored quantities are described by $\underline{m}^t$.

In the process of specifying REQ, we usually separate the specification of the ideal behaviour from the specification of precisions and tolerances. First, we specify how an infinitely fast and precise system should behave. Then we should validate the specification to gain sufficient confidence that this behaviour is what we want. After this, we specify (separate from the "ideal" relation REQ) how precise the system must measure each monitored variable, and how much tolerance is allowed for the values of each controlled variable. This is important, in particular, for variables with continuous sets of values. But it is also important for the timing constraints of otherwise completely discrete systems.

2.1.2   Requirements for the Software for an Embedded System

A first design step separates the software requirements from the requirements on the input devices (sensors) and on the output devices (actuators). The input devices set the software's input variables $\underline{i}^t$ according to the monitored variables, and the output devices set the controlled variables according to the software's output variables $\underline{o}^t$ (Fig. 2.1, middle).

We structure the software requirements in a particular way in the inverted four-variable model in order to ease maintenance (Fig. 2.1, bottom). We assume that the requirements on the software and the requirements on the input and output devices change rather independently. We introduce estimates $\overline{m^t}$ and $\overline{c^t}$ for the monitored and controlled variables $\underline{m}^t$ and $\underline{c}^t$. The software requirements specification SoRS consists of the relations D_IN, D_OUT, and $\overline{\text{REQ}}$. D_IN relates the input variables $\underline{i}^t$ to $\overline{m^t}$, and D_OUT relates $\overline{c^t}$ to the output variables $\underline{o}^t$. Accordingly, the input and output devices are specified by the inverse relations of D_IN and D_OUT. The relation $\overline{\text{REQ}}$ is quite similar to REQ. Usually, $\overline{\text{REQ}}$ is just an extension of REQ. REQ describes only "ideal" behaviour. $\overline{\text{REQ}}$ also must specify how to deal with failures of input and output devices.

We can express both discrete and continuous behaviour using the inverted four-variable model; the discrete part can be specified by a state transition system. The above variables are time-functions, and the relations are relations between vectors of time-functions. A time-function maps points in time to values. The relations can refer to the entire time-functions, in particular to past values. This allows to specify continuous changes of the controlled variables that depend on continuous changes of the monitored variables. We can specify discrete behaviour, too, if we define events. An event occurs when a predicate over some variables changes its boolean value. We can use a state transition system based on such events to specify the discrete part of the behaviour of the controlled variables. The original inverted four-variable model uses a tabular notation to express the state transition system. We will use the Z notation for this in Section 2.2.2 below.

We usually specify precisions and tolerances here analogously as for the system requirements REQ. After we have gained confidence in the specifications of ideal

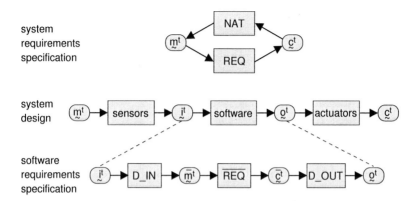

Figure 2.1: Structure of the software requirements in the inverted four-variable model.

D_IN, $\overline{\text{REQ}}$, and D_OUT, we add specifications of precisions for all read values and tolerances for all written values of D_IN and D_OUT. In particular, we always need timing constraints. By comparing these constraints with the constraints on REQ, we can check the feasibility of constructing a system that satisfies the end-to-end constraints.

2.1.3 Scope of the Approach

The inverted four-variable model is suited best for engineering systems, such as process control, automation, and embedded systems, where the environmental quantities represent physical properties (e. g., temperature, pressure, current, or position). This is because there are two necessary prerequisites for applying the (inverted or classical) four-variable approach [Pet00]:

1. The environmental quantities can be expressed as functions of time that are either piecewise-continuous (for real-valued quantities), or finitely variable (for discrete-valued quantities).

2. The acceptable behaviour can be characterized by a relation on the environmental quantities.

The environmental quantities cannot be expressed as functions of time if either this just cannot be done effectively, or if it is not useful to do so. It cannot be done *effectively*, for example, for a compiler. A compiler monitors the source code and controls the generated machine code. In principle, both can be described, for example, by two arrays of characters. But this would not help at all for describing their relationship effectively in terms of a flat mathematical relation. It is not *useful* to express the environmental quantities as functions of time, for example, for a compiler, again. A compiler has only two relevant instants of time. These are the start and the termination. Therefore, the four-variable approach is unsuitable for "information processing" systems in particular.

The acceptable behaviour cannot be characterized by a relation on the environmental quantities if there are non-behavioural properties, if there are internal properties, or if the requirements are not preserved under sub-setting of behaviours. Examples for non-behavioural properties are maintainability and code size. An example for an internal property is the number of times that an instruction is executed. We could express the latter only by including appropriate quantities as environmental quantities. However, for this the system must be changed such that they become observable externally.

A less obvious limitation is that the requirements must be preserved under sub-setting of behaviours. This means that if the possible behaviours of system A are a subset of the possible behaviours of system B, then A must be acceptable when B is acceptable. An example of a requirement that is not preserved under sub-setting is that "the average response time over all behaviours must be x milliseconds". This is different from a similar requirement over a single behaviour, which can be expressed. However, such statistical properties usually can be approximated reasonably well and specified with reference to a lengthy execution.

For some special properties, such an approximation is not possible. These are possibilistic properties. They are important for security. An example is: "if behaviour A is possible, then behaviour B must also be possible". This is not the same as $A \in \mathrm{REQ} \Rightarrow B \in \mathrm{REQ}$. What is acceptable in an implementation is different from what is possible. Usually, REQ is non-deterministic, but the implementation is not. Intruders must not be able to infer information from the possibility of A and the impossibility of B.

2.1.4   Relation to the Classical Four-Variable Model

The inverted four-variable model is a variant of the classical four-variable model by Parnas and others [PaMa95]; it allows particularly well to encapsulate the details of the hardware-software interface. Both approaches have in common the notions of monitored, controlled, input, and output variables and the separation of the system requirements into requirements on the input devices, on the software, and on the output devices, compare Figures 2.1 and 2.2.

The difference is that the inverted four-variable model additionally has the notions of the estimated monitored variables and the estimated controlled variables. This allows to encapsulate the details of the interface between hardware and software into requirements modules for the device interfaces. We will need this encapsulation in Chapters 5 to 8 below.

In the classical four-variable model, the software requirements specification is a relation over variables concerned with the details of the device interfaces. The relation SOF directly relates the input variables $\underline{i}^t$ to the output variables $\underline{o}^t$. The requirements on the input devices are specified explicitly by the relation IN between the monitored variables $\underline{m}^t$ and the input variables $\underline{i}^t$, and the requirements on

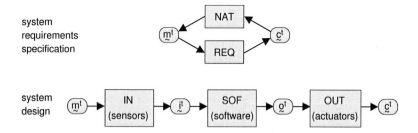

Figure 2.2: Structure of the system requirements in the classical four-variable model.

the output devices are specified explicitly by the relation OUT between the output variables $\underline{o}^t$ and the controlled variables $\underline{c}^t$.

It is possible to encapsulate the details of the device interfaces in the software requirements specification SOF, too, but it is more awkward. We can specify the relation as a relational composition of an "input relation", an "abstract behaviour relation", and an "output relation". This composition then introduces the necessary abstract variables. But in the inverted four-variable model, the software requirements specification already *is* such a relational composition of three relations. We can save the work of structuring the software requirements specification manually to encapsulate the details of the device interfaces.

A consequence of using the inverted four-variable model is that we don't specify the requirements on the input devices and output devices explicitly anymore. Instead, we specify the inverse relations D_IN and D_OUT. A prerequisite is therefore that it is practical to invert D_IN and D_OUT again in order to obtain the requirements specification for the hardware.

A prerequisite for using the inverted four-variable model for families of requirements is that the monitored and controlled entities are stable in the family, and that only the devices for monitoring and controlling them change. This prerequisite is often satisfied for engineering systems. For example, in a light control system, the level of illumination is always important, while the actual devices for measuring the brightness and for producing light can change. The same holds for the telecommunications domain which we will discuss in Section 7.6 and in Chapter 8 below. The users' desire to send and receive messages, or to make voice connections, will always be there. Only the actual devices and the actual protocols for interacting with these devices will change. Our argument for the telecommunications domain relies on a suitable choice for the environmental quantities. We will discuss the idea of "variables in the users' heads" further in Chapter 8 below.

2.1.5 The SCR Toolset

The SCR toolset [HABJ05, HBGL95] provides industrial-strength tool support for the inverted four-variable model. The toolset was and is developed by the U.S. Naval

Research Laboratory (NRL) as part of the Software Cost Reduction project (SCR), in the group of C. Heitmeyer. There is a suite of tightly integrated tools.

The basic tools are a specification editor, a simulator, a dependency graph browser, and a consistency checker. The specification editor is for creating a requirements specification in SCR's tabular format. The simulator helps to validate that the specification satisfies the customer's intent. The dependency graph browser helps to understand the relationships between different parts of the specification. The consistency checker analyzes the specification for properties such as syntax and type correctness, determinism, case coverage, and lack of circularity.

There is also a set of advanced analysis tools for application properties. The property checker Salsa uses binary decision diagrams (BDDs) [Bry86] to analyze propositional formulae and formulae containing enumerated type variables, and it uses a constraint solver to reason about linear integer arithmetic. Besides checking application properties, Salsa additionally can analyze a specification for determinism and case coverage like the consistency checker. The SCR invariant generator constructs invariants from the specification. These then can be validated with the customers. The model checker SPIN [Hol97] also has been integrated into the SCR toolset. The model checker proves application properties by a complete state space exploration. It works completely automatic. However, usually it needs manual effort to find suitable abstractions. Without suitable abstractions, the well-known state space explosion problem prevents the tool to complete its analysis. Finally, the verifier TAME is an interface to the theorem prover PVS [SORSC01]. It serves to automatically prove application properties by logical reasoning. For this, it also uses invariants that have been stated explicitly in the specification, or that have been derived by other tools.

The SCR graphical user interface builder can enhance the SCR simulator. It allows to build quickly a graphical front end and to attach it to the simulator, therefore producing a rapid prototype for demonstrating and validating the required behaviour.

Automatic code generation from the requirements specification is possible in some cases. For this, the APTS transformational system [Pai94] has been integrated into the SCR toolset. Of course, this cannot handle complex algorithms.

There is the prototype of an automated test tool. It generates test cases automatically from the requirements specification. A test case consists of a sequence of system inputs and system outputs. Since SCR specifications are always deterministic, we only have simple, deterministic test cases. (However, the inverted four-variable model in general does not restrict itself to deterministic requirements specifications.)

2.2 The Formalism Z

Z is a formalization of set theory; we can use it to specify a state transition system. Z allows to specify a mathematical theory. Common conventions for Z allow to interpret the mathematical theory of a specification as a state transition system.

Z is standardized by the International Standardization Organization (ISO) [Z02]. Before this official standardization, Z was defined for many years by Spivey's reference manual [Spi95]. The standard now provides a more detailed, well-structured definition of the syntax and semantics of Z.

There is a large number of tools available for Z, see the Z home page [Bow05]. For the work in this book, we use the tool CADiZ [To$^+$02], in particular (see Section 7.7 on tool support).

2.2.1 Specifying a Mathematical Theory

Z allows to specify a mathematical theory. A specification has a formal meaning in terms of names and values. Every expression in Z has a type; the types can be checked by an automated tool for consistency. We have atomic mathematical objects, which can be put together to more complex objects. There is a rich mathematical toolkit which provides us with a large body of the usual mathematical notation in a well-defined way.

Formal Meaning. We talk about names and values. The formal meaning of a specification in Z is a set of *models*. A model associates one value to each of a set of names. For example, consider the following specification in Z (taken from [Z02]):

$$
\begin{array}{|l}
n : \mathbb{N} \\
\hline
n \in \{1, 2, 3, 4\}
\end{array}
$$

This specification introduces one name, n, with four possible values, 1, 2, 3, and 4. The meaning of this specification is the following set of four models:

$$\{\{n \mapsto 1\}, \{n \mapsto 2\}, \{n \mapsto 3\}, \{n \mapsto 4\}\}$$

The above specification consists of one *axiomatic definition*. An axiomatic definition introduces names in its upper part. The lower part specifies constraints on the values for the names.

Types. Every expression in Z has a *type*. Types are important because an automated tool can calculate the types of all the expressions in a specification and check that they make sense. For example, the equation

$$(0, 1) = \{1, 2, 3\}$$

does not make sense, there is a type error. The left hand side is an ordered pair, and the right-hand side is a set.

A type is an expression of a restricted kind: it is either a given set name, or a compound type built up from simpler types using one of a small collection of type constructors. The value of a type is a set called the carrier of the type. By abuse of language, we often say that an object is a member of a type when it is a member of the carrier of the type.

Atomic objects.   A *basic type* or *given set* contains atomic objects. An atomic object has no internal structure of interest. For example, we can specify a set of file names:

[*FNAME*]

This allows us to specify, for example, that each file must have a file name, and that the names of all files must be distinct. But this specification will not describe how a file name is constructed from characters. There are also some predefined basic types, for example the integers $\mathbb{Z}$ and the natural numbers $\mathbb{N}$.

Complex objects.   More complex objects can be put together from the atomic objects. There are three kinds of composite types: *set types*, *Cartesian product types*, and *schema types*. A set type may be specified either by listing its elements, or by giving a characteristic predicate. A Cartesian product type is a set of tuples.

A schema type is a powerful means to specify complex composite objects. A schema type is a set of *bindings*. If p and q are distinct identifiers, and x and y are objects of types t and u respectivly, then there is a binding $z = \langle\!\langle p == x, q == y \rangle\!\rangle$ with components $z.p$ equal to x and $z.q$ equal to y. This binding is an object with the schema type $\langle\!\langle p : t; \; q : u \rangle\!\rangle$.

There is a notation for specifying a schema type. For example, the following specification introduces a schema type *rectangle* with three components. The predicate in the lower part can be used to specify restrictions on the set of bindings of this schema type.

```
┌─ rectangle ────────────────────────────────────────────┐
│  width : ℕ                                              │
│  height : ℕ                                             │
│  circumference : ℕ                                      │
├────────────────────────────────────────────────────────┤
│  circumference = 2 * width + 2 * height                 │
└────────────────────────────────────────────────────────┘
```

Free types are a convenience notation for specifying explicitly enumerated types and for specifying recursive structures such as lists and trees. The meaning for this notation is defined by a transformation to the previous Z constructs. An example is the following (taken from [Spi95]):

$TREE ::= tip \mid fork \langle\!\langle \mathbb{N} \times TREE \times TREE \rangle\!\rangle$

This type contains the values tip, $fork(1, tip, tip)$, $fork(2, tip, tip)$, $fork(1, fork(1, tip, tip), tip)$, $fork(1, tip, fork(42, tip, tip))$,   and so on.

Mathematical toolkit.   There is a rich *mathematical toolkit* which is defined based on the above primitives. The mathematical toolkit provides us with a large body of the usual mathematical notation in a well-defined way. Figure 2.3 presents some of the mathematical notation of Z. In particular, we list those notation which we use in this book. Please refer to the standard [Z02] for more details.

$X \times Y$	Cartesian product	$X \rightarrowtail\!\!\!\rightarrow Y$	partial injection
$\varnothing$	empty set	$X \twoheadrightarrow Y$	total surjection
$\mathbb{P}\, X$	powerset	$X \rightarrow\!\!\!\twoheadrightarrow Y$	partial surjection
$\mathbb{F}\, X$	finite powerset	$X \rightarrowtail\!\!\!\twoheadrightarrow Y$	bijection
$\mathbb{F}_1 X$	finite powerset without	$X \nrightarrow\!\!\!\rightarrow Y$	finite function
	the empty set	$X \nrightarrow\!\!\!\rightarrowtail Y$	finite injection
$X \leftrightarrow Y$	relation	$f \circ g$	functional composition
$\operatorname{dom} r$	domain of a relation	$\mathbb{A}$	arithmos
$\operatorname{ran} r$	range of a relation		(any kind of number)
$r \, {}_9^\circ \, s$	relational composition	$\mathbb{Z}$	integers
$X \lhd r$	domain restriction	$\mathbb{N}_1$	natural numbers without 0
$r \rhd X$	range restriction	$\langle 1, 2, 3 \rangle$	sequence
$r^{\sim}$	relational inversion	$\#X$	number of members of a set
$r (\!| X |\!)$	relational image	$\operatorname{seq} X$	(finite) sequence over a set
$X \rightarrow Y$	total function	$\operatorname{seq}_1 X$	non-empty sequence
$f(x)$ or $f\, x$	function application	$\operatorname{iseq} X$	injective sequence
$X \nrightarrow Y$	partial function	$s ^\frown t$	concatenation of sequences
$X \rightarrowtail Y$	total injection		

$$\{\, x, y : \mathbb{N} \mid x = y \; \bullet \; (x, y) \,\}$$ set comprehension

$$\forall \, x : \mathbb{N} \mid x > 6 \; \bullet \; x * x > 42$$ universal quantification

$$\exists \, x : \mathbb{N} \mid x < 5 \; \bullet \; x * x = 9$$ existential quantification

Figure 2.3: Some mathematical notation of Z.

2.2.2 Conventions for Specifying a State Transition System

Common conventions for Z allow to interpret the mathematical theory of a specification as a state transition system. A specification in Z on itself is just a mathematical theory over mathematical variables. The specification is of practical use only if it is linked to the real world. Due to the informal nature of the real world, this link must be informal. We often like to describe an embedded software system by a mathematical state transition system.

There are common conventions for specifying a state transition system using the general mathematics of Z [Spi95, Chap. 5.1]. Z has no formal means for specifying a state transition system itself, like, e. g., CSP [Hoa85]. Nevertheless, the conventions allow to specify an embedded software system rigorously.

Following these conventions, we describe the state space of the transition system by the set of values that a Z schema may take. We describe the state transition relation by other, special Z schemas called operations. And we describe the set of initial states by one more Z schema. Informal text must make clear which Z schema fulfills which of these purposes.

Operations are special Z schemas since they refer to the pre- and post-state through a naming convention. Another naming convention allows to specify input and output values for state transitions. The conventions are that variables describing the post-state are primed, pre-state variables are unprimed, input variables are decorated with a question mark, and output variables are decorated with an exclamation point. Other identifiers must not be decorated in this way.

We demonstrate the conventions at a very simple example. We specify a counter. Its (externally visible) state space is defined by the schema *Counter*:

```
┌─ Counter ─────────────────────────────────────────────
│ value : ℕ
├───────────────────────────────────────────────────────
│ value ≤ 100
└───────────────────────────────────────────────────────
```

The only operation of the counter is *Add*. The amount of increment is in the input variable "*jump?*", and the new value is in the output variable "*new_value!*".

```
┌─ Add ─────────────────────────────────────────────────
│ ΔCounter
│ jump? : ℕ
│ new_value! : ℕ
├───────────────────────────────────────────────────────
│ value′ = value + jump?
│ new_value! = value′
└───────────────────────────────────────────────────────
```

Note that the notation $\Delta Counter$ is a shorthand for including both *Counter* and *Counter′* at this point. (Note further that the notation $\Xi Counter$ additionally would have demanded that *Counter = Counter′*.)

The initial state of the counter is *init_Counter*:

```
┌─ init_Counter ────────────────────────────────────────
│ Counter
├───────────────────────────────────────────────────────
│ value = 0
└───────────────────────────────────────────────────────
```

An informal description must link the values of variables, inputs, and outputs to the real world. In the above example, linking the natural numbers used to the states of some physical counting device is obvious. But the values of basic types and free types may need more explanation. For example, an elevator specification with the free type definition

$$dir ::= up \mid down$$

does not yet make clear whether *up* and *down* denote buttons that can be pressed, or whether they denote indicator lights that can be lit.

The precise semantics of transitions must be stated. According to Spivey's convention [Spi95, Chap. 5.1], the state transition relation may be non-deterministic; there may be several possible post-states. All transitions must terminate successfully. (If there is a pre-state with no post-state, anything may happen.) There is no "parallel execution" of transitions; all transitions are atomic.

We can assign two different interpretations to transitions. On the one hand, we can say that the state transition relation is the disjunction of all transitions specified, and that the system evolves from one state to the next state by performing one of the possible transitions. On the other hand, we can say that the system evolves by events that happen. An event is specified by a transition, then. The event has a name and is distinguishable from other events. The effect of the event is specified by the post-states of the transition. The event may happen only if the current state is in the set of pre-states. Additionally, an event belonging to the environment may happen only if the environment agrees, and the system must not refuse it. We call this an input event. For output events, it is the other way around.

In this work, we use the second interpretation. The reason is that we specify communication systems in this book, and these systems are strongly event-oriented. It would be possible to follow the other interpretation, too, though. In any case, the interpretation chosen must be stated clearly.

The second interpretation allows for systems without any externally visible state space. In this case, any definition of a state variable is just an auxiliary definition. The example in Appendices A, B, and C is such a system. Note that auxiliary definitions in a requirements specification do not prescribe anything for an implementation of the requirements specification. For an auxiliary variable in the requirements, there need not appear any corresponding variable in the implementation. For example, the history variables in the specification in the appendix help to express things concisely, but they cannot be implemented efficiently.

2.3 Using the Inverted Four-Variable Model for Specifying in Z

We can use Z to specify the relations in the inverted four-variable model. The original inverted four-variable model uses a tabular notation to express a state transition system. But we can also use other formal notations when following the inverted four-variable model. In particular, we can use Z to specify state transition systems. For this, we can use the conventions from the previous section. Following the inverted four-variable model when using Z has the advantage of worked-out guidelines for linking the mathematical theory to the real world.

When we apply the inverted four-variable model with Z, we must separate the externally visible state space of the software into input and output variables, we must separate the transitions into those made by the software and those made by the environment, and we must structure the software transitions into the three parts $\overline{\text{REQ}}$, D_IN, and D_OUT. We can achieve the separations of the variables and of the transitions by informal descriptions. One easy way is to introduce suitable naming conventions. For example, all schemas whose names start with "*in_*" shall describe the transitions of the software's environment that are linked to events denoting changes of the input variables. The name of an event shall always be the same as the name of the corresponding schema. We will define more naming conventions in a moment.

An "*in_*" input event is caused by the software's environment; the restrictions in the corresponding transition schema must be ensured by the software's environment. After an input event, the software usually must update its estimates of the monitored variables within a certain time. This is the relation D_IN. We can model this by specifying a suitable invariant. The invariant is over two sets of variables. The first set is either a set of input variables or a set of auxiliary variables that reflect the input event. In the example in the appendices, we use auxiliary history variables here. The second set is either a set of estimated monitored variables or another set of auxiliary variables that reflect a monitored event. In the example in the appendices, we use auxiliary history variables here, again.

The only exception in the appendices where we will use a real input variable and a real estimated monitored variable, not auxiliary variables, is for the time. The passing of time is not event-oriented. We use the naming convention that the name of an input variable starts with "*vin_*" and that the name of an estimated monitored variable starts with "*vmon_*".

We can abstract the changes to the (auxiliary) estimated monitored variables by introducing monitored events. Our naming convention is "*mon_*" for such monitored events. These monitored events are caused by the software; to be more precise, they belong to D_IN. These events occur when the software has computed the estimates of the monitored variables. (This holds for the software requirements specification only. In the system requirements specification monitored events are caused by the environment of the system.)

We like to couple the monitored variables/events and input variables/events through invariants because this supports an incremental, constraint-oriented specification style. We will discuss this further in Section 7.5.2 below.

A prerequisite to the approach with monitored events is that any change to an estimated monitored variable does not happen at the exact time of the input event causing it. But this is true for any real software system, it always needs time to compute something.

We will use implicit output variables here. Communication systems are strongly event-oriented. Therefore, we introduce output events. An output event is an abstraction of a change to the output variables. We can specify the values of the output variables indirectly by stating constraints on output events. The effect is a strongly event-oriented specification.

We describe the state changes that are abstracted to an output event by an output transition. Our naming convention is that the names of the schemas of output transition start with "*out_*". The parameters of the output event specify the details of the change to the (implicit) output variables. Accordingly, output transitions are system transitions. To be more precise, they belong to D_OUT.

We complete the separation of D_IN, $\overline{\text{REQ}}$, and D_OUT by introducing (auxiliary) estimated controlled variables and the corresponding controlled events and controlled transitions. Our naming convention is "*ctrl_*". This is analogous to the distinction between input variables and monitored variables. The controlled events belong to $\overline{\text{REQ}}$.

We also introduce another kind of event, the operation. The interplay of input events and output events is handy to model communication systems. But some kinds of interaction of a system with its environment can be modelled more concisely with operations. An operation roughly is an output event followed by an input event. An important example where operations are suitable are function calls in programming languages. Even though we are concerned with embedded, communicating systems, this is important. The underlying software platform of a system is part of its environment, and we must be able to specify the interface between the system and this part of the environment, too. Such function calls are special since the system is inactive until the function call returns, typically after a quite short time. Distinguishing between the invocation event and the return event would complicate the description unnecessarily.

We therefore define an operation as an abstraction of specific changes to output variables followed by other, specific changes to input variables. The input parameters of the operation specify the changes to the output variables of the system, and the output parameters specify the changes to the input variables of the system. An operation is part of the specification of the environment NAT of the system; we assume that the environment always performs suitable changes to the input variables. (If this is not possible, the specification has a contradiction.) We identify operations by the convention that operation names start with "*op_*".

Examples are in Appendix A. The section *text_string_base* on page 246 specifies the operations *op_strI*, *op_strlen*, and *op_strcat* on text strings. The section *comm_io_behaviour* on page 254 specifies the input event *in_submit* and the output event *out_deliver*. The section *comm_behaviour* on page 253 specifies the estimated monitored event *mon_submit* and the estimated controlled event *ctrl_deliver*. The section *time_base* on page 249 specifies the input variable *vin_curr_time* and the corresponding estimated monitored variable *vmon_curr_time*.

Chapter 3

Maintaining Families of Rigorous Requirements

A family of requirements is a set of requirements specifications for which it pays off to study the common requirements first and then the requirements present in few or individual systems only. Because we are interested in the maintenance of such families, we concentrate on families of requirements where only a subset of the family is specified explicitly in the beginning, and where more members are specified explicitly incrementally over time. Domain Engineering helps to exploit the commonalities of a family. There is some initial work by others on how rigorous requirements should be organized to facilitate later changes. We are convinced that a family of requirements can and should be put under configuration management, analogously to software. Advanced, knowledge-based techniques can support the software configuration process if the product is particularly complex.

3.1 An Evolution Process Pattern for Maintaining Families of Requirements

In this book, we concentrate on the maintenance of families of requirements; during such maintenance, a family evolves in a typical process pattern. Initially, we analyze the domain (more or less thoroughly), and we specify and then implement one or a few systems. Over time, customers demand new or other features. Therefore, we specify explicitly and then implement more members of the family. Over more time, we iterate this many times.

In this process, implicit family members become explicitly specified. The initial analysis of the domain determines which systems are potential family members, and which systems can never be part of the family. Also, the requirements of one family member, or of a few, are specified explicitly in the beginning. We call these the *explicit family members*. We call the other potential family members the *implicit family members*. Over time, we make explicit more and more implicit family members, because they are needed by a customer (Fig. 3.1).

We are interested in intensional versioning, as introduced in Sect. 3.4.2 below.

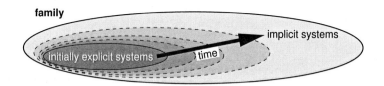

Figure 3.1: Explicit and implicit members of a family.

That is, we don't only want to collect and document those requirements specifications that we have written at some time. We want to have fragments of requirements specifications, and we want to compose them freely into new complete requirements specifications. This is because we want to compose "features" freely. Section 7.1 discusses this further.

The fragments of requirements specifications will be either explicit or implicit. In Chap. 5 and 6, we will introduce "properties" and "requirements modules" as suitable fragments. Initially, many of these fragments are not specified precisely, they are still implicit. Only the domain analysis determines the set of potential fragments. Over time, more and more fragments become explicitly and precisely specified. A fragment must be made explicit when it is needed for composing a new explicit requirements specification of which it is a part.

A new family member can be generated from the family automatically as soon as all necessary fragments have been specified explicitly. Obviously, an important goal is that we need to specify only a few new fragments explicitly for being able to generate the next family member of interest.

This approach allows to have a large set of family members, but it requires work only for those family members that are actually needed, plus the fixed work for the initial domain analysis. This initial work is smaller than making all family members explicit in the beginning. Nevertheless, it must be deep enough to ensure that all systems of interest are actually members of the family.

For example, in our LAN message service family application in Sect. 6.5 below, we specified explicitly only that messages are delivered timely, correctly, and by broadcast. But these three explicit properties are separated and can be removed individually to make place for other delivery strategies. Some obvious, but still implicit delivery strategies are individual addressing, delivery to a fixed address such as a logging agent, delayed delivery, message blocking, and message re-routing. Telephone voice conversation is not in this family, because it is connection-oriented communication. The family is restricted to connection-less messaging.

3.2 Domain Engineering

Domain Engineering helps to exploit the commonalities of a family. Domain engineering is part of software product-line engineering. Weiss and Lai [WeLa99] present an industry-proven approach for software product-line engineering, a family-based

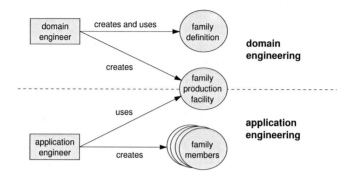

Figure 3.2: Family-based software development processes (after [WeLa99]).

software development process. We will summarize it briefly here, as far as it is concerned with domain engineering, and we will give an overview of an application. Furthermore, we will introduce to an application of domain engineering to tramway control systems which we are currently performing ourselves.

In family-based software development processes, the software engineer's role is split into two parts (Fig. 3.2): the domain engineer, who defines a family and creates the production facilities for the family, and the application engineer, who uses the production facilities to create new family members. Correspondingly, the two parts of the approach are known as *domain engineering* and *application engineering*.

3.2.1   The FAST Approach, With an Application

The approach of Weiss and Lai is known as Family-oriented Abstraction, Specification, and Translation (FAST). The FAST process was developed and is in use withing Lucent Technologies, a major North-American telecom provider. Many product-lines have been created there already for their software production. A few examples are command recognition, database views, and runtime equipment reconfiguration.

We now describe the basic assumptions underlying FAST and the steps for creating an engineered family with FAST, and we give an overview of an application of FAST to a commands and reports family.

Basic Assumptions

Three basic assumptions underlie the FAST approach, and also other domain engineering approaches:

The redevelopment hypothesis. Most software development ist mostly redevelopment. In particular, most software development consists of creating variations on existing software systems. Usually, each variation has more in common with other variations than it has differences from them. For example, the different versions of a telephone switching system may differ in the algorithms that they use to compute telephone bills or in some specialized features that they offer to the end user, but all of them may offer the same features for processing calls and may use the same type of equipment.

The oracle hypothesis. It is possible to predict the changes that are likely to be needed to a system over its lifetime. In particular, we can predict the types of variations of a system that will be needed. Manufacturers of telephone switches know from their experience that different customers will want to use different billing algorithms. It is a pattern that governs their business.

The organizational hypothesis. It is possible to organize both software and the organization that develops and maintains it so as to take advantage of predicted changes. For example, experienced manufacturers of telephone switches try to design their software so that the billing algorithm can be changed independently of other aspects of the system, such as the way calls are routed.

Our ability to predict change is critical in constructing families. But it is not an all-or nothing proposition. The better we are at it, the easier it will be to produce family members that meed customers' needs now and in the future. Our confidence in our ability to predict change should rule the size of our investment. There are several reasonably good guides for future change, according to Weiss and Lai: past change, the marketing organization, early adopters, and experienced developers.

Creating an Engineered Family

Weiss and Lai identify four stages towards an engineered family: For a *potential family,* one suspects sufficient commonality. For a *semifamily,* the common and variable aspects have been identified. A *defined family* is a semifamily plus an economic analysis of exploiting it. An *engineered family* is a defined family plus an investment in processes, tools, and resources.

The FAST approach uses the following steps for creating engineered families:

- Identify collections of programs that can be considered families.

- Design the family for producibility – design a process for producing family members concurrently with creating a common design for family members. The idea is to make it easy to produce any family member by following the process, which includes steps for applying the common design.

- Invest in family-specific tools.

- For each family, create a way to model family members for two purposes:

  1. To help the developer to validate the customer's requirements by exploring the behaviour of the model.

2. To provide a description of the family member from which the deliverable code and documentation for the family member can be generated.

Because we generate the deliverable code directly from the model of the family member, we know that the behaviour of the deliverable code corresponds to the behaviour of the model (if the tools are correct).

The model is expressed in the form of a language. Weiss and Lai call it an *application modelling language* (AML). Other terms frequently used are *domain specific language* (DSL) and *application specific language* (ASL).

The FAST process explicitly bounds change. We must not only document what can change, but also what cannot change within a family. Only this allows to have abstractions that are common to all family members.

Application: the Commands and Reports Family

Weiss and Lai describe the successful application of the FAST approach to a commands and reports (C&R) family in length. The family is part of Lucent's 5ESS telephone switch. To monitor and maintain the switch, technicians use an interface that allows them to issue commands to the switch and to receive reports on its status. There is also voluminous documentation on each command and report. The command set comprises thousands of commands and report types.

Weiss and Lai followed the standard FAST process (see Fig. 3.3). They analyzed the family and used the results to define a language, called SPEC (Specification of Executable Commands), for specifying family members. They also developed a toolset, called ASPECT (a SPEC translator), for analyzing SPEC specifications, for generating the compiled C&R descriptions maintained in the switch, and for generating the customer documentation.

Defining the C&R family means identifying potential family members and characterizing what they have in common and how they differ. Always the same is that a command to an 5ESS switch consists of a command code followed by parameters. Each command code consists of an action and an object. An example is a command code for reporting the status of a line that is connected to the switch. The action is reporting, and the object is the line. However, the particular actions, objects, and parameters vary. They vary over reasonably well-defined sets. And certain combinations are not included in the family. For example, removing the clock is not included, but setting the clock is included. All this was documented in a commonality analysis document. Weiss and Lai present excerpts of it in their book.

The SPEC language allows to express the command codes, their parameters, and the associated documentation by so-called property-lists. Writing in SPEC is easy and fast for people who work in the C&R domain, because SPEC uses familiar abstractions. The ASPECT translators generate both the code and the documentation from SPEC.

The ASPECT translators are a family themselves: they support multiple output formats, such as TROFF, HTML, text preview, SGML, and Postscript. This family approach payed off well. HTML was not yet invented when the family was designed.

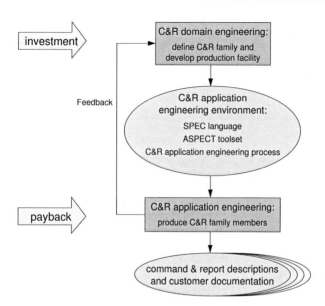

Figure 3.3: The FAST process applied to the Commands and Reports family (after [WeLa99]).

When this new output format needed to be added, only one new device driver module had to be added.

3.2.2 Application: Tramway Control Systems

We currently apply domain engineering in a project on tramway control systems. We not only generate the executable code from a specification in a domain specific language. We additionally automate the verification and testing process for these safety-critical systems. The ongoing two-year project is carried out by students of the University of Bremen as part of their curriculum.

A tramway control system controls the signals and the turnouts (= switches, in American English) in some region of the tramway tracks. Such a system shall set up a route for a tramway through the track network upon request from the driver. In particular, it must ensure that the route is safe, that no tramway on another route can collide with the tramway. The variability of the domain is in the different track networks. The current state of the art in industry is to design a new custom control system for each new track network. In particular, extensive and thus expensive tests are necessary, since these systems are safety-critical.

In our project TRACS [KSZ+04], we follow a new approach. This approach was devised by Haxthausen and Peleska [HaPe03b, HaPe02, HaPe03a]. There is only one

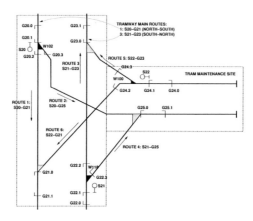

Figure 3.4: Network topology of a tram maintenance site (from [HaPe03b], with permission).

generic control system. It is instantiated with configuration data for a specific track network, and with drivers for the specific hardware used. The configuration data are generated automatically from a requirements specification. The requirements specification is written in a domain specific language. Thus it can be written by tramway network domain experts, and it can be validated by them. A domain-specific description consists of a description of the network topology, of the interlocking tables, and of the hardware devices. Figure 3.4 from [HaPe03b] shows a graphical representation of the network topology of a tram maintenance site. It consists of controllable turnouts (W100, W102, W118), signals (S20, S21, S22), sensors (G20.0, ..., G25.1), and track segments. The interlocking tables comprise a route definition table, a route conflict table, a point position table, and a signal setting table.

The tests for correct and safe operation are automated, too. This reduces the development costs substantially. The safety-critical domain demands particularly thorough tests. The test cases are generated from the requirements specification, too. They ensure that the data compiler for the configuration data worked correctly, and that the generic control system works correctly with this data. Additional hardware-in-the-loop tests cover the hardware drivers, the hardware/software integration, and the computer hardware. The tests are automated by a suitable testing tool [Ver04]. Additionally, the configuration data is tested exhaustively by a model-checking tool against the track network description and the associated safety properties. Thus we get a mathematical proof for the correctness of the specific run of the data compiler.

The ongoing project is carried out by about a dozen students of computer science [KSZ+04]. Such a two-year project is a mandatory part of the curriculum at the University of Bremen. The students shall solve a given task on their own, organizing themselves as a group. They can acquire the necessary knowledge in accompanying lectures. We supervise and guide this project together with Ulrich Hannemann. The idea for the project is due to Jan Peleska. At the time of this writing, the project was about halfway through. Therefore, we cannot yet report on a successfully running implemented system.

3.3 Organizing Requirements for Change

There is some work on how rigorous requirements should be organized to facilitate later changes. The CoRE (Consortium Requirements Engineering) method [Mil98, MiHo97, FBWK92, FJKFM93] is an extension to the four-variable model (Sect. 2.1) that adds a mechanism from object-orientation; a further extension of CoRE by Faulk [Fau01] addresses families of requirements, in particular. Thompson *et al.* [ThHe02, THE00] propose hierarchical families of requirements for the case where the members have different degrees of commonalities, and they apply a rather restricted, early version of this approach to the four-variable model and a formal language. And there is of course other work that is also related in some way to organizing requirements for change.

3.3.1 CoRE Method

The CoRE (Consortium Requirements Engineering) method is an extension to the four-variable model that adds a mechanism from object-orientation; a further extension of CoRE by Faulk addresses families of requirements, in particular.

Standard CoRE Method

The CoRE method [Mil98, MiHo97, FBWK92, FJKFM93] is an extension to the four-variable model (Sect. 2.1) that adds a mechanism from object-orientation.

The CoRE method is based on the classical four-variable model, and on the SCR method in particular, which have been discussed in Sect. 2.1. CoRE was developed by the Software Productivity Consortium. The method adds additional structure to the requirements document by grouping variables, modes and terms into "classes". This borrows from object-orientation. A class has an interface section and an encapsulated section. Entities not needed by other classes are hidden syntactically inside the encapsulated section. Classes may not be nested. CoRE documents the dependencies between classes explicitly by a dependency graph. Despite claims towards object-orientation, the CoRE method does not have instantiations of a class, inheritance, nor parameterized classes.

There is no formal semantics for the CoRE method [FJKFM93]. Furthermore, there is only little tool support. Croxford and Sutton [CrSu96] report that a CASE tool is used to maintain the CoRE data dictionary and to perform automatic well-formation checking of the CoRE model. Redmiles [Red97] presents a "design critic" agent which continually checks the specification during writing, using heuristics.

Nevertheless, there was a successful large-scale industrial application of CoRE at Lockheed [CrSu96, Ame02]. The Lockheed C130J or Hercules II Airlifter was a major updating of one of the world's most long-lived and successful aircraft. It included a completely new avionics fit, including new software. CoRE was applied in the development of the main mission computer software. The software amounts to some 200K lines of source code. Amey [Ame02] reports on a substantial increase in code quality and an associated reduction in cost. Testing revealed very few remaining errors, such that the effort for correcting them was unusually low.

The application of CoRE to a Flight Guidance System rendered valuable experience with respect to requirements changes [Mil98, MiHo97]. The authors found that the requirements for the user interface should have been separated from the requirements for the essential nature of the system, since the user interface is more likely to change. (We will come back to this issue in Chap. 8.) Furthermore, they found in particular that planning for change in a single product is not the same as planning for change in a product family [Mil98]. The requirements should have been organized entirely different for the latter.

Extension of CoRE for Families of Requirements

An extension of CoRE by Faulk [Fau01] addresses such families of requirements. Faulk is interested in the systematic reuse of requirements for embedded, mission- and safety-critical systems. His long-term goal is to develop a systematic approach to specifying requirements for embedded-system product lines, then rapidly generating demonstrably correct requirements specifications for applications in the product line.

The process of Faulk proceeds in defined steps from the commonality analysis of the product line to a Product-line Requirements Specification (PRS). Faulk envisages an application of his process in an overall product-line development process such as FAST [WeLa99] (see Sect. 3.2.1). Faulk's process consists of the following steps: 1) Group together requirements that vary together and separate those varying independently. 2) Create a model of the decisions that characterize a family member and of any constraints on their relative order. 3) Construct a CoRE-style requirements specification applying the information-hiding principle to localize and encapsulate related variations. 4) Specify how requirements vary as a function of the values of the variabilities. 5) Trace the variabilities to conditional inclusion statements in the product-line requirements specification.

The resulting product-line requirements specification has the form of an annotated CoRE model. There are three meta-text constructs: *decision variables* represent variabilities in the decision model; they can be used in expressions. A *nested if-then-else* construct is used to select portions of the specification for inclusion or exclusion; the condition of the construct is an expression containing decision variables. *Text replacement variables* denote a particular variation. On instantiation of a family member, they are replaced by one concrete value each.

These three constructs proved sufficient for the case study which Faulk performed. Faulk plans to extend the syntax further only when a clear need has been demonstrated.

The product-line requirements specification is structured by Faulk according to two purposes. First, the requirements that vary together should be in one place, so that they can be specified, understood, or changed relatively independently. Second, there should be an overall class structure that is common to all members of the product line.

The following structuring heuristics are applied by Faulk: 1) Requirements that hold for all members of the family or that vary for all members are placed first and are then grouped according to subject. 2) When the inclusion of one requirement depends on another, the former is subordinated to the latter in the domain definition. 3) A unique identifier is assigned to each commonality and to each variability, reflecting its type and place in the domain definition; this supports traceability in subsequent development steps.

Recursive subordination yields a hierarchy of requirements. The structuring hierarchy relation is the dependency relation among requirements. (In Section 6.1.1, we will discuss different kinds of hierarchy relations, and we will criticize the idea of making different relations equal.)

A decision model represents the choices that distinguish the members of a family. Faulk used in his case study a simple tabular representation of the underlying decision tree. The table carries over the subordination scheme of the domain definition.

A case study on a real family of systems was performed by Faulk. Faulk applied his approach to a portion of a commercial avionics product line: the Collins Flight Control System family produced by Rockwell Collins Avionics. The work covered the mode control logic of the flight guidance system. The specification in CoRE by Miller [Mil98], discussed above, provided input for Faulk's case study.

Much further work remains to be done into this interesting direction. There is no rigorous definition of the extension of the CoRE notation. (The same holds for the CoRE notation itself.) Only the above subordination kind of constraints between variabilities can be expressed. There is no tool support for the generation of individual family members. The envisaged integration into an overall product-line development process such as FAST is still to be done. The analysis of the family document for properties like consistency and completeness remains a goal of Faulk. Even the appropriate kinds of analysis and the means for it remain open research issues.

3.3.2 Hierarchical and n-Dimensional Families by Thompson *et al.*

Thompson *et al.* [ThHe02, THE00] propose hierarchical families of requirements for the case where the members have different degrees of commonalities, and they apply a rather restricted, early version of this approach to the four-variable model and a formal language.

In early work, Thompson *et al.* [THE00] use the four-variable model with the formalism RSML^{-e} and investigate a suitable structure of a requirements specification for reuse within a product family. They work in the mobile robotics domain. They want to reuse the same control requirements across different platforms where the hardware, i.e., sensors and actuators, may vary.

They acknowledge the work on (standard) CoRE (Sect. 3.3.1), but criticize that its structuring mechanism is based on the physical structure of the system as well as on which pieces of the system are likely to change together. These two criteria might conflict. They also refer to the FAST approach (Sect. 3.2.1) as useful; but they find that it does not explicitly address the structuring of product requirements.

Thompson *et al.* modify the classical four-variable model of Parnas (Sect. 2.1.4) and obtain something similar to the inverted four-variable model of Bharadwaj and Heitmeyer (Sect. 2.1.2). Thompson *et al.* split the software requirements relation SOFT into three pieces, IN^{-1}, OUT^{-1}, and $SOFT_{REQ}$. The relation IN^{-1} takes the measured input and reconstructs an estimate of the physical quantities. The relation OUT^{-1} maps the internal representation of the controlled variables to the output needed for the concrete actuators. The relation $SOFT_{REQ}$ now is essentially isomorphic to the system requirements relation REQ. $SOFT_{REQ}$ therefore need not change if it is reused on a new platform, only the relations IN^{-1} and OUT^{-1} must be changed. In contrast to Bharadwaj and Heitmeyer, Thompson *et al.* explicitly model *both* IN and IN^{-1} (and OUT and OUT^{-1}). Bharadwaj and Heitmeyer [HeBh00] discuss some further differences.

This work still has some restrictions. The authors use a formal specification language. But it is not clear how they maintain those parts of the requirements that are shared over the family. There appears to be no support for this. Furthermore, the kind of variability is restricted. Only the details of the hardware/software interface may change, but not the abstract control requirements.

Later work of Thompson *et al.* [ThHe02] has interesting ideas on a more general kind of variability, but does not apply it to a formal language or to the four-variable model anymore. They investigate hierarchical product families and n-dimensional product families.

Hierarchical product families help with near-commonalities. Thompson *et al.* state that current techniques for product-line engineering work well if the systems in the family share significant commonalities, and if values can be assigned straight-forwardly for the variabilities for each family member. A near-commonality is a commonality for most of the family members, but with one or a few exceptions. Therefore, Thompson *et al.* propose the concept of a hierarchical product family. They use a set-theoretic view. At the top level, there are some commonalities that hold for the entire family, and there are also some variabilities that apply to the entire family. But then they form sub-families. A sub-family is a subset of the top-level family. The sub-family may have additional commonalities and variabilities, as long as they don't conflict with those of the higher-level family. There can be a recursive, hierarchical decomposition into further sub-families. Thompson *et al.* also allow two sub-families of a family to overlap. In this case, we have no tree structure anymore.

n-dimensional product families shall help with dependencies among variabilities. An n-dimensional product family provides different views on the family. Thompson *et al.* investigate two dimensions concretely, which are the hardware dimension and the behavioural dimension. The top-level family is structured into sub-families along each of the dimensions. This allows to express constraints on the viability of family members. For example in their robot product line, the optional door navigation behaviour requires the optional enhanced obstacle detection hardware. The authors specify a two-dimensional viability matrix for their robot product line.

The authors do not refer to Parnas' hierarchical (design) modules [PCW85], even though they cite this article in their earlier work [THE00]. Parnas' kind of hierarchy of modules is closely related; we will discuss it in Sect. 5.1.1 below. This hierarchy is also related to the dimensions of the robot domain of Thompson *et al.*: Parnas has a hardware-hiding module and a behaviour-hiding module at the top level. This corresponds to the hardware dimension and the behavioural dimension of Thompson *et al.* Additionally, Parnas has a software decision module, which is not relevant for specifying requirements. We will discuss this in Sect. 5.3.1 below.

In an outlook, Thompson *et al.* [ThHe02] identify the need to provide a more detailed description of the formal foundations of their approach, and they would like to apply the approach to a formal specification language.

3.3.3   Other Related Work

There is of course other work that is also related in some way to organizing requirements for change. This includes so-called feature models for requirements which originally come from software product lines, the structuring of requirements into a hierarchy, and the clustering of requirements for specific purposes.

Feature Models by Riebisch *et al.*

Riebisch *et al.* use "feature models" for configuring members of a family of software requirements, design elements, and implementation items [Rie03]. Feature models originally were invented by Kang *et al.* for software product lines [KCH+90] (see also Sect. 3.2). A feature model helps to configure an individual software product from the family. Riebisch *et al.* extend this approach by also *linking features to requirements*, and to design elements. Therefore, they also maintain a family of requirements, besides the family of software products. However, Riebisch *et al.* are not working with rigorous requirements, like, e. g., the CoRE approach above.

A feature is defined as "representing an aspect valuable to the customer" by Riebisch *et al.* [Rie03]. There are functional features, interface features, and parameter features. A feature model gives a hierarchical structure to the features. There can additionally be concept features in the hierarchy. A concept feature is an abstract feature.

A feature model provides an overview over the requirements, and it models the variability of a product line. A feature model is used for the derivation of the customer's desired product and provides a hierarchical structure of features according to the decisions associated with the features.

Three different kinds of hierarchical relations over features were discovered by Riebisch *et al.*. These relations are refinement, decomposition, and a "requires" relation. Riebisch *et al.* decided to structure the requirements according to the "requires" relation, because they consider it the most important relation. It supports the selection process of the customer during the configuration of a product. Features with more influence on other decisions are arranged nearer to the top of the hierarchy.

If the other kinds of hierarchy are in conflict with this relation, then they must be expressed as external dependencies. We will come back to the issue of the right

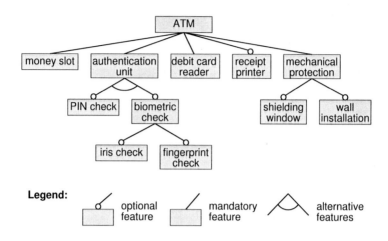

Figure 3.5: An example feature model in the FODA approach (after [Rie03]).

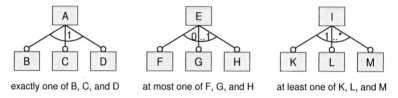

Figure 3.6: Grouping neighbouring features using multiplicities (after [Rie03]).

kind of hierarchy in Section 5.3 and in Section 7.2.

A graphical notation for features models was introduced by Kang *et al.* in their FODA approach [KCH+90]. Figure 3.5 presents an example feature model in FODA. Other feature model approaches extend this graphical notation. FeatuRSEB [GFd98] distinguishes between OR and XOR alternatives. Generative Programming [CzEi00] combines OR, XOR, and alternatives with designating the member features as mandatory or optional. But Riebisch *et al.* found this notation to be ambiguous. They therefore introduced *multiplicities* to overcome this problem [RBSP02, Rie03]. Figure 3.6 shows how neighbouring features can be grouped using multiplicities.

Classical feature models serve to configure software, not software requirements. It is Riebisch *et al.* who attempt to link the software requirements to the feature model, too [Rie03]. They also attempt to structure the architecture of the software according to its feature model [SRP05].

There is also an extension of UML/OCL for expressing feature relations by Riebisch *et al.* [SRP03]. The Object Constraint Language (OCL) of the Unified Modelling Language (UML) [OMG03, RJB98] (see Sect. 4.3 below) can be used to express additional constraints on UML models. Riebisch *et al.* add a construct "selected(<feature>)", in particular. It allows to adjust constraints on the presence of a feature, and it allows to express dependencies between the presence of features. All the more advanced graphical feature model constructs by Riebisch *et al.* are mapped onto this new OCL construct.

However, there is no precise definition of the OCL extension. The authors define the new construct by some examples only [SRP03, Sect. 4]. Similarly, there is no tool support yet.

Requirements Hierarchies by Savolainen and Kuusela

Savolainen and Kuusela [SaKu01] attempt to structure a family of software requirements in a rather practical way. They assume that the creation of domain assets starts simultaneously together with the application development of the first family variant. Thus, they must handle both general domain specifications and family variant specifications together.

The authors distinguish two sets of family properties. *Deductive properties* are based on the requirements defined for the products currently in the family. *Declarative properties* are based on the designer's intention and are expected to hold through the entire lifetime of the product family. Deductive properties are common, partial, or unique. Declarative properties are mandatory, optional, alternative, or multiple.

Near-commonalities of product-line requirements lead to a hierarchy of requirements. A sub-family has additional commonalities, compared with the entire family. This leads to a product requirements refinement hierarchy and a family requirements refinement hierarchy. Hoever, none of these is supported by a formal description or by tools.

There can be inconsistencies between different requirements. The authors investigate a consistency relation between the two kinds of hierarchies. The goal is to correct a detected inconsistency manually, based on the context of the inconsistency.

Requirements Clustering

Hsia and Gupta [HsGu92] structure software requirements for data-dominant systems into clusters. Their goal is the incremental delivery of a single system. A data-dominant system has its emphasis on maintaining the integrity of its data, for example a library information system, as opposed to a control-dominant system.

The clustering identifies all requirements that can be considered to be sensible parts of an increment. Requirements in the same cluster are delivered in the same increment. Requirements from different clusters are delivered in different increments. This approach is rather similar to Parnas' information hiding modules, which also enable extension and contraction of software (see Sect. 5.1.1 below). However, Hsia and Gupta appear to have re-invented the idea, since they do not cite Parnas' work. In contrast to Parnas, Hsia and Gupta do not have hierarchical information hiding modules.

The authors describe the requirements of a data-dominant system formally using Abstract Data Types (ADTs). Then they apply a requirements clustering algorithm.

The algorithm groups the requirements by objective criteria on the ADTs. No subjective decisions by the specifiers are needed. The idea is that requirements pairs that *change* one or more common ADTs belong into the same cluster. Finally, the system can be implemented incrementally along the clustering.

Future work includes tool support for the algorithm, and the investigation of the impact of requirements changes on the method. The latter point emphasizes that the method is intended to develop a single system, not a family of systems.

Palmer and Liang [PaLi92] also structure the software requirements for a single system into clusters. Their goal is to find problems in the requirements, such as imprecision, conflict, inconsistency, ambiguity, and incompleteness. They are concerned with requirements in natural language only. They aim at facilitating the manual inspection of the requirements by providing suitable small, related sets of requirements for the inspection process.

The authors devise a clustering algorithm. It is based on keyword indexing of the natural language. In a second tier, similarities between requirements are detected through clustering on keywords. The authors performed their algorithm manually (and only partially) in a case study since there was no tool support yet.

3.4   Software Configuration Management Definitions

A family of requirements can and should be put under configuration management, analogously to software. Configuration management is indispensable for any systematic work with any kind of families. Configuration management is a mature discipline, but only for software, not yet for requirements. We will show how we can configure and compose requirements to complete family members in Chapter 7. But before we can come to this, we will need another three chapters to lay the grounds. Here, in this section, we present the basic definitions from configuration management for *software*. They contribute to the idea of families, but not yet for requirements. We will relate the definitions to requirements configuration management in Section 7.1 below. We have to postpone this because we need to introduce to our product space in requirements configuration management first. In particular, we need the concept of the requirements module from Chapter 5 and the associated concrete supporting mechanisms from Chapter 6. After all this is available, we also will present our concrete mechanisms for requirements configuration management in the remainder of Chapter 7.

Software configuration management (SCM) contributes valuable basic definitions to the maintenance of requirements. SCM is a mature discipline. However, the problem of *combining* software versions consistently is still hard. Consistency usually is determined by domain-specific techniques outside the SCM area. SCM restricts itself mostly to textual aspects.

Conradi and Westfechtel [CoWe98] survey version models for software configuration management. In this section, we present an excerpt of this 51-page article with the aspects that are relevant for our work. We omit the discussion of specific version models, of their classification, of implementation aspects, of related work, and in particular the extensive description of a large number of SCM systems. We mostly cite the definitions of Conradi and Westfechtel. These citations are rather literally, by their nature. But we cut out a large part of the explanatory text between the definitions for brevity. For more information, please refer to the complete work of Conradi and Westfechtel [CoWe98]. The editing is our work; any problems with understanding the definitions should be attributed to us, not to the original authors.

A version model defines the objects to be versioned, version identification and organization, as well as operations for retrieving existing versions and constructing new versions. Software objects constitute the *product space*, their versions are organized in the *version space*. Many systems, including most commercial ones, are *file-based*. Various *language-based* approaches have been developed as well.

This section is structured similar to the original article. Before introducing versions, the product space is described in Sect. 3.4.1. Subsequently, we discuss the version space without making any assumptions about the product space (Sect. 3.4.2). The interplay of product and version space is addressed in Sect. 3.4.3. Section 3.4.4 is devoted to intensional versioning (i. e., construction of versions based on rules describing consistent combinations).

3.4.1 Product Space

The product space describes the structure of a software product without taking versioning into account. The product space can be represented by a *product graph* whose nodes and edges correspond to software objects and their relationships, respectively.

Software Objects

A *software object* records the result of a development or maintenance activity. Identification is an essential function provided by SCM. Thus, each software object carries an *object identifier* (OID).

Relationships

Software objects are connected by various types of relationships. *Composition relationships* are used to organize software objects with respect to their granularity. For example, a software product may be composed of subsystems, which in turn consist of modules. Objects that are decomposed are called *composite objects* or *configurations*. Objects residing at the leaves of the composition hierarchy are denoted *atomic objects*. Note that an "atomic" software object is still structured internally; that is, it has a fine-grained content. The root of the composition hierarchy is called the *(software) product*. As a least common denominator, a composite object is defined as an object *o* that represents a subgraph of the product graph.

Dependency relationships (simply called dependencies in the following) establish directed connections between objects that are orthogonal to composition relationships. The source and the target of a dependency correspond to a *dependent* and a *master object*, respectively. A dependency implies that the contents of the dependent must be kept consistent with the contents of the master.

3.4.2 Version Space

A *version model* defines the items to be versioned, the common properties shared by all versions of an item, and the deltas, that is, the differences between them. Furthermore, it determines the way versions sets are organized. To this end, it introduces dimensions of evolution such as revisions and variants, it defines whether a version is characterized in terms of some changes relative to some baseline, it selects a suitable representation of the version set (e.g., version graphs), and it also provides operations for retrieving old versions and constructing new versions.

Versions, Versioned Items, and Deltas

A *version* v represents a state of an evolving item i. v is characterized by a pair $v = (ps, vs)$, where ps and vs denote a state in the product space and a point in the version space, respectively. The term *item* covers anything that may be put under version control.

Versioning requires a *sameness criterion*; for example, an OID in the case of software objects. Within a versioned item, each version must be uniquely identifiable through a *version identifier* (VID). A version can also be identified by an expression, which is the identification scheme used by intensional versioning.

All versions of an item share common properties called *invariants*. At one end of the spectrum, versions virtually share only a common OID. At the other end of the spectrum, versions must share semantic properties. For example, version control in algebraic specification [EFH+89] enforces that all versions of a module body realize the shared interface.

The difference between two versions is called a *delta*. Deltas can be defined in two ways: a *symmetric delta* between two versions consists of properties specific to both; or a *directed delta*, also called a *change*, is a sequence of (elementary) change operations which, when applied to one version, yields another version.

It is usually unrealistic to assume that all versions of module bodies realize the same interface (this assumption is made, e.g., in the algebraic approach already cited [EFH+89] and in the Gandalf system [KaHa83]). A way out of this dilemma is *multilevel versioning*; that is, a version may have versions themselves. For example, in Adele [Est85] a module has multiple versions of interfaces each of which is realized by a set of body versions. DAMOKLES [DGL86] generalizes this idea and supports recursive versioning; that is, any version may be versioned in turn.

Extensional and Intensional Versioning

A versioned item is a container for a set V of versions. *Extensional versioning* means that V is defined by enumerating its members. Extensional versioning supports retrieval of previously constructed versions. *Intensional versioning* is applied when flexible automatic construction of consistent versions in a large version space needs to be supported. Instead of enumerating its members, the version set is defined by a predicate. In this case, versions are implicit and many new combinations are constructed on demand.

The difference between extensional and intensional version may be illustrated by comparing SCCS [Roc75] and RCS [Tic85] to conditional compilation as, for example, supported with the C programming language [KeRi78]. Extensional and intensional versioning are by no means mutually exclusive, but can (and should) be combined into a single SCM system.

Intents of Evolution: Revisions, Variants, and Cooperation

Versioning is performed with different intents. A version intended to supersede its predecessor is called a *revision*. Versions intended to coexist are called *variants*. Versions may also be maintained to support *cooperation*. In this case, multiple developers work in parallel on different versions.

State-Based and Change-Based Versioning

Version models that focus on the states of versioned items are called *state-based*. In state-based versioning, versions are described in terms of revisions and variants. In *change-based* models, a version is described in terms of changes applied to some baseline. To this end, changes are assigned *change identifiers* (CID). Change-based versioning provides a nice link to change requests. A version may be described in terms of the change requests it implements.

"State- versus change-based" is orthogonal to "extensional versus intensional." In *change-based intensional versioning*, changes are combined freely to construct new versions as required. Therefore a *change* is considered a partial function $c : V \rightarrow V$, where V denotes the set of all potential versions of some item. A version v is constructed by applying a sequence of changes $c_1 \ldots c_n$ to a baseline b:

$$v = c_1 \circ \ldots \circ c_n(b) = c_n(\ldots c_1(b) \ldots)$$

3.4.3   Interplay of Product Space and Version Space

A version model needs to address the interplay between product space and version space as well.

AND/OR Graphs

AND/OR graphs [Tic82] provide a general model for integrating product space and version space. An AND/OR graph (Fig. 3.7) contains two types of nodes, namely, AND nodes and OR nodes. Analogously, a distinction is made between AND and OR edges, which emanate from AND and OR nodes, respectively. An unversioned product graph can be represented by an AND/OR graph consisting exclusively of AND nodes/edges. Versioning of the product graph is modelled by introducing OR nodes. Versioned objects and their versions are represented by OR nodes and AND nodes, respectively.

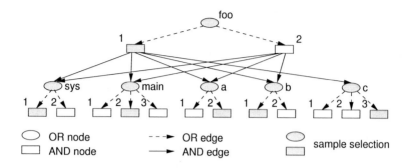

Figure 3.7: An intertwined AND/OR graph (after [CoWe98]).

AND edges are used to represent both composition and dependency relationships. A relationship is *bound* to a specific version if the corresponding AND edge ends at an AND node; otherwise it is called *generic*. A *configuration* is represented by a subgraph spanned by all nodes that are transitively reachable from the root node of the configuration. If all AND edges belonging to this subgraph are bound, the configuration is called bound as well; otherwise it is called generic. A bound configuration can be constructed from a generic configuration by eliminating the OR nodes, that is, by selecting one successor of each OR node reached during traversal from the root node.

We may classify version models according to the *selection order* during the configuration process: *product first* means that the product structure is selected first; subsequently, versions of components are selected. This approach suffers from the restriction that structural versioning cannot be expressed. *Version first* inverts this approach: the product version is selected first and uniquely determines the component versions. *Intertwined* (Fig. 3.7) means that AND and OR selections are performed in alternating order. Again, this selection scheme supports structural versioning.

3.4.4 Intensional Versioning

Intensional versioning deals with the construction of new versions from property-based descriptions. Intensional versioning is very important for large version spaces, where a software product evolves into many revisions and variants and many changes have to be combined. In order to support intensional versioning, an SCM system must provide for both combinability – any version has to be constructed on demand – and consistency control – a constructed version must meet certain constraints. The construction of a version may be viewed as a selection against a versioned object base. The selection is directed by *configuration rules*, which constitute an essential part of a version model, and is performed both in the product space and the version space.

Problem: Combinability Versus Consistency Control and Manageability

Configuration rules are used to configure consistent versions from a versioned object base. Rules are required to address the *combinability* problem. The number of potential versions explodes combinatorially; only a few are actually consistent or relevant. The combinability problem has to be solved in any version model.

The challenge of intensional versioning consists of providing for *consistency control* while still supporting combinability. The space of all potential versions is much larger than the space of consistent ones. The problem of consistency control can be addressed both in the version space and in the product space. In the version space, configuration rules are used to eliminate inconsistent combinations; in the product space, the knowledge about software objects, their contents, and their relationships is enriched in order to check and ensure product constraints. SCM systems tend to solve the problem in the version space because they frequently only have limited knowledge of the product space (typically, software objects are represented as text files).

Even if a sophisticated tool for constructing a version is employed, the user must be warned if a new version is created that has never before been configured. Although old versions can be assigned levels of "confidentiality" (e.g., tested or released), a new version cannot be trusted blindly. Therefore the configured version is subject to quality assurance (e.g., testing). Potentially, changes to the constructed version need to be performed (*correction delta*).

Conceptual Framework for Intensional Versioning

Figure 3.8 illustrates Conradi's and Westfechtel's conceptual framework for intensional versioning. A *configuration rule* guides or constrains version selection for a certain part of a software product. Thus a configuration rule consists of a *product part*, which determines its scope in the product space, and a *version part*, which performs a selection in the version space.

A *versioned object base* combines product space and version space and stores all versions of a software product. The versioned object base is augmented with a *rule base* of stored configuration rules.

A *query* consists of a set of submitted configuration rules, each composed of a product part and a version part. A *configurator* is a tool that constructs a version by evaluating a query against a versioned object base and a rule base. The constructed version has to satisfy both *version constraints* and *product constraints*.

Configuration Rules

Configuration rules take on different forms depending on how the version space is structured. Figure 3.9 provides some typical examples that refer to the revision, variant, and change space, respectively. In the *revision space* category, configuration rules refer to the time dimension. In the *variant space*, configuration rules refer to values of variant attributes. In the *change space*, Rule (5) specifies a version in terms of the changes to be applied. Rules (6) and (7) specify further relationships

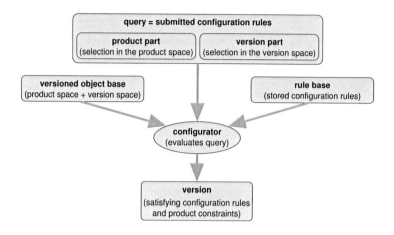

Figure 3.8: Intensional versioning (after [CoWe98]).

that describe consistent change combinations. Rule (6) states that change $c2$ implies $c1$. Rule (7) states that changes $c1$, $c2$, and $c3$ are mutually exclusive. The product part of a configuration rule describes the scope of a configuration rule in the product space.

Configuration rules can be ordered in *strictness classes*. A *constraint* is a mandatory rule that must be satisfied. Any violation of a constraint indicates an inconsistency. A *preference* is an optional rule that is applied only when it can be satisfied. Finally, a *default* is also an optional rule, but is weaker than a preference: a default rule is applied only when no unique selection could be performed otherwise.

In addition, rules may be given *priorities*. Rules with high priorities are considered before low-priority rules. A priority may be assigned explicitly or may be defined implicitly by textual ordering. Priorities may be combined with strictness classes such as by assigning priorities to preferences.

Finally, we may distinguish between *stored* and *submitted* configuration rules.

Merge Tools

Merge tools combine versions or changes. They may be classified as follows. *Raw merging* simply applies a change in a different context. A *two-way merge tool* compares two alternative versions $a1$ and $a2$ and merges them into a single version m. To this end, it displays the differences to the user who has to select the appropriate alternative. A two-way merge tool can merely detect differences, and cannot resolve them automatically. To reduce the number of decisions to be performed by the user, a *three-way merge tool* consults a common baseline b if a difference is detected. If a change has been applied in only one version, this change is incorporated automatically. Otherwise, a conflict is detected that can be resolved either manually or

revision space

(1) t = max

(2) no = 1.1.1.1

variant space

(3) os = Unix ∧ ws = X11 ∧ db = Oracle

(4) ¬ (os = DOS ∧ ws = X11)

change space

(5) c1 c2 c4

(6) c2 ⇒ c1

(7) c1 ⊗ c2 ⊗ c3

Figure 3.9: Version parts of configuration rules.

automatically (the latter is not recommended).

Merge tools can be characterized by the semantic level at which merging is performed (i.e., their knowledge about the product space): *Textual merging* is applied to text files. It works well when small, local changes to large well-structured programs are combined and changes have been coordinated beforehand so that semantic conflicts are unlikely to occur. *Syntactic merging* exploits the context-free (or even context-sensitive) syntax of the versions to be merged. Syntactic merging has been realized only in a few research prototypes. *Semantic merging* takes the semantics of programs into account. It is a hard problem to come up with a definition of semantic conflict that is neither too strong nor too weak (and is decidable). Semantic merge tools have not (yet?) made their way into practice.

An SCM System With Feature Logic

From the more than 20 SCM systems that Conradi and Westfechtel describe, we select only one here, because it is based on feature logic.

ICE [ZeSn95] is derived from conditional compilation and represents a versioned object base as a set of fragments that are tagged with control expressions. ICE is based on *feature logic*: a feature corresponds to an attribute whose value is defined by a feature term. For example, [ws : X11] means that the ws feature has the value X11. In general, a feature term denotes a set of potential values and may be composed by a wide range of operators such as unification, subsumption, negation, and the like [Zel96]. Probably the most important of these is unification, which is used to compose configurations (the feature terms of component versions are unified). A configuration is inconsistent if unification fails (empty intersection of value sets as, e. g., in [ws : X11] ⊓ [ws : Windows]).

3.5   Knowledge-Based Software Configuration

Advanced, knowledge-based techniques can support the software configuration process if the product is particularly complex.

Knowledge-based configuration is a advanced solution technique for those domains where the configuration constraints are particularly complex and hard to resolve. Knowledge-based configuration comes from the area of artificial intelligence. Traditionally, it is applied to various hardware domains. One example are mechanical drives for printing machines, sorting machines, automated saws and so on [GHH+02]. The basic problem is to find a configuration in a huge product space that meets a large number of customer-specified, potentially conflicting constraints. In the terms of the previous section, this is a complex case of intensional versioning.

For example, the Drive Solution Designer by Günter *et al.* [GHH+02] supports the sales engineer of a drive-selling company in creating an offer for a drive while visiting a customer. The product space has the size of 10^{21}. The tool guarantees the consistency of the result, thus radically speeding up the placement of the offer. Before, an expert back at the company site had to check the envisaged offer. This took three to thirty hours of working time. The tool uses a heuristic, *structure-based configuration* approach in order to handle the particularly complex domain. The approach was originally developed in the Prokon project and in its predecessor TEX-K [Gün95, CGS91]. The approach makes use of the component structure of the domain. The approach is based on three different knowledge representations: the knowledge about the objects in the domain is represented in an ontology; the dependencies between objects and their relations and attributes are represented by constraints in a meta-constraint modeling language; and knowledge about the control process is described declaratively by strategies.

The ConIPF project applies knowledge-based configuration to software product lines [HKW04, WKHM04, HoKr03]. The approach is similar as above, but now it is applied to complex software, not to complex hardware. The project uses structure-based configuration, too. The authors assume that a software product line already has been developed completely. They apply knowledge-based configuration in order to bind the variabilities of the software product line while respecting customer-specified constraints. These constraints are called requirements on the solution.

A difference between our aim and the ConIPF project is that that the latter configures software, but not software requirements. The notion of requirements is different. For the goals of the ConIPF project, one only must know sufficiently much about the software components to be able to configure them. One does not need to describe the requirements on the software completely. In contrast, we indeed describe the family of software requirements completely and then configure individual requirements specifications.

Nevertheless, it should be possible to apply knowledge-based configuration to a family of software requirements, too. This might be helpful if the family is so complex that simple configuration approaches do not suffice anymore.

Chapter 4

Object-Oriented Principles and Mechanisms for Families of Programs

The object-oriented paradigm offers structuring principles and mechanisms for organizing a family of programs. Many of these can be used for families of requirements,
too. A family of programs is a special case of reuse. Historically, reuse was a major
goal of object-orientation. Good object-oriented design follows structuring principles
that facilitate reuse. Object-oriented languages offer mechanisms for composition
that can be used to follow the basic structuring principles for reuse. The Unified
Modelling Language (UML) [OMG03, RJB98] is the current standard notation in
object-oriented analysis and design; the UML offers the structuring mechanisms discussed.

4.1 Structuring Principles for Reuse

Good object-oriented design follows structuring principles that facilitate reuse.
Object-orientated design is often used for agile software development. In this context,
"reuse" happens at a finer granularity than entire products. Nevertheless, the fundamental problems of reuse are universal to software engineering, as are the principles
for mastering them.

We take the presentation and definition of the structuring principles from Martin
[Mar03]. There is a host of literature on object-oriented design. Nearly every author
uses slightly different definitions and wordings. We decided to use the presentation
of Martin because it fits the structure of this section nicely. It is a current, deep,
and comprehensive presentation of the basic structuring principles.

Martin [Mar03] presents five basic structuring principles of agile, object-oriented
design. The basic principles are the

- single responsibility principle, the

- open-closed principle, the

- Liskov substitution principle, the

- dependency inversion principle, and the

- interface segregation principle.

The basic principles are supplemented by six more principles for splitting a large software system into packages.

4.1.1　The Single Responsibility Principle

A class should have only one reason to change.

DeMarco [DeM79] and Page-Jones [PJ88] originally called this principle "cohesion".

Martin defines a responsibility to be "a reason for change". If you can think of more than one motive for changing a class, then that class has more than one responsibility.

The rationale for the single responsibility principle is that each responsibility is an axis of change. If a class has more than one responsibility, then the responsibilities become coupled. Changes to one responsibility may impair or inhibit the ability of the class to meet the others. This kind of coupling leads to fragile designs that break in unexpected ways when changed.

A corollary of the principle is that an axis of change is an axis of change only if the changes actually occur. In agile software development, it is not wise to apply the principle if there is no symptom.

4.1.2　The Open-Closed Principle

Software entities (classes, modules, functions, etc.) should be open for extension, but closed for modification.

Meyer [Mey88] coined the open-closed principle.

The goals of openness and closedness appear to be at odds, but they can be reconciled by abstraction. A module must be open to adding new behaviours, i.e., to changing what the module does. A module must be closed for modification, i.e., the source and the binary code of it must not be changed. We can make a module both open and closed by finding suitable abstractions. These are represented by abstract base classes in object-oriented languages.

There are two common patterns to satisfy the open-closed principle, the strategy pattern and the template method pattern. The strategy pattern decouples a client class from changes to a server class. The strategy pattern introduces an abstract interface for the client. Both the client class and the server class now depend on the abstract interface class. In particular, the client class does not depend on the server class anymore. The template method pattern separates a generic policy from implementation details. A policy class provides concrete public functions that implement a policy of some kind. As before, these policy functions describe some work that needs to be done in terms of some abstract interfaces. However, the abstract interfaces are part of the policy class itself. They are implemented in the subclasses of the policy class.

The closure for modification cannot be complete; therefore it must be strategic. There will always be some kind of change against which a module is not closed. We can invent abstractions only for changes that we can anticipate. And "adding the hooks" is expensive. It takes development time and effort to create the appropriate abstractions. Those abstractions also increase the complexity of the software design. We must guess the most likely changes and then construct abstractions to protect us from those changes.

4.1.3   The Liskov Substitution Principle

Subtypes must be substitutable for their base types.

Liskov [Lis88] first formulated this principle.

The Liskov substitution principle gives a design rule for the use of inheritance as a mechanism for the open-closed principle. The primary mechanisms behind the open-closed principle are abstraction and polymorphism. In statically typed languages like C++ and Java, one of the key mechanisms that supports abstraction and polymorphism is inheritance.

The term "is a" is too broad to act as a definition of a subtype. The true definition of a subtype is "substitutable", where substitutability is defined by either an explicit or implicit contract.

An example of a violation of the Liskov substitution principle is about a "rectangle" class and a "square" class. Assume that we have a rectangle class, with a width and a height. We now need a square class. We decide that a square "is a" rectangle and let the square class inherit from the rectangle class. The square class adds and enforces the invariant that the width and the height of it are the same. But the rectangle class may have the implicit, contradicting invariant that the width and the height can change independently of each other. Some code may first set the width and then the height, and legitimately expect that the width remains unchanged by setting the height. This expectation will be violated when the code is applied to a square. The "is a" relationship is about behaviour. Therefore, a square definitely is not a rectangle.

Design by contract [Mey88] is a technique to make "reasonable assumptions" by users explicit. In the language Eiffel, a routine can (and should) have a precondition and a postcondition. These are two predicates. When the routine is called, it guarantees that the postcondition will be true upon completion, provided that the precondition was true upon invocation. It is the duty of the caller to ensure the satisfaction of the precondition. A class can also have invariants. All routines must guarantee the invariants to be true in all stable states. A derived class may only weaken a precondition, strengthen a postcondition, and strenghten an invariant.

In the example about the rectangle and the square, design by contract prevents the problem. The set-height method of the rectangle class then has the explicit postcondition that the height is set to the new value, *and* that most other properties of the rectangle remain unchanged, in particular including its width. When we then let a square class inherit from the rectangle class, the conflict is obvious. The additional, explicit class invariant of the square class weakens the postcondition of the set-height method and makes it false for any change of value. Therefore, any implementation of this method for the rectangle class explicitly violates the postcondition for the square class. This is easy to see for the specifier of the square class.

Contracts can also by specified by unit tests. Authors of client code will want to review the unit tests so that they know what to reasonably assume about the classes they are using.

There are heuristics that give some clues about Liskov substitution principle violations. They all have to do with derivative classes that somehow *remove* functionality from their base classes. The heuristics are: look for degenerate functions in derivatives (a degenerate function does less or is even empty), and look if a derivative throws an additional exception.

Beyond Martin, we conclude that the mechanism of inheritance is of less use than it appears at first sight. We cannot simply adapt an "almost right" class to our needs by inheritance. If we use inheritance for subtyping and follow the Liskov substitution principle to support the open-closed principle, then a subclass may only concretize the still unspecified behaviour of its superclass.

4.1.4   The Dependency Inversion Principle

Abstractions should not depend upon details. Details should depend upon abstractions.

The dependency inversion principle helps to reuse policies (business rules, ...), which are the most difficult things to reuse. In a naive layered architecture, the (uppermost) policy layer depends on the mechanism layer, and the mechanism layer depends on the utility layer. Therefore, the policies depend on the utilities. The policies are unlikely to be portable.

The problem is solved by inverting the dependency. The policy layer provides a policy service interface (and depends on it). The mechanism layer implements this interface (and also depends on the interface). Therefore, the mechanism layer now depends on the policy layer.

A more naive interpretation of the dependency inversion principle is the heuristic: "depend on abstractions". In more detail, this means: No variable should hold a pointer or reference to an instance of a concrete class. No class should derive from a concrete class. No method should override an implemented method of any of its base classes.

This heuristic is naive, since we need the heuristic only if the base class is volatile. If it is not going to change much, it does little harm to depend on it. For example, Java's String class is nonvolatile.

We can achieve the inversion of dependencies by dynamic or by static polymorphism. For example, a regulator class may dynamically get a thermometer class and a heater class as parameters. In the language C++, we can use templates to achieve static polymorphism. The latter is less flexible, needs more recompilation, but is a bit more efficient.

4.1.5   The Interface Segregation Principle

Clients should not be forced to depend upon methods that they do not use. Interfaces belong to clients, not to hierarchies.

The interface segregation principle deals with the disadvantages of "fat" interfaces. Classes that have "fat" interfaces are classes whose interfaces are not cohesive. A disadvantage of a "fat" interface is that a client applies a backward force on an interface. For example, if a client is extended, it may need slightly more functionality provided through the interface; say, one more parameter. This can demand for a modification of the interface because of the change to one of its clients. If there are many clients for the interface, all of them may be affected. The interface segregation principle acknowledges that there are objects that require noncohesive interfaces; however, it suggests that clients should not know about them as a single class. Instead, clients should know about abstract base classes that have cohesive interfaces.

We can achive interface segregation by delegation or by multiple inheritance. For example, assume that we have a Door class, and that we want to write a TimedDoor class. The TimedDoor should sound an alarm when the door has been left open for too long. We already have a Timer class; when an object wishes to be informed about a timeout, it calls the Register function of the Timer. Its arguments include a pointer to a TimerClient object whose TimeOut function will be called when the timeout expires. In a naive solution with single inheritance, TimedDoor inherits from Door, which in turn must inherit from TimerClient. This allows the TimedDoor to be notified of the TimeOut. But we should not inherit the definition of TimerClient in the original Door class. This would make all other kinds of doors depend on TimerClient, too. We can solve the problem by delegation. The TimedDoor creates a DoorTimerAdapter object, which inherits from TimerClient, and which delegates the TimeOut event back to the TimedDoor. Alternatively, we can solve the problem by multiple inheritance. TimedDoor inherits both from Door and TimerClient. The latter is the preferred solution of Martin.

4.1.6   Principles for Packaging

Large software applications need some kind of high-level organization. Classes are too finely grained to be used as the sole organizational unit for large applications. We need *packages*. Martin presents three principles of package cohesion and three principles of package coupling. The former help us to allocate classes to packages. The latter help us determine how packages should be interrelated.

The Release-Reuse Equivalence Principle:

The granule of reuse is the granule of release.

The release-reuse equivalence principle gives the reuser safety. He can decide himself when to switch to a new release. One only reuses things that are packaged and can be tracked with release numbers.

The Common Closure Principle:

The classes in a package should be closed together against the same kinds of changes. A change that affects a closed package affects all the classes in that package and no other packages.

This is the single-responsibility principle restated for packages.

The Common Reuse Principle:

The classes in a package are reused together. If you reuse one of the classes in a package, you reuse them all.

The common reuse principle helps us to decide which classes should be placed into a package. The principle says that classes which are not tightly bound to each other with class relationships should not be in the same package. There is a dependency relation at the level of packages, too. Every time a used package is released, the using package must be revalidated and rereleased.

The Acyclic Dependencies Principle:

Allow no cycles in the package dependency graph.

The acyclic dependencies principle allows a developer team to adopt the advances of other teams at their own pace. No global synchronization of the teams is required. All packages are released individually.

The Stable Dependencies Principle:

Depend in the direction of stability.

Any package that we expect to be volatile should not be depended on by a package that is difficult to change. Otherwise the volatile package will also be difficult to change.

Stability is related to the amount of work required to make a change. A package with lots of incoming dependencies is very stable because it requires a great deal of work to reconcile any changes with all the dependend packages.

The Stable Abstractions Principle:

A package should be as abstract as it is stable.

The stability of a package should not prevent it from being extended. An instable package should be concrete since its instability allows the concrete code within it to be easily changed.

The stable abstractions principle and the stable dependencies principle combined amount to the dependency inversion principle for packages.

4.2 Basic Mechanisms for Composition

Object-oriented languages offer mechanisms for composition that can be used to follow the above basic structuring principles for reuse. The three basic mechanisms are

- genericity / parameterized types,

- object composition and delegation, and

- inheritance (of classes or of interfaces).

The first two of the mechanisms are used outside of object-orientation, too, of course. Then, "object composition" becomes the composition of some other kind of module.

All kinds of composition need some unit of code grouping; in object-orientation, the unit usually is the "class".

The mechanisms for composition are related; we can achieve the same goal by different mechanisms. In particular, inheritance can always be substituted by at least one of the two non-object-oriented mechanisms for composition. We discuss this in the end of this section.

4.2.1 Genericity

Genericity means that a module/class can have parameters, in particular type parameters.

Genericity can be accompanied by static polymorphism. The language Ada is an example for this. Static polymorphism means that the admissible types for a parameter all have an operation with a specified name, but with a different implementation for each type. The operation's name is the same for the operations of all types. One of the operations is chosen when the parameter is instantiated. This must happen at compile time. The template mechanism of the language C++ is similar.

4.2.2 Object Composition and Delegation

Object composition achieves new, complex functionality by putting simpler modules/objects together. The simpler modules must have well-defined interfaces. Object composition is black-box reuse.

Delegation (in the sense of, e.g., [GHJV95]) means that a first module/object receives a request for an operation, but forwards this request to a second module/object for the actual processing. The first module/object includes a reference to itself in its request, such that the second module/object can manipulate the first's state. Delegation facilitates the composition of behaviour at runtime, including a change of the composition structure.

4.2.3   Inheritance

Inheritance is a syntactic mechanism present in all object-oriented languages; it is complemented by polymorphism and dynamic binding. Inheritance allows to reuse parts of a superclass in a subclass. We can distinguish inheritance of classes and inheritance of interfaces. Inheritance of classes is reuse of code. Inheritance of interfaces is subtyping.

(Dynamic) polymorphism is the ability of an entity to refer to different classes at runtime. Inheritance restricts the set of possible classes (in a typed language) [Mey88].

Dynamic Binding means that the dynamic form of an object determines at runtime which of the several versions of a polymorphic operation is used.

4.2.4   Relationship of the Mechanisms

The mechanisms are related; we can achieve the same goal by different mechanisms. Object composition and delegation together are equally powerful as class inheritance. Genericity is less powerful than inheritance. The side conditions determine what mechanism is best used in any particular case.

Object composition and delegation together are equally powerful as class inheritance, according to Gamma *et al.* [GHJV95]. Delegation can achieve the same dynamic binding as polymorphism in inheritance. Class inheritance has the advantage that it allows for default implementations of operations that can be redefined. (However, this can be dangerous if it violates the Liskov substition principle.) Object composition is more flexible when changing the composed behaviour at runtime. Readability and efficiency are a bit lower for object composition than for class inheritance. Class inheritance is white-box reuse, whereas object composition is black-box reuse. Gamma *et al.* therefore generally prefer object composition over class inheritance [GHJV95].

Genericity is less powerful than inheritance, finds Meyer [Mey88, Chap. 19]. Genericity allows static polymorphism (e.g., in Ada), but not dynamic polymorphism with dynamic binding. Ada does not allow to select the appropriate routine at runtime. The only way to simulate this is not acceptable because it violates basic principles. We can use variant records. But this distributes the secrets of a module and it also closes the module against extenstions. The other way around, we can express genericity with inheritance. But the discussion of Meyer demonstrates this to be awkward. Meyer's language Eiffel therefore offers both mechanisms, suitably restricted to avoid redundancy.

4.3   UML Notation for Composition

The Unified Modelling Language (UML) [OMG03, RJB98] is the current standard notation in object-oriented analysis and design; the UML offers the structuring mechanisms discussed. Additionally, it allows to document dependencies explicitly. (We will come back to dependencies later in this book.) It does not matter that the

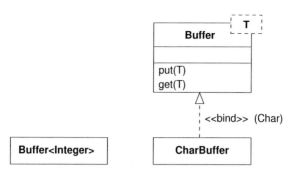

Figure 4.1: UML notation for a parameterized class (template) and two notations for binding it.

UML is a modelling language and not a programming language. We need the same structuring mechanisms when we describe a design with class diagrams.

A UML class is the descriptor for a set of objects with similar structure, behaviour, and relationships. UML provides a graphical notation for declaring and using classes. A class is drawn as a solid-outline rectangle with three compartments separated by horizontal lines. The top name compartment holds the class name and other general properties of the class; the middle list compartment holds a list of attributes; the bottom list compartment holds a list of operations [OMG03].

4.3.1 Genericity

A parameterized class (template) is the descriptor for a class with one or more unbound formal parameters. It defines a family of classes, each class specified by binding the parameters to actual values. Typically, the parameters represent attribute types; however, they can also represent integers, other types, or even operations. Attributes and operations within the template are defined in terms of the formal parameters so they too become bound when the template itself is bound to actual values. A small dashed rectangle is superimposed on the upper right-hand corner of the rectangle for the class. The dashed rectangle contains a parameter list of formal parameters for the class and their implementation types. To be used, a template's formal parameters must be bound to actual values. The relationship between the bound element and its template may be shown by a dependency relationship with the keyword ≪bind≫. The actual parameters are shown in parentheses after the keyword. The attribute and operation compartments are normally suppressed within a bound class, because they must not be modified. Alternatively, a bound element is indicated in text form as the template name followed by the actual parameters in angle brackets [OMG03]. Figure 4.1 shows examples.

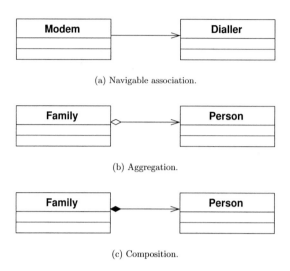

(a) Navigable association.

(b) Aggregation.

(c) Composition.

Figure 4.2: Three UML notations for object composition (after [Mar03]).

4.3.2   Object Composition and Delegation

Object composition can be represented in UML by object diagrams. The use of object diagrams is fairly limited in UML, mainly to show examples of data structures. An object diagram is a graph of instances, including objects and data values. A static object diagram is an instance of a class diagram; it shows a snapshot of the detailed state of a system at a point in time.

Class composition can be represented in UML by an association that is navigable, by an aggregation, or by a (UML) composition. An navigable association allows instances of a first class to send messages to instances of a second class. A navigable association is drawn as a solid path connecting the two classifier symbols, with an arrow attached to the second class's end of the path. An aggregation is a special form of an association. It represents (vaguely) some kind of whole/part relationship. An aggregation is drawn with a hollow diamond attached the the first class's end of the path. A composition is a special form of an aggregation. A composition implies that the "whole" is responsible for the lifetime of its "part". A composition is drawn with a filled diamond instead of a hollow diamond. Figure 4.2 shows an example for each of the three notations.

Delegation can be expressed in UML insofar as that we can specify that an operation of the forwarded-to object will be invoked. The actual parameters of the operation must include a reference to the forwarding object.

4.3.3 Inheritance

The UML offers notations for three important underlying concepts of inheritance and a notation for an important related concept. The underlying concepts are the interface, realization, and generalization; the related concept is the constraint (precondition, postcondition, or invariant). Inheritance in the raw form of Sect. 4.2.3 above is not supported; this is not required when the above basic structuring principles are followed. The random use of inheritance in its raw form would even break these principles.

A UML interface for a class specifies the signature of externally-visible operations. Each interface often specifies only a subset of all such operations of a class. Interfaces do not have an implementation. They lack attributes, states, or associations; they only have operations. An interface is formally equivalent to an abstract class with no attributes and no methods and only abstract operations. An interface may be shown using the full rectangle symbol with compartments and the keyword ≪interface≫. A list of operations supported by the interface is placed in the operation compartment. The attribute compartment may be omitted because it is always empty. An interface may also be displayed as a small "lollipop" shape. The shape consists of a circle and a solid line that is attached to a class that supports the interface. The name of the interface is placed below the circle. The operations provided are not shown in this notation. A class that uses or requires the operations supplied by the interface may be attached to the circle by a dashed arrow pointing to the circle [OMG03]. Figure 4.3 presents examples for both notations.

A realization relationship indicates that a class implements a type. The realizing class provides at least all the operations of the type, with the same behaviour, but it does not imply inheritance of structure (attributes or associations). A realization relationship is drawn as a dashed line with a solid triangular arrowhead [OMG03]. Figure 4.4 shows an example for a UML notation. The relation between an interface and its implementing class is also one of realization; the latter realizes the former.

Generalization is a taxonomic relationship between a more general element (the parent) and a more specific element (the child). The child must be fully consistent with the first element and adds additional information. It is essential that the child is substitutable for the parent. A generalization is drawn as a solid-line path from the child to the parent, with a large hollow triangle at the end of the path where it meets the more general element. Figure 4.5 shows an example for a UML notation.

Constraints allow design by contract. Constraints can be preconditions, postconditions, or invariants. Constraints can be expressed in the Object Constraint Language (OCL). The OCL is a formal language within the UML. The keywords "inv", "pre" and "post" denote the stereotypes of a constraint; respectively invariant, precondition, and postcondition. The optional keyword "context" can introduce the context for the OCL expression. The actual OCL expression comes after a colon. Figure 4.6 shows a simple example of the OCL notation.

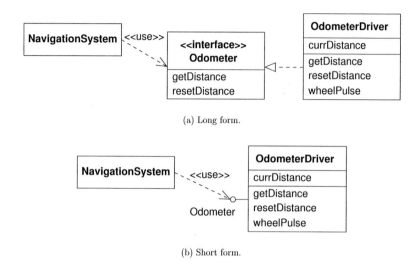

(a) Long form.

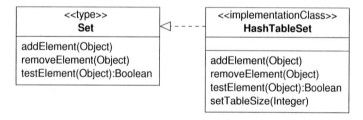

(b) Short form.

Figure 4.3: Two UML notations for an interface.

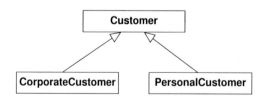

Figure 4.4: A UML notation for realization (after [OMG03]).

Figure 4.5: A UML notation for generalization.

```
context Company inv:
    self.numberOfEmployees > 50
```

Figure 4.6: A simple example of the Object Constraint Language (OCL) of UML (after [OMG03]).

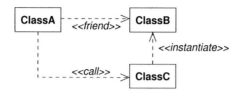

Figure 4.7: UML notation for dependencies (after [OMG03]).

4.3.4 Dependency Relationship

A dependency relationship indicates that a change to one model element may require a change to another model element. A dependency is shown in UML as a dashed arrow between the two model elements. The model element at the tail of the arrow depends on the model element at the arrowhead. Figure 4.7 shows an example. The following kinds of dependency are predefined and may be indicated with the respective keyword in guillemets: access, bind, derive, import, refine, trace, and use. The "use" dependency means that one element requires the presence of another element for its correct implementation or functioning. It may be stereotyped further to indicate the exact nature of the dependency, such as calling an operation of another class, granting permission for access, instantiating an object of another class, etc. [OMG03]. We will come back to the "use" dependency later in this book.

Chapter 5

Information Hiding Requirements Modules

A family of requirements can be organized into requirements modules to make it easier to maintain; however, existing formal languages do not fully support this. Requirements modules mean encapsulation in the information hiding sense. A requirements module is a set of properties that are likely to change together. We need a hierarchy of requirements modules to structure a large number of requirements. This approach conforms to the structuring principles for families of object-oriented programs in the literature. Several recent architectures for families of telephone switching systems already separate some inportant concerns into modules and thereby avoid some kinds of undesired feature interactions. But existing formal languages such as the well-known formalisms Z and Object-Z do not fully support hierarchical requirements structuring. We therefore will extend the formalism Z suitably in the next chapter. This extension will also be a necessary base for our feature construct in Chapter 7.

5.1 Information Hiding Definitions

Information hiding helps to structure a large software system design into modules such that it can be maintained. We now introduce some definitions from the literature as a base for our further discussion. We also point out that this section is about design, not yet about requirements.

5.1.1 Definitions

A *module* in the information hiding sense [Par72, Wei01, PCW85] is a work assignment to a developer or a team of developers. (There are *many* other meanings of this word, we use this meaning only here.) Such a work assignment should be as self-contained as possible. This reduces the effort to develop the system, it reduces the effort to make changes to the system later, and it improves comprehensibility. A successful software system will be changed many times over its life time. When some design decision must be changed, a change should be necessary in one module only. A design decision usually must be changed when some requirement changes.

The *secret* of a module is a piece of information that might change. No other module may rely on the knowledge of such a secret. Sometimes we distinguish between a primary and a secondary secret. A primary secret is hidden information that was specified to the software designer. A secondary secret is a design decision made by the designer when implementing the module that hides the primary secret.

The *interface* between modules is the set of *assumptions* that they make about each other. This not only includes syntactic conventions, but also any assumptions on the behaviour of the other modules. A developer needs to know the interface of a module only in order to use its services in another module.

There can be a *hierarchy of modules*. We need it for large systems. Its structure is documented in a *module guide*. The module guide describes the module structure by characterizing each module's secrets.

A fundamental *criterion for designing the module structure* of a software system is: identify the requirements and the design decisions that are likely to change, and encapsulate each as the secret of a separate module. If such a module is too large for one developer, the approach must be applied recursively. This leads to making the most stable design decisions first and those most likely to change last. The three top-level modules for almost any software system should be the hardware/platform-hiding module, the behaviour-hiding module and the software decision module. These modules must then be decomposed recursively, depending on the individual system. The structure presented in [PCW85] might serve as a template.

An *abstraction* of a set of entities is a description that applies equally well to any one of them. An *abstract interface* is an abstraction that represents more than one interface; it exactly and only consists of the assumptions that are included in all of the interfaces that it represents. A *device interface module* is a set of programs that translate between the abstract interface and the actual hardware interface [HBPP81]. Having an abstract interface for a device allows to replace the device during mainte-nance by another, similar model with a different hardware interface, without changing more than one module.

Information hiding enables to design software for ease of *extension and contrac-tion*. Design for change must include the identification of the minimal subset that might conceivably perform a useful service, and it must include the search for a set of minimal increments to the system [Par79]. The emphasis on minimality stems from the desire to avoid components that perform more than one function.

The *relation "uses"* among programs (i.e., pieces of code) describes a correctness dependency. A program A uses B if correct execution of B may be necessary for A to complete the task described in A's specification. We can facilitate the extension and contraction of a software, if we design the uses relation to be a hierarchy (i.e., loop-free), and if we restrict it as follows. A is allowed to use B only when all of the following conditions hold: (1) A is essentially simpler because it uses B. (2) B is not substantially more complex because it is not allowed to use A. (3) There is a useful subset containing B and not A. (4) There is no conceivably useful subset containing A but not B.

Information hiding is also a base for the design and development of *program families* (see Sect. 3.2). A set of programs constitutes a family, whenever it is worthwhile to study programs from this set by first studying the common properties of the set and then determining the special properties of the individual family member [Par76].

The single responsibility principle in *object-orientation* (see Chap. 4.1.1) is a reformulation of the information hiding principle, but with less details and with less advice. We will discuss this further in Sect. 5.4 below.

5.1.2   Families of Programs vs. Families of Requirements

A family of requirements needs a module structure, too, but the above kind of modules is not directly suitable. The above modules are a product of the software *design*. Their secret can be a requirement or a design decision. Their structure is a software design structure. Such artefacts of the software design do not belong into the software requirements. But we can adapt the idea.

5.2   Requirements Modules for Families of Requirements

A *requirements module* is a set of properties that are likely to change together. The likeliness of change of a property in a family is determined by its abstractness. The abstractness of a property in a family is determined by the share of the family in which the property is included in. A requirements module is an *abstract requirements specification*. An abstract requirements specification is a subset of properties of a single product. It will hold equally well for several or even all products of the product space.

The module structure for a family of requirements shall reduce the work to specify another member of the family. It shall restrict the addition of new requirements to a few places. And it shall help to ensure the consistency of the newly specified member.

5.2.1   Abstractness of a Property

Each of the properties is an *abstract requirement*. The property holds for all members of the family that include this property. This is in accordance with the definition of "abstract" above.

In principle, we could define a metric for the abstractness of a property. One property is more abstract than another if it is always included when the other is included, and at least for one more family member. A property is most abstract if it is included in all members of the family. We would need to assign concrete numbers for a complete metrics. Using the cardinality of the subset where the property is included is only one possibility. Any concrete metric should depend on the application domain. It should take the relative "importance" of family members into account.

In practice however, we will not use such a metric. It requires that we have access to the explicit specifications of all family members. This is not the case for the families of requirements in which we are interested. In practice, we can estimate the abstractness of a property only. However, we are only interested in qualitative, relative comparisons of abstractness, anyway. This suffices for the following considerations.

5.2.2 Likeliness of Change

We can regard the abstractness of a property as determining the *likeliness of its change*. When we step randomly from one family member to another one, the property will be added or removed with a likeliness that depends directly on its abstractness.

Please note that "likeliness of change" has a slightly different meaning with families of requirements than in design. A design module encapsulates details that are likely to change. "Change" in design means that the programs concerned are actually modified, the old version of the programs is discarded. There is no inherent configuration management in the classical information hiding approach. (Even though it can and should be added on top of it. See "families of programs" in Sect. 3.2). With families of requirements, we do not discard any property that we ever specified explicitly. We put it under configuration management. We include it in some versions of the requirements document, and we don't in others. Therefore, we do not need to protect a property against change in the classical sense.

We distinguish between the likeliness of change for a single property and the likeliness that a set of properties changes together. There can be a set of properties that is either included completely, or of which no element is included, for a large part of the family. In this case, there is a strong correlation of being included or not.

Both kinds of likeliness of change are important for a suitable requirements module structure. Properties that change together should be arranged together, in the description of the family of requirements. And the likeliness of change for a single property should determine whether other properties depend on it or not. The rationale for arranging properties together that change together is the historically proven success of the information hiding approach with design modules.

5.2.3 Right Size of Properties

The right size of the properties, when taken as the atomic objects of configuration management, depends on the size of the family. We must split up the requirements specification into small properties when a family of requirements has a large number of potentially specified members. We want to avoid to specify the same aspect A in two different properties. This can happen if we specify two aspects A, B in one property P_1 first and then need to specify A in another property P_2 again, because there is a family member that has A but not B.

In case of doubt, we should make a property in the requirements as small as possible while being useful. This is a safe strategy when we cannot overlook the entire set of family members easily. Such a specified property will be much smaller than the user of a new system or of a new feature usually thinks.

By small, we mean abstract in the above sense. A small property is part of the requirements of as many useful potential systems as possible. The goal is that each time a new member is specified, we will never need to copy and modify any existing property. The new member will only exchange one or more entire properties by one or more other properties.

5.3   A Hierarchy of Requirements Modules

We need a hierarchy of requirements modules to structure a large number of requirements. When we have a large number of requirements and therefore of requirements modules, we need some additional structure. It shall help the reader of a requirements document to find easily the module he/she is interested in. We structure the requirements modules analogously to the hierarchy of design modules [PCW85].

We propose to use a hierarchy of requirements modules. Each leaf module should consist of a relatively small number of properties that are quite likely to change together, as discussed above. These modules shall be grouped together into higher-level requirements modules. The criterion for grouping modules together is the same as above: the likeliness of changing together for the properties in these modules. This assumes that we have several degrees of correlation. The number of properties in a leaf module and the number of modules in a higher-level module should be so small that a reader can still grasp the structure of the module. If necessary, we repeat the grouping of modules recursively. At the top level, the properties of different modules should be most independent.

A criterion for the quality of the organization of the specified requirements modules is how many modules must be changed for obtaining another family member, on the average. These change costs must be weighted with the probability that the change actually occurs.

Having a hierarchy of requirements modules and sub-modules helps to make both small and larger changes. We assume that small changes are more probable than large changes. For a small change, it should suffice to change a small requirements sub-module far down in the hierarchy. For a larger change, we must touch a requirements module further up, which consists of several smaller sub-modules.

5.3.1   A Standard Hierarchy Structure

We propose a standard structure for a requirements module hierarchy. It has the same top-level structure as for design modules, which has historically proven to be suitable for almost all systems [Wei01]. There is only one major difference: the design module structure additionally has a software decision module. Such a module does not make sense for the requirements, obviously. Figure 5.1 summarizes the template requirements module hierarchy. We will present a concrete example of a requirements module decomposition in Sect. 6.5 below.

There usually should be two top-level modules: an environment module and a system behaviour module. The environment module specifies the relevant parts of the world that are assumed to exist by the system. If the pre-existing hardware

1. environment module

    1.1 computing platform module

    1.1.1 data type module

    1.1.2 (concurrent execution module)

    1.1.3 (distributed processing module)

    1.1.4 (...)

    1.2 device interface module

    1.2.1 device 1 module

    1.2.2 device 2 module

    1.2.3 ...

2. system behaviour module

    2.1 function driver module

    2.1.1 ...

    2.2 shared services module

    2.2.1 (...)

Figure 5.1: Template requirements module hierarchy.

or the pre-existing software changes, this module must be changed. The module hides the details of the world that vary for different family members. The system behaviour module specifies what the system to build effects in its environment. The module hides this behaviour as its secret. The behaviour is specified in terms of the abstractions provided by the environment module.

There is a cosmetic difference to the original names of the top-level modules [PCW85]: we renamed the "hardware-hiding module" to "environment module". In the original specification of the A-7 aircraft, the only environment of the software to build was the bare hardware. Hence the name of the module. Nowadays, there often is pre-existing software in the environment, too. An example is an operating system including a complete graphical user interface. Hence our more general name. Furthermore, as a consequence we slightly changed the name "behaviour-hiding module" to "system behaviour module". This gives us back the right contrast to the other module's name.

The second level from top should take the module hierarchy from [PCW85] as a template, too: the environment module should contain a computing platform module and a device interface module. The computing platform module hides those characteristics of the underlying computing platform that vary from one family member to another. In particular, it hides the details of the platform's native data types. If applicable, it also hides the platform's facilities for concurrent execution, for communication among the different, distributed locations of itself, and so on. The device interface module hides the varying details of the concrete peripheral devices that allow the software to achieve its goal in the physical world. There usually is one third-level module per device, the same detailed grouping rules as in [PCW85] apply.

Again there is a cosmetic difference in naming with respect to [PCW85]: We renamed the "extended computer module" to "computing platform module". The A-7 system ran on a single computer only, while nowadays many systems are distributed in nature. Hence our more general name.

The (top-level) system behaviour module should be composed of a function driver module and a shared services module that supports the function driver module. Each function driver module describes all properties of a set of closely related outputs. Outputs are considered closely related if it is easier to describe their values together than individually. The behaviour is specified in terms of the abstractions provided by the environment module, not in terms of concrete devices. Some aspects may be common to several function driver modules. If there is a change in that aspect of the behaviour, it will affect all of the function driver modules that share it. Such aspects should be grouped into third-level modules that are contained in the shared services module. In this case, the function driver modules shall contain a note that further properties can be found in the shared services module.

5.4 Object-Oriented Structuring Principles and Requirements Modules

The approach with a hierarchy of requirements modules conforms to the structuring principles for families of object-oriented programs in the literature; additionally, the requirements modules are grouped into a full-fledged hierarchy, while object-oriented code is grouped at the two levels of class and package only. We presented the principles from object-orientation in Chap. 4.1 above.

When we do a comparison, we have to keep two differences in mind: the slightly different domain and the different degree of detail. The structuring principles for families of object-oriented programs are formulated for design, not for requirements. Also, we first want to look at which basic principles we need and only then we want to introduce mechanisms. Several of the principles from object-orientation are formulated assuming that the mechanism of inheritance is available. We here do not (yet) assume this.

We now look at each of the structuring principles for families of object-oriented programs.

The single responsibility principle is a reformulation of the information hiding principle, but with less details and with less advice. The mechanism of the class is taken to realize the principle of a module. The guideline then is the same to put in only one secret / only one reason to change. But the single responsibility principle does not have the hierarchy of modules, the criterion for designing the module structure, and the clear definition that the interface between modules are the assumptions that they make about each other. In particular, the idea that a module may contain sub-modules is missing. The mechanism of inheritance in object-orientation is a rather different thing. Inheritance allows to delegate the processing of a message to a superclass and it allows to reuse the syntactic interface of a superclass, but it does not group classes together. More closely related is the mechanism of the package. A package contains a set of related classes (see Sect. 4.1.6 above).

The open-closed principle can be followed by finding suitable abstractions; finding suitable abstractions is at the heart of the criteria for designing a module structure. The emphasis of our approach on the likeliness of change is an emphasis on abstractness, and the sorting by the likeliness of change is a sorting by abstractness. We can apply the strategy pattern (compare Sect. 4.1.2 above) to satisfy the open-closed principle. The strategy pattern relies on abstract interfaces; we discuss their use with requirements modules in more detail in Sect. 6.4 below.

The Liskov substitution principle restricts the use of inheritance such that the open-closed principle is not violated; the Liskov substitution principle is not applicable here because we have not (yet) introduced the mechanism of inheritance anyway. Otherwise, our approach does allow to follow the open-closed principle, as just discussed. The technique of design by contract makes assumptions explicit, such that the Liskov substitution principle can be checked. Making assumptions explicit is part of our notion of interface: the interface is the set of assumptions that the modules make about each other.

The dependency inversion principle can be interpreted as the heuristic "depend on abstractions"; this is also a rule in the information hiding approach. An example are the device interface modules, as proposed in Sect. 5.3.1 above. We discuss abstract interfaces for requirements modules in more detail in Sect. 6.4 below. The notion of the "uses" hierarchy is an important part of the information hiding approach. The "uses" relation describes dependencies. We will present support for handling dependencies in Sect. 6.1 below.

The interface segregation principle is realized by our principle of splitting a "fat" interface into many small interface modules in Sect. 5.3.1 above, such that a client module must only depend on what it needs.

The six more principles for splitting a large software system into packages offer a simplified form of our hierarchical modules, but with only two levels of hierarchy: the class and the package.

> **The Release-Reuse Equivalence Principle** emphasizes that packages are self-contained, stable modules.

> **The Common Closure Principle** is the single-responsibility principle restated for packages.

> **The Common Reuse Principle** also says that a package shall be a cohesive module.

The Acyclic Dependencies Principle is closely related to the rule in information hiding that the "uses" relation shall be a hierarchy, i. e., free of cycles. Compare our support for handling dependencies in Sect. 6.1 below.

The Stable Dependencies Principle is closely related to our distinction between interface properties and secret properties in Sect. 6.3 below. This distinction prevents that unstable properties are depended upon.

The Stable Abstractions Principle and the stable dependencies principle combined amount to the dependency inversion principle for packages.

There is related work on object-orientation and information hiding. Andexer [And01] takes the documentation structure that was developed with the information hiding approach [PCW85] and applies it to object-oriented programs. The goal is the reduction of maintenance costs. Andexer also discusses Parnas' work on information hiding and how software should be structured, but he does not relate Parnas' work to the structuring ideas used within object-orientation.

5.5   Telephone Switching Family Architectures and Requirements Modules

Several recent architectures for families of telephone switching systems already separate some inportant concerns into modules and thereby avoid some kinds of undesired feature interactions. In Section 1.2.4, we already introduced to naive feature orientation, and we showed why it is attractive but also can promote undesired feature interactions. The Intelligent Network (IN) is the telephone switching industry's currently implemented response to the demand for new features. It follows a rather naive approach of feature orientation. Several more recent architectures separate some important concerns better. Nevertheless, we find that some undesired feature interactions can still happen in the new architectures; therefore we will come back to the idea of features in Chapter 7 below.

5.5.1   The Intelligent Network

The Intelligent Network (IN) [ITU01, GRKK93, DuVi92] is the telephone switching industry's currently implemented response to the demand for new features. We already introduced to it in Sect. 1.2.4 on naive feature orientation. We now show some prominent examples where our principles for requirements structuring are violated.

The specification of the Intelligent Network is oriented along execution steps. It is hard to specify a property of the IN without saying a lot about the exact sequencing of steps. The Basic Call Process consists of explicit automata with explicit triggering points, and the Service Independent Building Blocks of a feature are chained together by the explicit sequencing of the Global Service Logic. This violates the principle of making any single requirement as small and abstract as possible, and composing the base system and the features from these atomic properties.

The Service Independent Building Blocks (SIBs) provided in the standard [ITU97b] are designed to be general in the sense that they offer a lot of functionality. For example, the Charge SIB performs a special charging treatment for a call, and the Algorithm SIB applies a mathematical algorithm to data to produce a data result. Any details of the operations are controlled by run-time parameters. Any concrete system requirements document must specify which charging or calculating operations these SIBs support, respectively. From then on, it is likely that there will come up another operation not yet supported. This will require a change of the SIB concerned. This in turn threatens to break all other features using this SIB. SIBs therefore are usually not a unit of most abstract requirement.

The Basic Call Process itself violates the principle of making any single requirement as small and abstract as possible. It specifies many different aspects at the same time, as could be seen above. Instead of allowing for small requirements to be taken out and in, a monolithic specification provides hooks for changes of its behaviour. Few properties of its behaviour will be valid for all sets of features. It is hard to design a feature on top of this monolithic base system that will not break for some combination of features. If the base system would consist of smaller, explicitly stated properties with explicitly stated dependencies, then it would be easier to see which features are affected when a new feature removes a certain property.

One example is the step from the two-party call to the n-party session. The Basic Call Process is written in terms of the two-party call. Nevertheless, the Intelligent Network allows to combine several call legs. The n-party call is necessary for such features as Consultation Call, Conference Call, and Call Forwarding. Many features and SIBs are designed with the two-party call in mind, though. For example, the Screen SIB compares a data value against a list. If it is used to specify originating call screening, the screening can fail. Call Forwarding can translate the dialled number several times before making a connection. A single instance of the Screen SIB will check only one of the numbers. Even though the Basic Call Process insinuates that there is exactly one terminating side (Fig. 1.3), this property is not true for all systems.

The user interface is likely to change, nevertheless its concerns are spread out. This is so despite there being a User Interaction SIB that is intended to perform the user interaction for one feature. Most of the IN features need to interact with a user. This interaction must be possible through a scarce physical interface: twelve buttons, a hook switch, and a few signal tones. Ten of the buttons are used already by the base system. Physical signals must therefore be reused in different modes of operation. But the definitions of several features implicitly assume exclusive access to the user's terminal device. There is no single requirement that specifies the scheme how multiple features coordinate the access. The above interaction between a calling card feature and a voice mail feature is a consequence. Both features assume exclusive access to the "#" button. Details of the user interface are specified at the bottom of the requirements, even though they are likely to change. We discuss this in more detail in Chapter 8.

5.5.2   An Agent Architecture

An agent architecture is outlined by Zibman et. al. [ZWO+96]. It separates several concerns explicitly. There are four distinct types of agents: user agents, connection agents, resource agents, and service agents. This separates user and terminal concerns. The terminal resource agent encapsulates the user interface details, such as the signal syntax. The distinct user and connection agents separate call and connection concerns. The user agents bring the session abstraction with them. The connection agents coordinate multiple resource agents. The resource agent separates resource management from both session control and from the services.

It was a design goal that the introduction of new services should not require modifications of existing software. Therefore POTS is represented by a single service agent even though POTS really comprises several distinct concerns.

5.5.3   Tina, Race, and Acts

The Tina initiative (Telecommunication Information Network Architecture) [MaCo00, Ab+97], the Race project (Research and technology development in Advanced Communications technologies in Europe), and the Acts project (Advanced Communications Technologies & Services) developed and improved a new service architecture for telecommunications.

These projects have added most of the interesting new abstractions explicitly to the resulting architecture. For example, the explicit distinction between a user and a terminal device splits up the host of properties that can be associated with a directory number in the Intelligent Network. Therefore, the requirements of the base system are more structured than for the Intelligent Network. The drawback is that the architecture is quite far away from the structure of current systems, and a transition would be expensive.

5.5.4   The DFC Virtual Architecture

The DFC (Distributed Feature Composition) virtual architecture is proposed by Jackson and Zave [JaZa98]. It is implemented in an experimental IP telecommunication platform called BoxOS [BCP+04, ZGS04].

The DFC architecture allows to compose features in a pipe-and-filter network. The filter boxes are relatively simple. This is in accordance with the principle of small requirements. Also, several new abstractions are explicitly supported, for example multi-party sessions and the distinction among users, the different roles they play, and the different terminal devices they may use.

A strong point of BoxOS is that it can inter-operate with the existing telephone network. However, part of its functionality is lost for these calls, naturally.

5.5.5   Aphrodite

Aphrodite is an agent-based architecture for Private Branch Exchanges that has been implemented recently [Pin03].

Each entity, device and application service is represented as an agent. Agents are therefore abstractions. The often-changing details of the behaviour of an agent are specified as policies. Policies can be changed easily since they are stored as data in a table.

It is an explicit goal to make features small. For example, "transfer" is no longer a feature, but made up of three different smaller features: "invoke transfer", "try transfer", and "offer transfer". Another stated goal is to make the assumptions explicit that features make. Also, many new abstractions are already incorporated in the base system as "internal features".

5.5.6 Feature Interactions in the New Architectures

Some undesired feature interactions can still happen in the new architectures, such as Tina, though. This is so despite that Tina avoids several kinds of feature interactions which can occur in the IN, for example in the users' interface and due to limited network support. Violated assumptions or conflicting goals can still cause undesired feature interactions.

Kolberg and Magill [KoMa98] report that many undesired feature interactions known from the IN world can still happen between Tina services. Calling Number Delivery (CND) could be implemented in Tina. It allows its users to see the identification of the inviting party. Independently, Calling Number Delivery Blocking (CNDB) could be implemented. It allows its users to block the delivery of the identification information. When a user with CNDB invites a user with CND, it cannot be decided who has priority, and whether the identification information should be revealed. Tina does not provide any mechanisms to prevent such interactions, where user goals conflict.

We will come back to the idea of features in Chapter 7 below.

5.6 Support for Requirements Modules and Families in Existing Formalisms

Existing formal languages such as the well-known formalisms Z (see Sect. 2.2) and Object-Z [Smi00] do not fully support structuring by hierarchical requirements modules and by requirements families. Formal languages can be used to document requirements rigorously. Rigorous requirements are necessary to ensure the dependability of the software system. Embedded software systems are often expected to be dependable. The formalism Z is a well-known notation to describe properties of an information system precisely; however, we can express a module hierarchy and a family only informally. Object-Z is the most popular of several extensions of Z that add object-oriented mechanisms; however, it is not easier to express a module hierarchy in Object-Z than in plain Z, and it is *more* difficult to express a family. This is due to the fact that the standard object-oriented mechanisms have been added in Object-Z, but no package mechanism. A package mechanism would have made the ease of expression in Object-Z similar to plain Z. A host of other formal languages exists; we select Z here because it is comparably widely used. None of these other languages fully support structuring by hierarchical requirements modules, too.

5.6.1   Modularity and Families in the Formalism Z

The formalism Z (see Sect. 2.2) is a well-known notation to describe properties of an information system precisely; however, we can express a module hierarchy and a family only informally. Z offers basic support for modularity. But there is no formal way to express a multi-level hierarchy of modules. We can express a family of requirements by a suitable convention. But there are some limitations when we want to extract a single member of the family into a separate document automatically.

The Formalism Z

Z is a formalization of set theory; we can use it to specify a state transition system. Z allows to specify a mathematical theory. A specification has a formal meaning in terms of names and values. Every expression in Z has a type; the types can be checked by an automated tool for consistency. We have atomic mathematical objects, which can be put together to more complex objects. There is a rich mathematical toolkit which provides us with a large body of the usual mathematical notation in a well-defined way. Common conventions for Z allow to interpret the mathematical theory of a specification as a state transition system. Following these conventions, we describe the state space of the transition system by the set of values that a Z schema may take. We describe the state transition relation by other, special Z schemas called operations. And we describe the set of initial states by one more Z schema. See Section 2.2 for details.

Z is standardized by the International Standardization Organization (ISO) [Z02]. Before this official standardization, Z was defined for many years by Spivey's reference manual [Spi95]. The standard now provides a more detailed, well-structured definition of the syntax and semantics of Z. The standard also provides a few extensions to Spivey's Z. One of these extensions is a structuring means for a specification document.

Modularity

Z offers basic support for modularity. A schema allows to group variables together. A paragraph is the basic formal unit of structure for Z. A section and a specification are higher-level formal units of structure. The parents construct serves to specify the dependency relation among sections.

A schema   allows to group variables together. A schema is a signature together with a property of the signature. For the moment, we might think of the components of a schema as being simply the variables in its signature. Roughly speaking, the signature and property parts of a schema correspond to the declaration and predicate written in the text of the schema. The scope of a declaration of a schema is local to the schema.

But Z also allows global variables that are declared outside any schema. For example, the symbols "+" and "<" from the mathematical library are technically such global variables. We can introduce global variables by an *axiomatic description*. The global variables together with with their types form a global signature [Spi95].

A paragraph is the basic formal unit of structure for Z. A Z specification document consists of interleaved passages of formal text and informal prose explanation. The formal text consists of a sequence of paragraphs. A paragraph can be, for example, one type definition, one axiomatic description, or one schema definition. Spivey's Z already uses paragraphs [Spi95].

A section and a specification are higher-level formal units of structure. These are extensions by the ISO standard. The aim is to offer modest but useful functionality; it is considered as a starting point [Art95]. A *specification* consists of *sections*, which in turn consist of paragraphs. The meaning of a formal Z specification is the set of named theories established by its sections. Each section adds one named theory to the set established by its predecessors. A named theory associates a section name with a set of models.

The section construct allows for a constraint-oriented, incremental style of specification. Each section has a self-contained formal meaning. Any initial sequence of sections can be taken as the set of requirements for a variant of the specified system. Each further section adds more constraints on the system (and new declarations).

The specification and section constructs are optional. If they are not used, the entire set of paragraphs is considered to be a specification with one big section. This makes the ISO extension compatible to Spivey's Z.

The parents construct serves to specify the dependency relation among sections. The parents construct is part of the section construct. It lists the names of other sections of which the current section is an extension. Therefore, a section need not be an extension of the previous section; the sections may be arranged independently of their dependencies. Also, a section may have more than one parent section. In this case, the sets of models of the parents' theories are merged by a kind of logical conjunction.

Hierarchy of Modules

There is no formal way to express a multi-level hierarchy of modules. That is, there is no way to group related lower-level modules together into higher-level modules. It can be done informally only. We can have a hierarchy of informal chapters, sections, subsections and so on around the formal Z sections. But such an informal hierarchy is already sufficient to arrange together the formal sections according to their likeliness of change.

Families

We can express a family of requirements by a suitable convention. For this, we use the section construct together with the parents construct. The dependency relation is a hierarchy, i. e., acyclic. We can use the convention that each bottom leaf section in the hierarchy is one member of the family. Such a leaf section composes the desired properties from other, non-bottom sections through its parent construct.

Extracting a Family Member

We can extract a single member of the family into a separate document automatically, with some limitations. We must use the above convention that the leaves in the dependency hierarchy of sections each specify one family member. We then can indicate the family member desired through the name of the corresponding leaf section. A suitable tool can follow the dependency relation in order to identify all sections included in this family member. The tool then can copy the document with the family into another document, while deleting those sections that are not included.

A limitation is that we cannot select the appropriate informal text automatically. Each sections terminates implicitly at the start of the next section. There is no separate formal termination symbol. Where one section ends and another section starts, it is not clear how the informal text between these two formal parts should be split up. In particular, if there are higher-level, informal chapters, any informal closing remarks of the first section are merged inseparably with any following informal chapter heading. Furthermore, there is no way of determinining whether an informal chapter has become completely empty by the section de-selection process. Such an empty chapter should be removed, too. This avoids confusing empty chapter headings, possibly with informal introductory remarks to non-existing sections.

5.6.2   Modularity and Families in the Formalism Object-Z

Object-Z [Smi00] is the most popular of several extensions of Z that add object-oriented mechanisms; however, it is not easier to express a module hierarchy in Object-Z than in plain Z, and it is *more* difficult to express a family. Object-Z offers a basic support for modularity, too, but it is different from the one in plain Z. Object-Z is similar to plain Z in that there is no formal way to express a multi-level hierarchy of modules. Object-Z offers no easy way to express a family of requirements formally; it falls back behind plain ISO Z with this respect. Accordingly, there is no mechanizable way to extract a single member of a family into a separate document.

The Formalism Object-Z

Object-Z is a conservative extension of Spivey's version of Z [Spi95]; Object-Z adds the mechanisms of class, object, inheritance, and polymorphism. All syntax and semantics of Spivey's Z is also part of Object-Z. According to Smith [Smi00], a primary motivation for Object-Z was the need to enhance the structuring means in

Z for medium- to large-scale systems; a more fundamental motivation was the desire to investigate the integration of formal techniques with object-orientation.

A *class* groups together variables and operations on them; a class has an explicit syntactic interface. A class definition contains a single state schema, its initial state schema, and operation schemas. A class definition also contains a visibility list. It explicitly defines which variables and operations can be referred to from outside the class. Therefore, a class has an explicit signature (here not meant in the formal sense of Z). Class definitions may not be nested.

An *object* is an instance of a class. An object is identified uniquely by an object identity. An object is a persistent entity and continues to exist despite changes to its state. Object-Z has a reference semantics; a variable can have an object identity as its value. Object-Z does not support the creation and destruction of objects. Each object exists even if it is never actually referenced.

A class can *inherit* from another class. Multiple inheritance is allowed. The state schema, the operations, ... of an inherited-from class are merged with those of the inheriting class. Only the visibility list is never inherited and must be re-stated suitably for each subclass. The syntax for inheritance is simple. The names of the superclasses are written, without any further keyword, after the visiblility list and before the local definitions. Renaming allows to make arbitrary changes to a superclass in a subclass. The merging of schemas essentially only allows to restrict the superclass's schemas further. But by renaming operations (and variables), we can add entirely different operations (and variables) in the subclass under the same names.

Polymorphism allows a variable to contain an object that belongs to any one class from a particular inheritance hierarchy. An object itself always belongs to a unique class. The said inheritance hierarchy comprises a given class and all the classes which inherit, directly or indirectly, from this class. The syntactic interface of each subclass of the hierarchy must include all the variables, operations, ... of the given class. Otherwise, the specification is not well-formed.

The tool support for Object-Z includes the type checker Wizard [Joh96] and typesetting macros for LaTeX [Kin90]. There is also a number of other tools, e.g., for graphical editing and for animation. The Object-Z home page provides a current overview [Smi04].

Modularity

Object-Z offers a basic support for modularity that is different from the ISO standard Z. Object-Z does not provide the formal section construct from the ISO standard. Object-Z is based on the old version of Z by Spivey. Object-Z offers the class construct as the primary mechanism for modularity. Nevertheless, a paragraph is still the basic formal unit of structure for Object-Z. Formally, Object-Z adds the class as a new kind of paragraph. Therefore, Object-Z still allows all the different kinds of paragraphs of Z to be used, outside of any class. A paragraph can be, for example, one type definition, one axiomatic description, or one schema definition.

A modular specification can be achieved in Object-Z only by following a stylistic convention and under a limitation. One must abstain to use other kinds of paragraphs than classes. But this rises a difficulty with generic class definitions. A generic class definition needs globally defined actual parameters for instantiation. The actual parameters of a generic class are expressions defined in terms of previously defined global types and constants, and class names (and, if the inheriting class is also generic, in terms of the inherited-from class's formal parameters). Such previously defined global items would break the modularity. A solution is to also avoid generic class definitions in Object-Z. (At least with actual parameters that are not classes.) Meyer has shown that we can simulate genericity by inheritance (see Sect. 4.2.4). But he also observed that this is a bit awkward, in particular for unrestricted genericity [Mey88, Sect. 19.4].

Hierarchy of Modules

Object-Z is similar to plain Z in that there is no formal way to express a multi-level hierarchy of modules. Class definitions may not be nested. The mechanism of inheritance is a rather different thing, as we already argued in Sect. 5.4 above. Inheritance allows to delegate the processing of a message to a superclass and it allows to reuse the syntactic interface of a superclass, but it does not group classes together. More closely related is the mechanism of the package. A package contains a set of related classes. But the mechanism of the package is missing in Object-Z entirely. We only can have an informal hierarchy of modules, like in Z. We can have a hierarchy of informal chapters, sections, sub-sections and so on around the formal Object-Z classes. Anyway, the formal mechanism of the package only offers the two levels of the class and the package (Sect. 4.1.6).

Families

Object-Z offers no easy way to express a family of requirements formally; it falls back behind plain ISO Z with this respect. We cannot use the convention that the bottom leaf sections in the section dependency hierarchy denote the individual family members. Object-Z does not have the section construct of ISO Z. And we cannot sensibly use the class construct instead. If we said that each leaf class in the inheritance hierarchy denotes one family member, then each family member would consist of a single, large, monolithic class. Having only one single class would contradict the very idea of object-orientation. But there is no other formal construct in Object-Z for composing a set of classes together. In particular, there is no package construct.

Of course, we can describe a family of requirements informally. We just need to list informally which paragraphs and which informal text belongs to each family member.

Extracting a Family Member

There is no mechanizable way to extract a single member of a family into a separate document. This is because the family members can be described informally only. If one needs tool support nevertheless, one would have to add at least some ad-hoc extension of Object-Z that identifies the parts of the family members suitably.

Chapter 6

Supporting Mechanisms and Patterns for Requirements Modules

Several mechanisms and patterns for requirements modules can support the maintenance of requirements modules. Two mechanisms are explicit configuration constraints and explicit interfaces, a pattern is the abstract interface. Explicitly documenting, minimizing and checking the configuration constraints on requirements helps to get consistent configurations; we show how we can document such constraints in the formalism Z. We extend the formalism Z by a hierarchical module structure; via a further extension this is a necessary base for our feature construct in the next chapter. Explicit interfaces between requirements modules help to control dependencies between them; we also add them to our extension of the formalism Z. The pattern of the abstract interface between requirements modules helps to avoid dependencies on those requirements that change. We demonstrate our approach on an example, a family of LAN message services.

6.1 Explicit Configuration Constraints on Requirements

Explicitly documenting, minimizing and checking the configuration constraints on requirements helps to get consistent configurations; we show how we can document such constraints in the formalism Z. Configuration constraints limit the combinability of properties in a requirements document; the most common constraint is that one property depends on the presence of another property. We can minimize the dependencies among properties by several techniques. When we specify the configuration constraints explicitly and formally, this allows for a syntactic consistency check, possibly with tool support. Finally, we show how we can express dependencies in the formalism Z.

6.1.1   The Dependency Relation Among Properties

Configuration constraints limit the combinability of properties in a requirements document; the most common constraint is that one property depends on the presence of another property. The requirements dependency relation needs a careful definition: we must not equal it with the requirements module hierarchy, and we must not define it over higher-level requirements modules.

Definition: a property P_2 *depends* on a property P_1, if P_2 is not well-formed without the presence of P_1.

In particular, declarations cause dependencies. For example, P_1 introduces a variable monitored by the system, such as the position of a button. P_2 determines the system behaviour depending on the value of this variable. P_2 would not make sense without the variable being declared. Such declarations can both be about variables representing concrete physical values or about variables representing some abstraction.

Our definition helps to ensure that all configurations which we ever generate will consist, by definition, of well-formed properties. For this, we must generate only configurations which respect the dependency relation. This is the configuration constraint that when a property is part of this configuration, also all the properties on which it depends must be part of the configuration. By explicitly forbidding a dependency of property P_2 on property P_1, we can demand that the absence of P_1 must not prevent P_2 from being well-formed. The mechanism of the explicit module interface below will allow us to forbid dependencies. This allows us to ensure that all potential configurations will be well-formed, without actually generating and checking all of them individually.

The requirements dependency relation is quite different from the requirements module hierarchy; we must take great care to not confuse them. In general, there is not necessarily a correlation between two abstract requirements depending on each other, and being likely to change together. For example, Figure 6.7 on page 113 shows both the dependency relation and the requirements module hierarchy of the LAN message service family example introduced in Sect. 6.5 below. In this example, property broadcast_message_delivery depends on property comm_params_base, but they are absolutely unlikely to change together. They are from two different top-level modules. The former is an optional, easily changing requirement on the system behaviour. The latter is a basic device abstraction that probably never will change. On the other hand, property c_text_string and property pascal_text_string are from the same sub-module and are likely to change together, but they do not depend on each other. The are likely to change together because it is usually not useful to add both properties to the same system. The relationship of requirements modules and requirements dependencies is similar to the relationship of design modules and the design "uses" relation among programs. (See Sect. 5.1 above.)

We must not define the requirements dependency relation over higher-level requirements modules. The dependency relation is among properties, not among modules. Otherwise, we would introduce additional, artificial dependencies. For example in Figure 6.7 on page 113, many properties depend on property comm_params_base, and property comm_params_base in turn depends on property time_base. If the dependency instead would be on the entire module time, then all the many properties would depend on the easily-changing property time_milliseconds, too.

6.1.2 Minimizing the Dependencies Among Properties

We can minimize the dependencies among properties by several techniques. We can try to localize the dependencies inside modules. We can look for properties with a high degree of dependency on other modules and try to fix this. We can avoid circular dependencies. We can restrict dependencies to the (explicit) interfaces of requirements modules only.

Localizing Dependencies Inside Modules

We can try to localize the dependencies inside modules. This was the subject of the previous chapter. If all modules have cohesion, then there is only a small number of inter-module dependencies.

Looking For and Fixing a High Degree of Dependency

We can look for properties with a high degree of dependency on other modules and try to fix this. A property that depends on many other properties is probably not minimal and could be split up. Each property must be formulated such that is a minimal useful increment. The search for minimal increments is an adaption of the corresponding strategy for design information hiding modules, as discussed in in Sect. 5.1 above. It is also another formulation of the single responsibility principle in object-orientation (see Sect. 4.1.1 above).

The dependencies are, in our experience, a good means to check the minimality of properties. In our LAN message service family example in Figure 6.7 on page 113 in Sect. 6.5 below, only two properties depend on more than two other properties. These properties introduce the basic parameters for communication events. We could have split them up further, too. But since these basic parameters are so very basic, we could not imagine a system that does not need all of them. Therefore, we kept the specification a little simpler. All remaining properties indeed depend on two other properties at most.

There is related work on measuring dependencies by Martin [Mar03] for agile programming, even though the goal is different. For object-oriented programs, Martin counts the program dependencies that enter and leave a package. This renders a stability metrics. A package with many incoming dependencies is very stable because it requires much work to reconcile any changes with all the dependend packages. Martin follows the stable dependencies principle (see Sect. 4.1.6) by recommending that any package that we expect to be volatile should not be depended on by a package that is difficult to change. Otherwise the volatile package will also be difficult to change. In the programming language C++, dependencies are typically represented by #include statements. In the programming language Java, we can count import statements and qualified names.

Avoiding Circular Dependencies

We can avoid circular dependencies. The dependency relation among the properties should be a partial order, that is, a *hierarchy*. Circular dependencies are bound to make many properties depend on many other properties. The technique of sandwiching (see [Par79, p. 289] for sandwiching of programs) can help to resolve circular dependencies: if P_1 depends on P_2, and P_2 depends on P_1, it might be possible to split up P_1 into P_{1_1} and P_{1_2}, such that P_{1_2} depends on P_2 (and on P_{1_1}) and P_2 depends on P_{1_1}. Such sandwiching can also be viewed as an application of the dependency inversion principle (see Sect. 4.1.4): in this case, P_{1_1} is the abstraction that becomes the common interface for P_1 and P_2.

Restricting Dependencies to the Interfaces of Modules

We can restrict dependencies to the (explicit) interfaces of requirements modules only. For this, we must introduce the notion of an interface for a requirements module first. This is worth an entire section on its own. We therefore postpone the details of this issue to Sect. 6.3 below. This allows us to complete the discussion of dependencies among properties first.

6.1.3   Checking the Configuration Constraints

When we specify the configuration constraints explicitly and formally, this allows for a syntactic consistency check, possibly with tool support. Such an automatic check supports the maintainers of a family of requirements. Without it, they must either have a very good overview knowledge of the entire family, or they must do manual checks for any change or addition. This will be difficult for a large, complex family. To specify explicit configuration constraints means to specify an explicit dependency relation among properties, in particular. If a depended-on property is not present in a configuration, while the depending property is present, this is inconsistent. A tool can reject outright any attempt to select such a configuration. We will present some tool support for such a dependency analysis in Chap. 7.7 below.

The best time to document a dependency is when it is created. The original author of a property probably has the best understanding of the property.

6.1.4   Support for Dependencies in the Formalism Z

We now show how we can express dependencies in the formalism Z. We can specify dependencies among properties by using the section/parents construct. For this, we follow the convention that each formal section holds exactly one property each. This is a rather natural convention.

From now on, we will always refer to the ISO version of Z [Z02], not Spivey's Z [Spi95]. Only the ISO version of Z offers the constructs for modularity we need, as discussed in Sect. 5.6.1 above.

A section and a specification are higher-level formal units of structure, as already said in Sect. 5.6.1. A specification consists of sections, which in turn consist of the different kinds of paragraphs. The parents construct serves to specify the dependency relation among sections. The parents construct is part of the section construct. It lists the names of other sections of which the current section is an extension. Therefore, a section need not be an extension of the previous section; the sections may be arranged independently of their dependencies. Also, a section may have more than one parent section. In this case, the sets of models of the parents' theories are merged by a kind of logical conjunction.

The section/parents construct can express a dependency relation in the sense of Sect. 6.1.1. First, if a section S_2 needs another section S_1 to be well-formed, then S_1 must be in a parents relationship with S_2 (either directly or by transitive closure). Second, the parents relation is cleanly separated from the submodule/supermodule relation, as required in Sect. 6.1.1. (If we use an informal submodule/supermodule relation as proposed in Sect. 5.6.1.) Third, the dependency relation is defined over sections, i.e. properties, not over higher-level modules. This avoids the introduction of additional, artificial dependencies. Therefore, all conditions on the definition of a dependency relation from Sect. 6.1.1 are met.

6.2 Adding Formal Hierarchical Modules to the Formalism Z

We now extend the formalism Z by a hierarchical module structure; via a further extension this is a necessary base for our feature construct in the next chapter. This extension itself only fixes a minor limitation of Z. We add a "chapter" construct on top of the existing "section" construct of Z. A chapter groups sections together. It may also group other chapters together. This allows for a full hierarchy of chapters, sub-chapters, and sections. A chapter is different from a section in that it has no parents construct. This is because the dependency relation should be defined over individual properties, i.e., sections, not over higher-level modules, i.e., chapters, as discussed in Sect. 6.1.1 above. One can derive the dependency relation for the chapters through forming a suitable hull of the dependency relation for the sections. The chapter construct has no formal semantics (for now); it is "syntactic sugar" only. It will get a semantics when we extend the language further and add interfaces between sections and between chapters in Sect. 6.3, and when we add a feature construct in Chap. 7.

We now first recapitulate the way the relevant part of the syntax and semantics of plain Z is defined. We then propose our extension of Z by a chapter construct.

6.2.1 Syntax and Semantics of Z

We now present the formal syntax and formal semantics of ISO Z's constructs for modularity [Z02]; an informal introduction can be found in Sect. 5.6.1 above. The standard defines the syntax and the semantics of Z in eight phases, see Tab. 6.1. The relevant phases for our purposes are mark-up, lexing, parsing, type inference, and the semantic relation. In order to ease reading, we present the first three phases in

Table 6.1: The eight phases of the definition of ISO Z.

definition phase	product
	source text
mark-up	↓
	sequence of Z characters
lexing	↓
	sequence of Z tokens
parsing	↓
	parse tree of concrete syntax sentence
characterizing	↓
	characterized parse tree of concrete syntax sentence
syntactic transformation	↓
	parse tree of annotated syntax sentence
type inference	↓
	fully annotated parse tree of annotated syntax sentence
semantic transformation	↓
	fully annotated parse tree of sentence of subset of annotated syntax
semantic relation	↓
	meaning in ZF set theory

reverse order here and start with the syntax first, that is, the parsing phase.

Syntax

A specification consists of sections, which in turn consist of paragraphs. A paragraph can be, for example, one type definition or one schema definition. A specification may consist directly of paragraphs instead of sections, too. (In this case, there is a single, implicit, anonymous section.) The parents construct is part of the section construct. It is optional; a base section may leave it out entirely. The relevant part of the BNF grammar of the concrete syntax is:

```
Specification  =  { Section }
               |  { Paragraph }
               ;
      Section  =  ZED , section , NAME , parents , [ NAME , { ,-tok , NAME} ] , END ,
                  { Paragraph }
               |  ZED , section , NAME , END , { Paragraph }
               ;
    Paragraph  =  ...
```

The non-terminal symbols that are written in MixedCase are defined within this grammar. The others are defined in the lexis.

Lexis

The lexical analysis phase groups Z characters to tokens. For example, the string of Z characters 'p', 'a', 'r', 'e', 'n', 't', 's' is converted to the token "parents". In particular, the Z character ZEDCHAR is converted to the token ZED, and the Z character ENDCHAR is converted to the token END. Both characters have their own Unicode [ISO93] code position.

Mark-Up

A mark-up allows to represent all of the many characters of Z on machines that have only a small character set. The definitive representation of Z characters is in 16-bit Unicode [ISO93]. A mark-up is a mapping to the Unicode representation. There is a mark-up for the typesetting system LaTeX [Lam86, MGB$^+$04] and a light-weight one for email in the standard. The mark-up phase additionally has a rather "high-level" duty, it takes care of the right order of sections.

LaTeX mark-up. The input "\begin{zsection}" is converted to the Z character ZEDCHAR, and the input "\end{zsection}" is converted to the Z character ENDCHAR. In context, a Z section heading thus looks like:

```
\begin{zsection}
\SECTION NAME \parents ...
\end{zsection}
```

Most keywords, like "parents", can be written straightforwardly. Usually, one simply prepends a backslash. An exception is the keyword "section", whose spelling collides with the LaTeX macro "\section{...}". This is why the above macro "\SECTION" is in uppercase.

Email mark-up. The input "%%Z" is converted to the Z character ZEDCHAR, and the input "%%" is converted to the Z character ENDCHAR. In context, a Z section heading thus looks like:

```
%%Z
section NAME parents ...
%%
```

Permutation of sections. The mark-up phase also takes care of the right order of sections. The later phases assume a definition-before-use order for sections. Nevertheless, this restriction is not necessary for the presentation to a human reader or to a tool. Therefore, the mark-up phase recognizes the section headers and then permutes the sections suitably.

Type Inference Rules

All expressions in Z are typed; the type inference rules allow for an automated check of the well-typedness of a Z specification. The type inference rules produce a set of constraints on a set of special variables. For a well-typed specification, the solution of these constraints must provide exactly one value for each of these variables.

Examples of such special variables are *type environments*, which are partial, finite functions that associate names to sets of type values, *section-type environments*, which associate names of declarations with a pair out of the name of the ancestral section that originally declared the name and its type, and *section environments*, which associate section names with section type environments.

The type inference rule for an entire specification describes the constraints on the section environments of the individual sections. Essentially, the section environment δ_{k+1} of each section i_k is equal to the section environment δ_k of its predecessor section i_{k-1}, merged with a mapping from its own section name i_k to its own section-type environment Γ_k:

$$\delta_{k+1} = \delta_k \cup \{i_k \mapsto \Gamma_k\}$$

The full type inference rule is [Z02, Sect. 13.2.1.1]:

$$\frac{\{\} \vdash^S s_{prelude} \,\, {}^{\circ}_{\circ}\, \Gamma_0 \quad \delta_1 \vdash^S s_1 \,\, {}^{\circ}_{\circ}\, \Gamma_1 \quad \dots \quad \delta_n \vdash^S s_n \,\, {}^{\circ}_{\circ}\, \Gamma_n}{\vdash^Z \quad s_1 \,\, {}^{\circ}_{\circ}\, \Gamma_1 \quad \dots \quad s_n \,\, {}^{\circ}_{\circ}\, \Gamma_n} \left(\begin{array}{l} \delta_1 = \{prelude \mapsto \Gamma_0\} \\ \vdots \\ \delta_n = \delta_{n-1} \cup \{i_{n-1} \mapsto \Gamma_{n-1}\} \end{array} \right)$$

The (more complex) type inference rule for a section imposes nine constraints. They link a section to its paragraphs, and they relate a section to its parents. Some of the constraints are: the name of the section, i, is different from that of any previous section; the names in the parents list are names of known sections; the section-type environment γ_0 is a merge of those of the parents; and the type environment β_0 is determined from the section-type environment γ_0. We omit the lengthier of the constraints here for brevity; see [Z02, Sect. 13.2.2.1] for the details.

Semantic Transformation Rules

There are no semantic transformation rules for specifications or for sections; but we will add one for our new chapter construct below. Z has semantic transformation rules for a few other constructs.

Semantics

The semantic relations define the meaning by sets of models in ZF set theory. The meaning of a Z specification is a function from sections' names to their sets of models. The meaning is an element of the set *SectionModels*, which is defined as:

$$SectionModels == \text{NAME} \nrightarrow \mathbb{P}\, Model$$

A model associates Z names with values from the semantic universe $\mathbb{U}$:

$$Model == \text{NAME} \nrightarrow \mathbb{U}$$

The above sets of models are formed by starting with the empty function and extending that with a maplet from a section's name to its set of models for each section.

As a consequence of this definition, there can be several meaningful units within a document. The meaning of a specification is not simply the meaning of its last section. Each section has its own meaning. Nevertheless, there is no formal way to indicate which section should be regarded as a meaningful unit, and which section exists only as a base for other sections.

6.2.2 Z_{Ch}: Extending Z by a Chapter Construct

We now propose our extension of Z by a chapter construct. We call the extended language Z_{Ch}. In the syntax grammar, we insert the chapter construct between the specification construct and the section construct. We also extend the lexis and the mark-up suitably. The latter, quite suprisingly, needs special care. We then add a type inference rule for chapter names. A new semantic transformation rule eliminates the new chapter construct after the type inference phase. Thus, the definition of the semantics remains unchanged; there is no formal meaning for a chapter (yet). Finally, we show an example of a usage.

Syntax

The modified part of the BNF grammar is:

$$
\begin{array}{rcl}
\text{Specification} & = & \{\,\text{Chapter}\ |\ \text{Section}\,\} \\
& | & \{\,\text{Paragraph}\,\} \\
& ; & \\
\text{Chapter} & = & \text{ZED}\,,\text{chapter}\,,\text{NAME}\,,\text{END}\,,\{\,\text{Section}\,\}\,, \\
& & \text{ZED}\,,\text{endchapter}\,,[\,\text{NAME}\,]\,,\text{END} \\
& | & \text{ZED}\,,\text{chapter}\,,\text{NAME}\,,\text{END}\,,\{\,\text{Chapter}\,\}\,, \\
& & \text{ZED}\,,\text{endchapter}\,,[\,\text{NAME}\,]\,,\text{END} \\
& ; & \\
\text{Section} & = & \dots \\
\text{Paragraph} & = & \dots
\end{array}
$$

Note that we introduced an explicit token that delimits the end of a chapter. Otherwise, the grammar would have become ambiguous. For example, take the string "chap sect sect". In such a string, it is not clear whether it should be parsed as "chap (sect sect)" or as "(chap sect) sect".

We add one context-sensitive rule to the syntactic grammar: the optional NAME after the token "endchapter", if it exists, must be the same as the NAME after the corresponding token "chapter". The optional NAME has no meaning; it shall be dropped after the syntax check. The repetition of the NAME is intended to improve readability when a chapter is long and the reader might have lost a part of the context.

All specifications in Z are also specifications in Z_{Ch} (with the same meaning). The only exceptions are those specifications in Z that use the two new keywords "chapter" and "endchapter". These specifications are not legal in Z_{Ch} anymore.

Lexis

We add the two new alphabetic keywords and associated tokens to the lexis. The lexis specifies a function from sequences of Z characters to sequences of tokens. The new keywords are "chapter" and "endchapter", obviously.

Mark-Up

We define suitable mark-ups for the new keywords; and we take care of sections that are permuted by the mark-up phase.

LATEX mark-up. Unfortunately, the LATEX macros "\chapter" and "\endchapter" are already reserved. We solve this in the same way as for the keyword "section". In the LATEX mark-up of Z_{Ch}, the input "\begin{zchapter}" is converted to the Z character ZEDCHAR, and the input "\end{zchapter}" is converted to the Z character ENDCHAR. The input "\CHAPTER" is converted to the string "chapter", followed by a space. In context, a Z_{Ch} chapter heading thus looks like:

```
\begin{zchapter}
\CHAPTER NAME
\end{zchapter}
```

Furthermore, the input "\ENDCHAPTER" is converted to the string "endchapter". In context, a Z_{Ch} chapter end thus looks like:

```
\begin{zchapter}
\ENDCHAPTER NAME
\end{zchapter}
```

Here, the chapter end is enclosed in the same LATEX environment as the chapter heading. This helps to ensure that the chapter heading and the chapter end are typeset in the same way.

We suggest that the LATEX environment zchapter might provide a suitable automatic, hierarchical chapter numbering scheme when typesetting. This can aid the reader. The environment might also set LATEX labels with the \label{...} macro. This allows references to the chapter numbers in the informal text from other parts. Furthermore, the already existing LATEX environment zsection might be adapted to be typeset similar to zchapter. When this is done, the already existing \parents command might be extended to switch back to normal font and to start a new paragraph. We implemented a LATEX style that follows this suggestion. We discuss it in Chapter 7.7.1.

Email mark-up. The email markup is straightforward. In context, a Z section heading looks like:

```
%%Z
chapter NAME
%%
```

Permutation of sections. The possibility that the sections are permuted in the mark-up phase complicates the extension. In Z_{Ch}, the mark-up phase must perform an additional transformation.

As discussed in Sect. 6.2.1 above, the mark-up phase additionally has a rather "high-level" duty, it takes care of the right order of sections. The mark-up phase recognizes the section headers and then permutes the sections in order to achieve a definition-before-use order for sections. This permutation of sections must be independent of the association of sections to chapters. We discussed the difference between the requirements dependency relation and the requirements module hierarchy in depth in Sect. 6.1.1 above. In the original input document, the sections of the requirements should be grouped into a hierarchy of requirements modules. But this grouping may be destroyed by the permutation of sections. We therefore have to extend the permutation process suitably.

In Z_{Ch}, the mark-up phase must perform an additional transformation. In the case when sections change order, it copies the applicable chapter headings in front of each individual section heading. As a consequence, each chapter heading may appear many times in the document. But each section is fully qualified with the chapters and sub-chapters that it is part of. Additionally, the mark-up phase must insert the corresponding "endchapter" markers. Of course, this demands that the mark-up phase not only parses the section headings as before, but that it also recognizes all chapter headings and that it keeps track of the hierarchical chapter structure.

We regard this additional transformation in the mark-up phase as a little unfortunate. It already includes a restricted lexing and parsing functionality in the mark-up phase. But it is an inevitable consequence of the decision of the authors of the Z standard to perform the permutation of the sections in the mark-up phase. Any other solution would have to change this first, and it would be a substantial deviation from the Z standard.

Type Inference Rules

We add a type inference rule for chapter names. It takes care that the chapter hierarchy is consistent, and that chapter names are different from section names.

Here, let c denote a chapter name (and not a digit within a NUMERAL phrase, as elsewhere).

Informally, the constraints on chapter names and section names are:

- The *chapter environment* Υ_c *of the chapter* c is a mapping from the chapter name c to the sequence of the names of the higher-level chapters in the chapter hierarchy which contain the chapter. The sequence is ordered top-down according to the hierarchy. The last element of the sequence is always c, the name

$$
\dfrac{\vphantom{X}}{\substack{\vdash^{c} \quad \text{ZED chapter } c_{1,1} \text{ END}}}
\left(
\begin{array}{l}
\Upsilon_{c_{1,1}} = c_{1,1} \mapsto \langle c_{1,1} \rangle \\[4pt]
\Upsilon_{c_{1,2}} = c_{1,2} \mapsto \langle c_{1,1}, c_{1,2} \rangle \\[4pt]
\quad\vdots \\[4pt]
\Upsilon_{c_{n,m-1}} = c_{n,m-1} \mapsto \langle c_{n,1}, \ldots, c_{n,m-1} \rangle \\[4pt]
\Upsilon_{c_{n,m}} = c_{n,m} \mapsto \langle c_{n,1}, \ldots, c_{n,m} \rangle \\[4pt]
\Psi = \{ \Upsilon_{c_{1,1}} \} \cup \{ \Upsilon_{c_{1,2}} \} \cup \ldots \cup \\[4pt]
\qquad \{ \Upsilon_{c_{n,m-1}} \} \cup \{ \Upsilon_{c_{n,m}} \} \\[4pt]
\Psi \subseteq (\operatorname{dom} \Psi \twoheadrightarrow \operatorname{ran} \Psi) \\[4pt]
\operatorname{dom} \Psi \cap \{ i_1, \ldots, i_n \} = \varnothing
\end{array}
\right)
$$

$\quad\quad$ ... $\quad$ ZED chapter $c_{1,l}$ END

$\quad s_1 \quad$ ZED endchapter END

$\quad\quad$ ... $\quad$ ZED endchapter END

$\quad$ ...

ZED chapter $c_{n,1}$ END

$\quad\quad$ ... $\quad$ ZED chapter $c_{n,m}$ END

$\quad s_n \quad$ ZED endchapter END

$\quad\quad$ ... $\quad$ ZED endchapter END

Figure 6.1: The added type inference rule for chapter names in Z_{Ch}.

of the chapter itself. The constraint is that for all chapters c, their chapter environment Υ_c is uniquely defined.

- The name of a chapter is different from that of any section.

We introduced the first constraint because any chapter name may appear multiple times in a specification. This is due to the possible reordering of sections in the mark-up phase allowed by the Z standard. Nevertheless, multiple appearances must leave the chapter hierarchy consistent.

We introduced the second constraint in order to have a common name space for chapters and sections. This is not strictly necessary. But we think that separate name spaces could be confusing for a reader.

The formal type inference rule is presented in Fig. 6.1. In the rule, i_k denotes the name of the section s_k. For simplicity, we assume that all section headings have been fully qualified with their chapter headings, in the way discussed above. Of course, there may be sections outside of any chapters. For them, no constraints arise among chapter names.

Semantic Transformation Rules

Z_{Ch} adds a semantic transformation rule that eliminates the chapter construct; this formally defines chapters to have no meaning of their own. This transformation is necessary to link the meaning of the sections to the meaning of the entire specification. The transformation could not be done at an earlier, syntactic phase because

---

1. chapter environment
1.1 chapter computing_platform
1.1.1 chapter data_types
1.1.1.1 chapter text_strings
1.1.1.1.1 section text_string_base
...

1.1.1.1.2 section c_text_string
...

endchapter text_strings
1.1.1.2 chapter graph_images
1.1.1.2.1 section graph_image_base
...

endchapter graph_images
endchapter data_types
...

endchapter computing_platform
...

endchapter environment
2. chapter system_behaviour
...

endchapter system_behaviour

Figure 6.2: A simplified example usage of Z_{Ch}, our Z extension for a chapter construct, extracted from the specification in Appendix A.

the type inference rules must be applied first. The formal rule is:

$$
\frac{\text{ZED chapter } c_1 \text{ END } \ldots \text{ ZED chapter } c_m \text{ END} \quad s}{\text{ZED endchapter END } \ldots \text{ ZED endchapter END}}
$$
$$
\Longrightarrow
$$
$$
s
$$

Example of a Usage

To illustrate our extension, Fig. 6.2 shows a simplified example of a usage from our family of LAN message services in Appendix A.

6.3 Explicit Interfaces Between Requirements Modules

Explicit interfaces between requirements modules help to control dependencies between them; we also add them to our extension of the formalism Z. The interface between requirements modules is the set of assumptions that they make about each other. A property that is likely to change should not be depended upon by properties from other modules; distinguishing between interface properties and secret properties of a module is a mechanism to avoid this. We add this mechanism to the formalism of Z, too.

6.3.1 Definition of an Interface Between Requirements Modules

Our notion of interface is not restricted to syntax. We follow the definition of an interface between design modules in Sect. 5.1.1 closely and define: the *interface* between requirements modules is the set of *assumptions* that they make about each other.

This not only includes syntactic conventions, but also any assumptions on the behaviour of the other modules. A developer needs to know the interface of a module only in order to use its services in another module.

6.3.2 The Mechanism of the Interface

Properties and also entire requirements modules must be marked with their likeliness of change. This helps a specifier to make new properties depend only on properties that are sufficiently stable.

One mechanism for this is to partition all properties in a module into interface properties and secret properties. An interface property must be present in all configurations where the module is present. A secret property may be missing in some of them. Similarly, a higher-level module can be partitioned into interface sub-modules and secret sub-modules. Again, the interface properties of interface sub-modules must always be present when the module is present, while they don't for secret sub-modules.

Explicit interfaces make syntactic checks possible. If dependencies are explicit, too, a syntactic check can ensure that there is no dependency on a secret property from outside its module. And it can ensure that there is no dependency on any of the properties of a secret sub-module from outside its module. In this way, we can prevent dependencies on properties that are likely to change.

This mechanism of interfaces and secrets is the same as in design. In design, an interface consists in the assumptions that the interfacing modules make about each other. That means that these properties must be true regardless of the changing secret details inside a design module. Programming languages that support interfaces provide a partial, syntactic check. This check ensures that at least no secret identifiers are referenced from outside of the design module.

We will present a concrete example of a family of requirements with explicit interfaces in Sect. 6.5 below.

6.3.3 Support for Module Interfaces in the Formalism Z

Z provides no mechanism to specify interfaces between requirements modules formally. This is because there is no formal way to express higher-level requirements modules in Z, as discussed in Sect. 5.6.1 above. With only one level of modules, there are no sub-modules that could be hidden. A requirements module is represented by the mechanism of the section. In Sect. 6.1.4, we introduced the convention that each formal section holds exactly one property each. This convention was necessary to express dependencies between properties formally in Z. Plain ISO Z provides no formal structure on top of sections.

Our extension Z_{Ch} from the previous section provides formal higher-level modules, but still no way to hide sub-modules.

Please note that Z schemas provide some degree of encapsulation, but that they are no candidate for representing a requirements module. The basic formal unit of structure for Z is the paragraph, see Sect. 5.6.1. A paragraph may contain one schema, but alternatively it may contain other things, too. For example, Z allows global variables that are declared outside of any schema.

6.3.4 Z_{CI}: Extending Z by a Chapter Interface Construct

We now propose our extension of Z_{Ch} by a chapter interface construct. We call this extended language Z_{CI}. In the syntax grammar, we allow to prefix a section or a chapter with the new keyword "private". We also extend the lexis and the markup suitably. We add a suitable type inference rule to restrict the access to private sections and chapters. Otherwise, the definition of the semantics remains unchanged. Finally, we show an example of a usage. We do not yet introduce a formal mechanism for actually selecting configurations; this is the subject of Chap. 7 below.

Syntax

We need to replace two rules in the BNF grammar of the concrete syntax of Z_{Ch}. The new rules optionally allow the new keyword "private" before the keywords "chapter" and "section".

$$
\begin{aligned}
\texttt{Chapter} \;=\; & \texttt{ZED}\,,[\,\texttt{private}\,]\,,\texttt{chapter}\,,\texttt{NAME}\,,\texttt{END}\,,\{\,\texttt{Section}\,\}\,, \\
& \texttt{ZED}\,,\texttt{endchapter}\,,[\,\texttt{NAME}\,]\,,\texttt{END} \\
\mid\; & \texttt{ZED}\,,[\,\texttt{private}\,]\,,\texttt{chapter}\,,\texttt{NAME}\,,\texttt{END}\,,\{\,\texttt{Chapter}\,\}\,, \\
& \texttt{ZED}\,,\texttt{endchapter}\,,[\,\texttt{NAME}\,]\,,\texttt{END} \\
; \\
\texttt{Section} \;=\; & \texttt{ZED}\,,[\,\texttt{private}\,]\,,\texttt{section}\,,\texttt{NAME}\,, \\
& \texttt{parents}\,,[\,\texttt{NAME}\,,\{\,\texttt{,-tok}\,,\texttt{NAME}\}\,]\,,\texttt{END}\,,\{\,\texttt{Paragraph}\,\} \\
\mid\; & \texttt{ZED}\,,[\,\texttt{private}\,]\,,\texttt{section}\,,\texttt{NAME}\,,\texttt{END}\,,\{\,\texttt{Paragraph}\,\} \\
;
\end{aligned}
$$

Lexis

We add the new alphabetic keyword and associated token to the lexis. The new keyword is "private", obviously.

Mark-Up

We define a suitable mark-up for the new keyword. In LaTeX mark-up, the input "\private" is converted to the string "private", followed by a space. The email mark-up is trivial: "private".

Type Inference Rules

We add a second type inference rule for chapter names to the one we introduced for Z_{Ch}; it restricts the access to private sections and chapters.

The type inference rule for Z_{Ch} remains; only the optional "private" token must be added in the phrase for a section. We omit this for brevity here.

We introduce the additional notion of a *chapter interface environment* Υ_c^I. It is similar to a chapter environment Υ_c. But the sequence of chapter names is replaced by a sequence of pairs of a chapter name and a flag. The flag indicates whether this chapter is private. We also add the notion of a chapter interface environment Υ_s^I for a section. It is constructed exactly analogously as for chapters. The set of all possible chapter interface environments for sections shall be ChapIfEnv.

Furthermore, we need two functions on chapter interface environments for sections. The *closest common super-chapter ccsc* for two sections s_a and s_b is that chapter name which appears in the sequences of both sections, and which does so in the latest position for both. If there is no common super-chapter, then the value of the function is $\top$. The *chapter path suffix cps* for a section s and a chapter name c is that suffix of s's chapter interface environment's sequence of chapter-flag pairs which starts after c. If the chapter name is $\top$, then the value of the function is the full sequence.

Informally, the additional constraints on chapter names and section names are:

- For all chapters c, their chapter interface environment Υ_c^I is uniquely defined.

- Access rules: Let section s_a be a parent of section s_b, and let chapter c be the closest common super-chapter of section s_a and section s_b. Then:

  - "An interface never depends on a secret": Let "s_b be an interface", that is, no element in the chapter path suffix for s_b and c is private. Then, "s_a must be an interface", that is, no element in the chapter path suffix for s_a and c is private.

  - "A secret can depend on a secret only if they are siblings": Let "s_b be a secret", that is, at least one element in the chapter path suffix for s_b and c is private. Then, "s_a must be an interface, except maybe at the top level", that is, no element in the tail of the chapter path suffix for s_a and c is private.

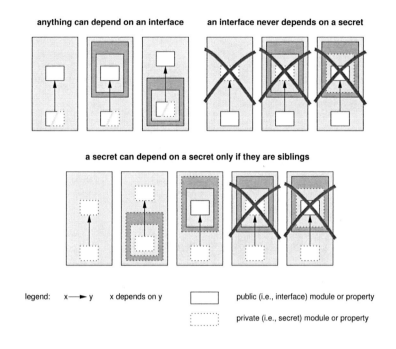

Figure 6.3: The access rules for Z_{CI} modules with interfaces.

We introduced the first constraint to ensure that multiple appearances of a chapter name are marked consistently as private or non-private.

Figure 6.3 visualizes the access rules with some typical cases. We introduced the first access rule to ensure that a stable property never depends on an unstable property. The second access rule permits that a module contains several private properties with dependencies among them. Otherwise, nothing could ever depend on a private property. They would not be useful anymore. But this access is restricted to direct siblings in the module hierarchy. In such a strictly local setting, it is easier to manage configuration problems.

The formal definition of our two auxiliary functions *ccsc* and *cps* is:

$ccsc : (\text{ran } \texttt{ChapIfEnv}) \times (\text{ran } \texttt{ChapIfEnv})$

$\forall x, y : \text{ran } \texttt{ChapIfEnv} \mid \text{dom ran } x \cap \text{dom ran } y = \varnothing \bullet ccsc(x, y) = \top$
$\forall x, y : \text{ran } \texttt{ChapIfEnv}, k, l : \mathbb{N}, c : \text{NAME} \mid$
$\quad c = \textbf{first } tail^k(x) \ \wedge \ c = \textbf{first } tail^l(y) \ \wedge \ ccsc(tail^{k+1}(x), \ tail^{l+1}(y)) = \top \bullet$
$\quad ccsc(x, y) = c$

(In this definition, we take advantage of the fact that each section name may appear at most once in every sequence of a chapter interface environment.)

$cps : (\text{ran ChapIfEnv}) \times \text{NAME}$

$\forall s \bullet cps(s, \top) = s$

$\forall x : \text{ran ChapIfEnv}, k : \mathbb{N}, c : \text{NAME} \mid c = \textbf{first } tail^k(x) \bullet cps(x, c) = tail^{k+1}(x)$

The formal type inference rule is presented in Fig. 6.4. In this rule, p is a phrase that is either the token "private" or empty. D is a paragraph phrase, as usual.

Semantic Transformation Rules

Z_{CI} modifies slightly the semantic transformation rule of Z_{Ch} that eliminates the chapter construct. The optional "private" token must be added suitably in the phrase for a section. We omit this for brevity here.

Example of a Usage

To illustrate our extension, Fig. 6.5 shows a simplified example of a usage from our family of LAN message services in Appendix A.

6.4   Abstract Interfaces Between Requirements

The pattern of the abstract interface between requirements modules helps to avoid dependencies on those requirements that change. Abstract interfaces allow to achive an inversion of the dependencies. However, having abstract interfaces needs some effort for finding suitable abstractions; it pays off when the specification of the family can be extended without restructuring. We conclude this section with an observation on abstract interfaces and inheritance.

6.4.1   Dependency Inversion

Dependencies on easily changing requirements cause problems; dependency inversion by abstract interfaces avoids this.

Some requirements easily change from one family member to another. If other requirements depend on them, then they must be changed, too, in order to keep the entire requirements specification consistent. It is better to avoid dependencies on such easily changing requirements. We can check for such undesired dependencies by encapsulating a changing requirement as a secret inside a requirements module, and by suitable type rules that deny access to secrets. We can *avoid the need to depend* on such a changing requirement by inverting the dependency. This is similar to the dependency inversion principle in object-oriented design (Chap. 4.1.4).

We can achieve such requirements dependency inversion by abstract interfaces for requirements modules. This is similar to the idea of abstract interfaces in design [HBPP81]. The mechanism of explicit requirements module interfaces in the language Z_{CI} from above allows us to express abstract interfaces for requirements modules. For each module, we specify those properties as its interface, i. e., as non-private, that are always there when this module is there. And we specify all the other, changing

$$\vdash^{c^I} \left|
\begin{aligned}
&\text{ZED } p_{1,1} \text{ chapter } c_{1,1} \text{ END} \\
&\quad \ldots \text{ ZED } p_{1,l} \text{ chapter } c_{1,l} \text{ END} \\
&\quad \text{ZED } p_1 \text{ section } i_1 \\
&\quad \text{parents } i_{1,1}, \ldots i_{1,q} \text{ END} \\
&\quad D_{1,1} \ldots D_{1,r} \\
&\quad \text{ZED endchapter END} \\
&\qquad \ldots \text{ ZED endchapter END} \\
&\ldots \\
&\text{ZED } p_{n,1} \text{ chapter } c_{n,1} \text{ END} \\
&\quad \ldots \text{ ZED } p_{n,m} \text{ chapter } c_{n,m} \text{ END} \\
&\quad \text{ZED } p_n \text{ section } i_n \\
&\quad \text{parents } i_{n,1}, \ldots i_{n,s} \text{ END} \\
&\quad D_{n,1} \ldots D_{n,t} \\
&\quad \text{ZED endchapter END} \\
&\qquad \ldots \text{ ZED endchapter END}
\end{aligned}
\right.
\left(
\begin{aligned}
&\Upsilon^I_{c_{1,1}} = c_{1,1} \mapsto \langle c_{1,1} \mapsto p_{1,1} \rangle \\
&\Upsilon^I_{c_{1,2}} = c_{1,2} \mapsto \langle c_{1,1} \mapsto p_{1,1}, c_{1,2} \mapsto p_{1,2} \rangle \\
&\qquad\qquad \vdots \\
&\Upsilon^I_{c_{n,m-1}} = c_{n,m-1} \mapsto \langle c_{n,1} \mapsto p_{n,1}, \quad \ldots, \\
&\qquad\qquad\qquad c_{n,m-1} \mapsto p_{n,m-1} \rangle \\
&\Upsilon^I_{c_{n,m}} = c_{n,m} \mapsto \langle c_{n,1} \mapsto p_{n,1}, \quad \ldots, \\
&\qquad\qquad\qquad c_{n,m} \mapsto p_{n,m} \rangle \\
&\Psi^I_c = \{\Upsilon^I_{c_{1,1}}\} \cup \{\Upsilon^I_{c_{1,2}}\} \cup \ldots \cup \\
&\qquad \{\Upsilon^I_{c_{n,m-1}}\} \cup \{\Upsilon^I_{c_{n,m}}\} \\
&\Psi^I_c \subseteq (\operatorname{dom} \Psi^I_c \nrightarrow \operatorname{ran} \Psi^I_c) \\
&\Upsilon^I_{s_1} = i_1 \mapsto \langle c_{1,1} \mapsto p_{1,1}, \quad \ldots, \\
&\qquad\qquad\qquad c_{1,l} \mapsto p_{1,l}, \quad i_1 \mapsto p_1 \rangle \\
&\qquad\qquad \vdots \\
&\Upsilon^I_{s_n} = i_n \mapsto \langle c_{n,1} \mapsto p_{n,1}, \quad \ldots, \\
&\qquad\qquad\qquad c_{n,m} \mapsto p_{n,m}, \quad i_n \mapsto p_n \rangle \\
&\Psi^I_s = \{\Upsilon^I_{s_1}\} \cup \ldots \cup \{\Upsilon^I_{s_n}\} \\
&\Pi = \{ \ i_1 \mapsto \{i_{1,1}, \ldots, i_{1,q}\}, \quad \ldots, \\
&\qquad i_n \mapsto \{i_{n,1}, \ldots, i_{n,s}\} \ \} \\
&\forall a, b : \operatorname{dom} \Pi; \\
&\quad c : \operatorname{dom} \Psi^I_c; \ \psi_a, \psi_b : \mathbb{P} \operatorname{dom} \Psi^I_s \mid \\
&\quad a \in \Pi(b) \wedge \\
&\quad c = ccsc(\Psi^I_s(a), \Psi^I_s(b)) \wedge \\
&\quad \psi_a = \operatorname{ran} \operatorname{ran} cps(\ \Psi^I_s(a), c\ ) \wedge \\
&\quad \psi_{at} = \operatorname{ran} \operatorname{ran} tail\ cps(\ \Psi^I_s(a), c\ ) \wedge \\
&\quad \psi_b = \operatorname{ran} \operatorname{ran} cps(\ \Psi^I_s(b), c\ ) \bullet \\
&\quad (\text{ private} \notin \psi_b \Rightarrow \text{private} \notin \psi_a\ ) \wedge \\
&\quad (\text{ private} \in \psi_b \Rightarrow \text{private} \notin \psi_{at}\ )
\end{aligned}
\right)$$

Figure 6.4: The additional type inference rule for chapter names in Z_{CI}.

---

1. chapter environment

1.1 chapter device_interfaces

1.1.1 chapter communicating_entities

1.1.1.1 private chapter user_interface

1.1.1.1.1 section user_base

...

1.1.1.1.2 private chapter graphical_user_interface

1.1.1.1.2.1 section gui_comm_base

...

1.1.1.1.2.2 private section gui_io_base

...

endchapter graphical_user_interface

endchapter user_interface

endchapter communicating_entities

endchapter device_interfaces

endchapter environment

Figure 6.5: An example usage of Z_{CI}, our Z extension for a chapter interface construct, extracted from the specification in Appendix A.

properties as secrets, i. e., as private. Similarly, we also specify those sub-modules as its interface that are always there, and the other sub-modules as secrets.

For example, take the LAN message service family introduced in Sect. 6.5 below. Figure 6.7 on page 113 shows both the dependency relation and the requirements module hierarchy. The **time** module hides the differences of the ways in which the access to time can be specified. The module's secret is the concrete kind of time scale used, and the concrete way in which the software can obtain information about the current time. The module provides the notion of time and of time differences, and it provides an abstract global clock. The chapter for this module contains the sections **time_base** and **time_milliseconds**.

The section **time_base** specifies an interface property that introduces a set of points in time and a set of time differences, with base operations on them. The time values are from the set of "arithmos", that is, they are some unspecfied kind of numbers. The arithmos include the natural, the integer, the rational and the real numbers. Also, the section declares a Z schema with a variable that holds the value of the current time, and it declares a Z schema with an operation that increments the current time (see page 249).

The section **time_milliseconds** is marked as private. It is therefore a secret of the module **time**. This section introduces additional constraints. It states that the time values are natural numbers in milliseconds (with no fraction), and that the system starts at 0 ms. This section is part of only some family members. Other family members could have a different section that specifies time to be discretized into

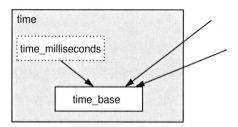

Figure 6.6: Dependency inversion for the time module: dependencies are on the stable interface only.

microseconds, or time that is rational-valued or real-valued.

Many dependencies enter module **time**, but they are all on the abstract interface property **time_base** only (Fig. 6.6). No part of the requirements specification depends on the changing property that time is discretized and in milliseconds.

Without caring for an abstract interface, we could have specified directly that time is in discrete milliseconds. But this would have precluded systems with rational-valued or real-valued time. Our choice of an abstract interface allows to change this aspect of the requirements specification easily, just by selecting a different secret property in the module **time**.

6.4.2 Finding Abstractions

Having abstract interfaces needs that we find suitable abstractions. Such an abstract property must always hold when the module is part of the requirements specification. We have to find out the commonalities of the aspect described in the module. This usually is a non-trivial intellectual task. It needs additional effort during the initial conception of the family of requirements. It pays off when the specification of the family can be extended without restructuring.

For example, in the above module **time**, we had to analyze which parts of the properties of time can change. This required domain knowledge and experience. When we thought about which Z type we should use for the value of the current time, we found that there are several ways of modelling time. In particular, there is discrete time and continuous time. Therefore, we left this particular aspect out of the interface property. We used the most general kind of numbers that the language Z offers, the arithmos.

6.4.3 Abstract Interfaces Need No Inheritance

We observe that the pattern of the abstract interface between requirements modules is independent of the mechanism of inheritance. We can apply this pattern even though the language Z_{CI} does not offer inheritance.

6.5   Example: A Family of LAN Message Services

We demonstrate our approach on an example, a family of LAN message services. We specified this family in the language Z_F. Z_F is a further extension of the language Z_{CI}; we will define Z_F in Sect. 7.4.2 below. After introducing to the functionality of such a LAN message service, we discuss the document structure and the module structure of the specification of the family, how the details of the boundary of the specified system are hidden, how we strived to make the property in a section "small", i.e., abstract, how we used a constraint-oriented style and explicit interfaces, and how we decoupled the properties of the specification using abstract interfaces. The actual specification is in Appendix A, on pp. 242–261. Figure 6.7 shows its module structure and its dependency relation.

6.5.1   Functionality of a LAN Message Service

The basic idea of such a service is that computer users on a local area network (LAN) can send each other short messages that are displayed immediately. Such a system is simpler than telephony because its communication is not connection-oriented, and because it is a closed system with no connection to a global telecommunications network. Nevertheless, it is related to telephony and has many of its challenges, too, since such a system also provides real-time communication means among a set of distributed users.

These systems can have less or more functionality. A very simple version just unconditionally opens a graphical window at the receiving side and displays one line of text. This can be convenient to alert one's colleagues on the same floor that one will cut a birthday cake in five minutes. Other family members can support individual addressing, message blocking, message re-routing, output on a text console, delayed messages, and so on. Therefore, all these aspects are likely to change from one family member to another. Again, this family of systems is similar to telephony with its large set of optional behaviour that might be available to a user.

Our specification is not intended to be complete. It contains the important abstractions, and it contains also some details in sub-modules. This shows how we can describe such details. But we do not elaborate all details, since we do not actually want to build such systems. A complete specification would not contribute much further to our demonstration of its structure. But it would need space beyond what fits into an appendix.

6.5.2   Document Structure

The document structure shall help the reader to locate the information quickly which he or she is looking for. A tree structure of the document shall enable an efficient search. Each node starts with an overview that shall allow to decide which is the relevant sub-node. Accordingly, the specification has a recursive, hierarchical tree structure. Each module is a "chapter" in the language Z_{CI}. The chapter heading has a formal meaning, as discussed above. Then follows a short informal overview of the chapter. Sub-chapters or Z_{CI} "sections" recursively contain the details. The sections

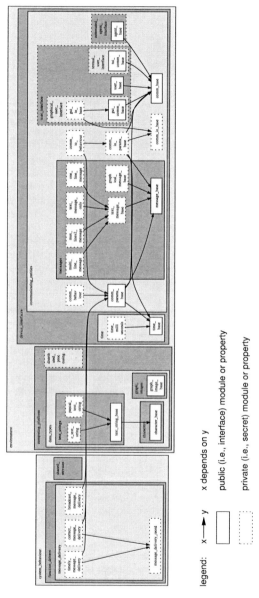

Figure 6.7: The dependency hierarchy and the requirements module hierarchy of the LAN message service family.

form the leaves in the hierarchy. Each section starts out with a section heading and a short informal overview, again. The details are specified with formal paragraphs of Z_{CI}.

Each formal paragraph is preceded by an informal explanation, for two reasons. First, the explanation shall help the reader to quickly get the idea of what the formulae are about. But the informal explanation sometimes does not discuss all tiny aspects. Therefore, the formal paragraph is always the authoritative version. Second, the informal text also links the formal constructs to real-world entities. The formal text does not do this at all, by its nature. But a formal specification can only be precise if it roots firmly in the real world. Achieving this is a task of the informal description. For example, we can specify formally that the variable vin_curr_time has discrete numbers as values. But only the informal text can specify that the variable denotes the current time, and that time is measured in milliseconds.

We made abstractions explicit and prominent. The informal first paragraph also describes the abstractions that the module provides, when applicable. This can help to locate a specific abstraction more quickly. For example, we not only write that the message module hides the differences between the various types of messages (e. g., text messages and graphical messages). We also explicitly write that the message module provides the notion of an abstract message. This helps if we want to write a property that refers to the notion of an abstract message, because we need to specify a dependency on its declaration.

We documented solved issues explicitly. A second informal paragraph solves issues about where a specific information can be found, where necessary. For example, in the computing platform module we write that "this module does not specify that part of the hardware which allows the software to achieve its goal in the physical world. This part can be found in the device interface module." And in the device interface module, we write that "this module does not specify that part of the hardware that is internal to the computing platform and that makes no contact with the physical world. This part can be found in the computing platform module."

6.5.3   Module Structure

The requirements module structure follows the template structure from Sect. 5.3.1 (see Fig. 5.1 on page 79). At the top level, the specification is divided into the requirements on the behaviour of the software system to build and into the requirements on its environment. The environment comprises the communicating entities, the messages they want to exchange, and the existing hardware and software that that can be made use of. The specification of the behaviour of the software system describes what the system does to the communicating entities and the messages, without referring to any details of the existing hardware or software. We expect that changes in the hardware devices will happen independently from changes to the high-level behaviour of the system. For example, a change from a textual user interface to a graphical user interface will be independent of whether there is a message broadcast scheme or an individual message addressing scheme.

The division of secrets determines the module structure. For each module, the informal first paragraph specifies what secret the module hides. Each secret is some requirement that might change. Separating and encapsulating secrets means separating and encapsulating aspects that can change independently. Since the module structure is based on secrets, it localizes changes and facilitates maintenance. For example, the top-level decomposition into an environment module and a system behaviour module is based on our expectation that changes in the hardware devices will happen independently from changes to the high-level behaviour of the system.

There would have been other, less advantageous ways to determine the module structure. We could have based it on the roles played by the individual modules in the overall system operation. We could have based it on the facilities provided by each module. Such a module structure would have been harder to maintain. It would be more probable that a change affects more than one module. This is because the module structure would not be oriented along what can change together. For example, we could have had a top-level module that specifies how a sender can send a message, and another one for a receiver. But if we change from a graphical user interface to a textual user interface, both would have to be changed. And if we introduce the concept of message re-routing, again both would have to be changed. Message re-routing can be initiated by the sender, by the receiver, or by a third party. If fact, the current way of specifying telephone switching systems by a top-level split into an originating side and a terminating side causes many difficulties as soon as more than two partners are involved, like in call forwarding (see Sect. 1.2).

6.5.4 Encapsulation of the System Boundary

The details of the boundary of the specified system are hidden in the environment module. There, they are further hidden in the sub-modules, starting with the device_interfaces module and the computing_platform module.

For example, the computing_platform module hides how much and which data types and distributed processing facilities are provided by the operating system of the underlying platform. If we change from an operating system that provides rich support to a nearly naked microprocessor, then this shift of the boundary between the system and its environment will be localized to the computing_platform module. Similarly, a change from C-Style text strings to Pascal-style text strings will be localized even further to the text_strings sub-module of the data_type module inside the computing_platform module.

We will discuss the encapsulation of the user interface in more detail in Section 8.3.2 below, in the chapter on the user interface module.

6.5.5 Size of a Property

We strived to make the property in a section "small", i.e., abstract. (Compare Sect. 5.2.3.) There should be only one reason for a property to change. This is the single responsibility principle (compare Sect. 4.1.1). It avoids that responsibilities become coupled, that is, it reduces dependencies.

For example, in the section text_message_base we specify that "there is a set of text

messages which are part of the set of messages", and in the section text_message_only
we specify that "nothing but a text message can be a message." Formally, the former
section declares that the set TEXT_MESSAGE is a subset of the set MESSAGE, and
the latter section adds the constraint that both sets are equal. We expect that there
are LAN message systems which allow nothing but text messages, but we also expect
systems that allow other kinds of messages, too. Therefore, we split the possibility
from the necessity. If graphical messages are added to the system, only the section
text_message_only must be removed. All the sections that depend on the section
text_message_base are not affected at all. Text messages are transferred exactly as
before.

Nevertheless, we sometimes put more than one aspect into one property. We did
this when we were absolutely sure that these aspects will *always* change together.
Then, the additional complexity of a split would not pay off.

For example, the section gui_comm_base introduces both GUI submission events
and GUI delivery events. We are sure that nobody will want to have a LAN message
system that allows submissions through a graphical user interface (GUI), but delivers
messages only via a text console. The same holds for a system that delivers messages
through the GUI, but accepts only text-based submissions from its users.

6.5.6 Constraint-Oriented Specification

The specification is written in a constraint-oriented style. (See Sect. 7.5.2 and 7.5.4
below.) Such a style helps to specify the individual requirements separately and to
then compose them in different ways as needed. We use the section construct for
expressing an individual constraint, in particular.

An example are the constraints on the number of text lines of a display. The
section text_message_base on page 251 states that each text message has a number
of lines, and that there is an upper limit on the number of lines:

$$TEXT\_MESSAGE : \mathbb{F}_1 \; MESSAGE$$
$$max\_lines : \mathbb{N}_1$$

$$msg2line\_no : TEXT\_MESSAGE \rightarrow 0 \; .. \; max\_lines$$

This section is a loose specification because the actual maximum number of text
lines is not yet fixed. Other sections add a suitable constraint, depending on which
of them is included in a family member. For example, the section max_lines2_message
adds the constraint that a message has at most two lines:

$$max\_lines = 2$$

The resulting family member is not loose anymore: text messages have up to two
lines of text.

Incremental constraints on *dynamically changing* state variables can be found in
the LAN message service specification too, of course. For this, we specify Z schemas

with variables instead of axiomatic definitions of constants, as we did above. Already plain Z allows to specify arbitrary constraints in the lower predicate part of a schema. We can use a schema with this to specify additional constraints on a previously define schema, exactly as we did in the lower predicate part of the second axiomatic definition above.

An example are the constraints on the history of message submission events. The section **comm_base** on page 252 introduces the variable hist_submit:

$$
\begin{array}{|l}
\underline{\;hist\_comm\;} \\
hist\_submit : \mathrm{iseq}\, EV\_SUBMIT \\
\ldots \\
\end{array}
$$

The section **comm_behaviour** on page 253 then adds a constraint on the dynamic behaviour of the variable:

$$
\begin{array}{|l}
\underline{\;mon\_submit\;} \\
m? : MESSAGE \\
s? : COMM\_ENTITY \\
\Delta hist\_comm \\
\hline
\exists\, e : EV\_SUBMIT \mid ev\_sub2msg(e) = m? \wedge ev\_sub2sender(e) = s? \bullet \\
\quad hist\_submit' = hist\_submit \frown \langle e \rangle \\
\ldots \\
\end{array}
$$

The section **comm_io_behaviour** on page 254 adds another constraint on the dynamic behaviour by specifying a (rather complex) invariant:

$$
\begin{array}{|l}
\underline{\;inv\_hist\_input\;} \\
hist\_comm \\
hist\_io \\
clock \\
\hline
\exists\, h\_i, h\_j : \mathrm{iseq}\, EV\_INPUT \mid h\_i \frown h\_j = hist\_input \wedge \\
\quad (\forall\, e : \mathrm{ran}\; h\_j \bullet ev\_input2time(e) + max\_mon\_delay > vmon\_curr\_time) \bullet \\
\quad hist\_submit \,\fatsemi\, ev\_sub2msg = h\_i \,\fatsemi\, ev\_input2msg \wedge \\
\quad hist\_submit \,\fatsemi\, ev\_sub2sender = h\_i \,\fatsemi\, ev\_input2sender \wedge \\
\quad \exists\, tshift : time \rightarrow time \mid (\forall\, t : time \bullet tshift(t) = t - max\_input\_delay) \bullet \\
\quad\quad hist\_submit \,\fatsemi\, ev\_sub2time = h\_i \,\fatsemi\, ev\_input2time \,\fatsemi\, tshift \\
\end{array}
$$

(This Z schema means that for each submission event that has been input, there has been exactly one corresponding estimated monitored event, except maybe for those input events which are too new; also, no other estimated monitored submission events are computed.)

There are also *dependencies of variables on dynamically changing other variables.* In the above Z schema, the function **ev_input2time** associates a time stamp to each

input message in the input history variable hist_input. The time stamp depends on
the current time value in the variable vmon_curr_time. Our formalism can express
arbitrary constraints on the dynamically changing values of variables.

We will discuss how constraints can be composed in Section 7.5 in detail. In
particular, Sect. 7.5.2 is about constraint-oriented specification in general, and Section 7.5.4 presents a pedagogical example that shows even more clearly that our
formalism is sufficiently general such that we can express arbitrary constraints on
dynamically changing values of variables.

6.5.7   Explicit Interfaces

Explicit interfaces of the requirements modules prevent the access to their changable
secrets. (Compare Sect. 6.3.) The interface between requirements modules is the set
of assumptions that they make about each other. A property that is likely to change
should not be depended upon by properties from other modules; distinguishing between interface properties and secret properties of a module is a mechanism to avoid
this.

For example, the chapter messages on page 251 hides the differences between the various types of messages. There is only one property common to
all family members: the section message_base states that there *is* a set of messages. This is the only interface section of the chapter messages. Numerous
private sections specify additional properties, but may not be present in some
family members: **text_message_base**, **text_message_only**, **one_line_message**,
multi_line_message, **max_lines2_message**, and **graphical_message_base**.

Sections outside of the chapter messages have no access to these additional properties. Therefore, they cannot rely on them for their own definitions. If some of the
additional properties are absent in a family member, the rest of the specification is
not affected.

Another example is the chapter time on page 249, which hides the differences of
the ways in which the access to time can be specified. Here is only one property
common to all family members, too: the section time_base states that there is a
set of points in time and a set of time differences, with base operations on them.
The section contains, among others, a definition of a data type for the time, and a
declaration of a variable holding the software's estimate of the current time:

$$time : \mathbb{P}\,\mathbb{A}$$

$$\underline{\quad clock \quad\rule{8cm}{0.4pt}}$$
$$vmon\_curr\_time : time$$

These definitions are part of all family members.

Some properties of the modelling of time vary from family member to family
member. They are specified as secrets of the time module. For example, the private
section time_milliseconds imposes further constraints on variable vmon_curr_time that
holds the current time. This section demands a discrete time scale (in milliseconds)
and an initial value of 0 ms:

$$time = \mathbb{N}$$
$$vin\_start\_time = 0$$

(The initial value of vmon_curr_time is set to vin_start_time in a schema not shown here.)

Sections outside of the chapter time have no access to to the predicate that states that time is represented by natural numbers. These sections must be formulated using the data type of Z's arithmos $\mathbb{A}$, which can be any kind of number whatsoever. For example, the section timely_message_delivery on page 260 expresses a constraint that couples the delivery of messages to the progress of time. This property is formulated using the operators "+" and "<" which are defined for all kinds of arithmos:

$$
\begin{array}{l}
\rule{0pt}{0pt}\_\ inv\_timely\_msg\_delivery _____ \\
hist\_comm \\
clock \\
\hline
\forall\, h\_s : \mathrm{iseq}\, EV\_SUBMIT \mid h\_s\, \mathrm{prefix}\, hist\_submit \wedge h\_s \neq \langle\rangle \wedge \\
\quad ev\_sub2time(last(h\_s)) + max\_msg\_delivery\_delay < vmon\_curr\_time \bullet \\
\quad\quad \exists\, reord : \mathbb{N}_1 \rightarrowtail\!\!\!\rightarrow \mathbb{N}_1 \mid reord = (\mathrm{dom}\, h\_s) \lhd reord\_delivery \bullet \\
\quad\quad\quad \mathrm{ran}(reord) \subseteq \mathrm{dom}\, hist\_deliver \wedge \\
\quad\quad\quad h\_s \,\fatsemi\, ev\_sub2msg = reord \,\fatsemi\, hist\_deliver \,\fatsemi\, ev\_deliv2msg
\end{array}
$$

(This schema says that after the maximum message delivery delay, any submitted message will have been delivered. For this, we consider only those submission events which are at least sufficiently old.)

6.5.8 Reducing Dependencies by Abstract Interfaces

We decoupled the properties of the specification by letting them depend on abstract interfaces only. (Compare Sect. 6.4.) The pattern of the abstract interface between requirements modules helps to avoid dependencies on those requirements that change. Abstract interfaces allow to achive an inversion of the dependencies.

An example ist the time module, again. The section time_base contains its abstract interface. It was a deliberate decision of ours to specify the data type of time by the general "arithmos" of Z, and to specify the concrete granularity of time in the separate, private section time_milliseconds. In this way, most properties depend on the stable interface only, not on some concrete granularity of time. We inverted the dependency and let the optional section time_milliseconds depend on the interface section time_base. (See also the longer discussion in Section 6.4.1.)

One can observe our success at decoupling by looking at the large communicating_entities module. In Figure 6.7 on page 113, we can see that the sections of the system_behaviour module are allowed to access only three sections of the communicating_entities module. (Look for solid boxes.) These are the sections comm_base, comm_params_base, and message_base. They provide the basic abstractions of the communicating entities, of the communication events, and of the messages. The sytem behaviour is specified only in terms of these abstractions.

Our success at decoupling is also underlined by the fact that the dependency hierarchy is flat. Figure 6.7 shows that it is wide, but that it is only three levels high. Also, most properties are not depended upon at all. This allows for easy changes and for many consistent subsets of properties.

Chapter 7

Configuring and Composing Family Members Using Features

We show how we can configure and compose requirements to complete family members; in this, we must distinguish the notions of a requirements module and of a feature to avoid feature interaction problems. We first show that the underlying concepts are related in software configuration management (SCM) and in requirements configuration management (RCM) for families of requirements; even though the vocabularies are really different. We find that a feature is a set of changes, not a requirements module. A selected configuration of requirements must be consistent; we can automatically check for and we can automatically reconcile at least some inconsistencies. We complete our support for families of requirements in the formalism Z by adding a suitable feature construct; it allows to specify a configuration. We then describe how we can compose the properties in the requirements to a complete system description. We illustrate our approach by presenting some features and family members for our family of LAN message services from Sect. 6.5 above. Configuring requirements family members needs tool support; some tools already exist, more are planned. We already collected considerable experience with a large case study of a telephone switching system and in an industry project where we had to maintain a set of communication protocol test specifications. This chapter ends with an outlook on several ideas for further research.

7.1 Requirements Configuration Management for Families of Requirements

We show that the underlying concepts are related in software configuration management (SCM) and in requirements configuration management (RCM) for families of requirements; even though the vocabularies are really different. For this, we take each relevant definition from Sect. 3.4 on SCM in turn and show which notion from RCM corresponds to it, and where the differences are, if any. As a result, we transfer the sound base of SCM to RCM.

7.1.1 Product Space

A software *product* in SCM maps to a complete *requirements document* in RCM; i. e., to the root of the module composition hierarchy. There is only one *composition relationship*: the *product graph* is the *hierarchy of requirements modules*. A *composite object* (or *configuration*) is a *requirements module* in RCM. An *atomic object* is a *property*. The *dependency relationship* is the *dependency* between properties.

7.1.2 Version Space

A *version* of a software product in SCM maps to a *family member* of a family of requirements specifications in RCM. A family member may either be a *revision* or a *variant*, as in SCM. But we are interested mostly in managing variants. We do not discuss the difficulties of distributing or undoing updates here. These difficulties are related to revisions.

A set of *changes* (or of *directed deltas*) in SCM maps to a *feature* in RCM. A feature extends a base system by an arbitrary increment of functionality, we found in Section 1.2.4 on naive feature orientation. A typical feature addition operator adds text in different places of the base system as needed. A feature is also inherently non-monotonous; most features really change the behaviour of the base system. Therefore, the notions of a change and of a feature match quite well. To be more precise, a feature maps to an entire set of changes, not only to one change; we discuss this in Sect. 7.2 below. A small difference is that a feature is (usually) defined as an increment to the base system only, while a change is more general. A change can be either defined for a base system, or it can need that other changes already have been applied.

A *feature oriented* requirements specification assumes a *change-based* version model, of course (not a *state-based* version model).

Extensional versioning means that the set of possible family members is defined by enumerating the family members. Extensional versioning supports retrieval of previously constructed family members. Even though this is important, we are interested even more in *intensional versioning*. We want to construct a (potentially new) family member on demand, by giving the set of names of features which the family member shall comprise. We want that the requirements specification for this family member then is constructed automatically from the specification of the family. As in SCM, the retrieval of known family members and the construction of new ones are not mutually exclusive, of course.

7.1.3 Intensional Versioning

We discuss the definitions of intensional versioning along Conradi's and Westfechtel's framework for intensional versioning in Fig. 3.8 on page 58. The *versioned object base* in SCM maps to the specification of a *family of requirements* in RCM. A *query* (or *submitted configuration rule*) maps to a *selection of feature names*.

There are different kinds of *stored configuration rules* in RCM. In feature-oriented approaches, explicit or implicit *priorities* are a common means for resolving conflicts when composing features. Many approaches for feature composition use some kind of feature stack ([AuAt97] is just one example). Events are passed top-down through such a stack until a feature is prepared to handle it. The pipe-and-filter network of the DFC architecture [JaZa98] is a generalization of this, and it has been implemented in an experimental IP telecommunication platform [BCP$^+$04, ZGS04]. Other kinds of *strictness classes* (i. e., *constraints*, *preferences*, and *defaults*) are used, too. For example, Amer *et al.* [AKGM00] resolve feature interactions using fuzzy policies.

A *configurator* in RCM is a tool that extracts an individual requirements specification from a family of requirements specifications. The *combinability problem* manifests itself in RCM as *feature interaction problems*. *Semantic merging* of changes is what we would like to have for the combination of features. But unfortunately, as in many SCM applications, there is no decidable definition for a semantic conflict that is neither too strong nor too weak.

7.1.4 Interplay of Product Space and Version Space

SCM offers three different *selection orders*: *product first*, *version first*, and *intertwined*. The product first selection order ist not relevant for families of requirements, since it does not allow structural versioning, i. e., adding and removing features. The version first selection order allows this, but we get a new configuration for every combination of module selections. This problem is called *version proliferation* in SCM. The intertwined selection order distinguishes between versions of modules and versions of configurations and does not have this problem.

An example for a version first selection order in RCM is: the description of a family member consists of a list of the names of all properties that are part of it. This is feasible. But the list will become unwieldy for large systems. In particular, such a list is not suitable for marketing.

Feature orientation allows for a more compact and marked-oriented description. A *base system* makes all those properties implicit that are part of many systems. Each *feature* consists of the changes to this base system, that is, it lists only those properties that are added to the base system and those properties that are removed from the base system. A feature description is made up by a system designer in the hope that it will meet the needs of customers. Each customer then selects a list of features and pays for them. This is two-level version first selection, with additional configuration rules for removing properties.

7.2 A Feature Is Not a Requirements Module

A feature is a set of changes, not a requirements module. Features and requirements modules are similar. Both concepts serve to group properties. But there are marked differences. Examples from telephony support our claim that a feature often affects different requirements modules of a well-designed requirements module hierarchy. The telephony system sketched in the examples avoids many kinds of undesired feature interactions. But we find that none of the telephone switching architectures that we discussed in Sect. 5.5 above distinguish between requirements modules and changes clearly.

7.2.1 The Differences

There are two marked differences between features and requirements modules:

1. A requirements module is a set of properties (i.e., *one* set), while a feature consists of both added and removed properties.

2. The properties of a module are selected because of their likeliness to change together, *averaged* over the entire family, while the properties of a feature are selected to fit the marketing needs of a *single situation*.

Forcing requirements modules and features to be the same is not advisable. A feature fits the marketing needs of one occasion only, even though perfectly. It is likely to not fit well for the remaining family members. A requirements module supports the construction of all family members well, even though it does not satisfy all the marketing needs of a particular occasion by itself. A few other requirements modules will be concerned, too. In contrast, adding one more feature on top of a large naively feature-oriented system will concern many other features.

A requirements module provides an abstraction, while a feature is a configuration rule for such abstractions.

A feature is an entire set of changes, not only one change. This is because a feature usually should be made up of changes to different requirements modules. For example, a feature should list the properties that are to be added or removed for all requirements modules concerned by that feature.

7.2.2 Examples from Telephony

Examples from telephony support our claim that a feature often affects different requirements modules of a well-designed requirements module hierarchy.

- The 800 feature allows a company to advertise a single telephone number, e.g., 1-800-123-4567. Dialling this number will connect a customer with the nearest branch, free of charge.

  This feature should be composed of properties from these three requirements modules: a module that provides addresses for user roles (example: the above 800 number for the pizza delivery role), a module that translates a role address into a device address based on the caller's address, and, entirely independently, a module that charges the callee. The feature removes the property that the caller is charged.

- The emergency call feature allows a person in distress to call a well-known number (911 in the U.S., 110 in Germany and in some other European countries, ...) and be connected with the nearest emergency center.

This feature will include the properties from the three requirements modules above, and from a few more. For example, there will be properties from a module that allows the callee to identify the physical line the call comes from. Of course, this feature also removes the property that the caller is charged.

- The follow-me call forwarding feature allows a person to register with any phone line and receive all calls to his/her personal number there.

  This feature includes properties from the module in the first example that provides addresses for user roles. The other modules are not needed. Instead, we need properties from a module that translates a role address according to a dynamic user preference. We also need properties from a further module to enable the user to set his or her preferences dynamically.

Successful marketing needs features such as the above ones. A "user role address" feature would probably sell much worse than the ubiquitous 800 feature.

Nevertheless, structuring the system only into the above features would not have been good. We could not have reused requirements modules across features, as we have done above. This would have been the naive feature-oriented approach.

7.2.3   Feature Interactions Avoided in the Examples

The telephony system sketched in the examples above avoids many kinds of undesired feature interactions. There is only one module that translates a role address into a device address. A consistent distinction between user roles and devices is important.

For example, undesired feature interactions between call forwarding and terminating call screening, as discussed in Sect. 1.2.4, disappear as soon as we make clear whether the screening acts on the device that made the connection or whether it acts on the user who initiated the session. The latter, of course, needs that users explicitly register with devices. If devices are screened, the phone should ring, if users are screened, the phone should not ring. The description of the features will make clear to the customers what they can expect.

A naive feature oriented system adds the translation in the call forwarding feature only, with entailing confusion and grief. For example in the Intelligent Network (IN) architecture discussed in in Section 1.2.4, call forwarding would most probably be realized by "glueing" two IN calls together. The terminating call screening would act on the second IN call only, thus omitting any checks on the first IN call. (See the more detailed discussion in Sect. 1.2.4.) But the actual rules would not be clear to the subscriber of terminating call screening.

7.2.4   No Clear Distinction Between Requirements Modules and Changes in Existing Approaches

None of the telephone switching architectures that we discussed in Sect. 5.5 above distinguish between requirements modules and changes clearly. We will now look at these architectures in turn.

The Intelligent Network (IN) architecture [ITU01, GRKK93, DuVi92] provides the notions of a Service Independent Building Block (SIB) and of a feature. But a SIB is no suitable module in our sense, as dicussed in Sect. 5.5 above. An IN feature composes SIBs. But it also comprises so-called service logic that "glues" the exits and the entries of the SIBs together. Therefore, an IN feature is not a set of changes in the configuration management sense.

The agent architecture by Zibman et. al. [ZWO+96] separates several concerns explicitly, but there is no on-demand composition of modules and thus no notion of change in our sense. There are only revisions of the complete system.

Similarly, the Tina initiative [MaCo00, Ab+97] also separates many important concerns explicitly. The deliverable on the Tina service architecture recognizes that life cycle support for objects needs configuration management [Ab+97, pp. 70]. But then, it states that this is mostly a research subject at this point.

The Race project does an important step and distinguishes in its Open Services Architecture (OSA) between OSA components and OSA service configurations [Tri95, p. 68, pp. 72]. An OSA component is meant for reuse, while an OSA service configuration specifies how a service is composed out of OSA components for one specific occasion. A service configuration is not meant for reuse. But OSA service configurations comprise also the specifications of interactions between OSA components. Therefore, an OSA service configuration is not a set of changes in the configuration management sense, but a kind of one-time component that is flagged as not reuseable.

The Acts project followed the Race project and developed and refined the Tina architecture (and also Race's OSA), in particular in the area of mobility [WLR98]. The result is called Open Service Architecture for an integrated fixed and Mobile environment (OSAM). Like in Tina's OSA, there is no configuration management for OSAM's "components".

The DFC virtual architecture by Jackson and Zave [JaZa98, BCP+04, ZGS04] mixes our notions of module and change. In their pipe-and-filter network, the filter boxes are called "features". But a filter box is not a set of changes. A filter box can be present or not; it is integrated implicitly by the DFC router when it is present. But there is no mechanism to include or exclude specific sets of such filter boxes. Also, a filter box has only some traits of a module in our sense. The filter boxes are relatively simple. This is in accordance with the principle of small requirements. But there is no mechanism for grouping filter boxes into larger units.

The agent-based architecture Aphrodite for Private Branch Exchanges [Pin03] has an entirely different view than us, it is hard to compare. An Aphrodite agent has some traits of a module in our sense. Important abstractions are represented by agents. Examples are devices, certain persons, certain roles, and fixed application services. But there is no grouping of agents. An Aphrodite feature has some traits of an atomic property in our sense. An Aphrodite feature is a small piece of code, and it is atomic. But it is atomic with respect to execution; it is not a property in the sense of requirements. An Aphrodite policy is some configuration data. Eeach agent has its own state machine and its own trigger table, filled with policies. The trigger tables allow for an extensive parameterization of the agents. Examples for parameter data are device IDs, role IDs, and time-of-day specifications. An Aphrodite feature can be invoked via such a trigger table.

7.3 Consistent Configurations

A selected configuration of requirements must be consistent; we can automatically check for and we can automatically reconcile at least some inconsistencies. A formal specification of the requirements enables automated consistency checks; we can turn some inconsistencies into type errors which tools can find efficiently. Differentiating the strictness of configuration rules helps to reconcile inconsistencies; we propose to distinguish between the essential properties and the changeable properties of a feature.

7.3.1 Checking the Consistency of a Family Member

A formal specification of the requirements enables automated consistency checks; we can turn some inconsistencies into type errors which tools can find efficiently. A configuration of behaviour requirements is consistent if there exists a non-empty set of behaviours that satisfies these requirements. There are different ways to prove a configuration to be consistent, at different costs. We can construct an implementation, we can write an existential proof, and we can perform much cheaper partial checks on whether a configuration is *not* consistent.

Full consistency proofs are usually expensive. It is usually expensive to construct an implementation. This is true at least if the implementation is not generated automatically from the requirements. An existential proof is even more expensive to write. The tool CADiℤ allows to prove theorems about specifications written in ISO Z [To+02]. However, such effort is invested better in providing an actual implementation.

We can encode cheap partial consistency checks as type rules. This makes type errors out of some inconsistencies. The most obvious configuration constraints to check are those that define the features. A feature both adds properties and removes properties. Two features therefore can be inconsistent about whether a property should be added or removed. We will provide corresponding formal consistency rules in Sect. 7.4.2 and we will discuss tool support in Sect. 7.7.

A specification of a single family member in ISO Z also contains some explicit configuration constraints: the parents relation between sections demands that every parent section that is named in some section header is also part of this family member. We can check this easily with the tool CADiℤ. It comprises a typechecker for ISO Z. The typechecker flags any violation of such configuration constraints.

Similarly, the typechecker of CADiℤ also detects conflicting type declarations for Z names in a requirements specification. This allows to detect some more inconsistent configurations without much effort.

7.3.2   Configuration Priorities

Differentiating the strictness of configuration rules helps to reconcile inconsistencies; we propose to distinguish between the essential properties and the changeable properties of a feature. We will introduce such a distinction for the formalism Z in Sect. 7.4 below.

Conflicting feature definitions that demand to both include and to exclude a property are an important special case of an inconsistent configuration. Such an inconsistency is an adverse feature interaction. For example in our family of LAN message services in Appendices A, B, and C, the feature note_to_all demands the property one_line_message to be included, while the feature scroll_text_message demands this property to be excluded.

A solution is to have different configuration priorities for the properties of a feature. We found that not all properties of a feature are equally important. Some properties are definitely necessary to meet the expectations evoked by the feature's name. But other properties are provided only in order to make the requirements specification complete and predictable for the user. For example, the feature note_to_all can be recognized no matter what the requirements say on how many lines a note can have.

We therefore propose that the specifier of a feature documents explicitly which properties are *essential properties* and which are *changeable properties*. If a feature demands the inclusion of a changeable property, but another feature demands the exclusion of this property, then the property is excluded without the configuration being inconsistent. The attribution of a priority is per feature, not per property. A property can be essential for one feature and be just ancillary for another feature. We will introduce such a distinction of priorities for the formalism Z in Sect. 7.4 below.

The idea can be generalized to arbitrary configuration priorities or even to a precedence partial order. However, we found that the basic distinction between essential and changeable properties already yields good results.

Related work on configuration priorities.   Our approach is related to the foreground/background model approach of Hall [Hal00, Hal98], which was developed independently of ours [Bre98]. Hall separates the description of a feature into its foreground behaviour, which is "essential" behaviour in our terms, and its background behaviour, which is "changeable" by another feature's foreground behaviour without causing a warning by his analysis tools. His goal is to perform feature interaction detection with *less* results; i.e., his tools do not report "spurious" interactions. A difference of the approaches is that Hall assigns priorities to transitions, while we assign priorities to properties.

7.4 Adding a Feature Construct to the Formalism Z

We complete our support for families of requirements in the formalism Z by adding a suitable feature construct; it allows to specify a configuration. We could specify family members in plain Z by an informal convention, but we cannot extend the convention to features. We therefore define an extension of the formalism Z for families of requirements; it includes a construct to specify a feature.

7.4.1 No Support for Features in Plain Z

We could specify family members in plain Z by an informal convention, but we cannot extend the convention to features. In Section 5.6.1, we found that we can extract a single member of the family into a separate document automatically, with some limitations. We must use the convention that the leaves in the dependency hierarchy of sections each specify one family member. We then can indicate the family member desired through the name of the corresponding leaf section. A suitable tool can follow the dependency relation in order to identify all sections included in this family member. A limitation is that we cannot select the appropriate informal text automatically.

But the extension of this convention does not work, that the sections above the leaf sections serve to specify features. We can use this extended convention to specify the properties that a feature includes. But we cannot express that a feature excludes some other properties. There is no means for non-monotonous extensions.

7.4.2 Z_F: Extending Z by Families and Features

We define an extension of the formalism Z for families of requirements; it includes a construct to specify a feature. We call the language Z_F. We define the language by a transformation that maps the specification of a family of requirements to an individual family member, depending on a list of selected features. Following our arguments in Sect. 7.1.4, we will use two-level version first intensional versioning, with additional configuration rules for removing properties. A feature is a list of sections added and a list of sections removed. The list of added sections is differentiated into essential and into changeable sections. The list of removed sections is not differentiated.

We define the language Z_F by a transformation from Z_F to Z_{CI} (as defined in Sect. 6.3.4), not by an extension to Z_{CI}. We do this because of the typing in Z (and in Z_{CI}). A single family member must have consistent types for all Z names, while we do not want this for an entire family. For example, we want to be able to specify that a variable has a different type in a different family member. The sections with these contradicting variable declarations cannot be part of the same family member. Therefore, we do not want to apply the type rules of Z to an entire family. The major difference between a family document and a family member document is that we can have several, even inconsistent versions in one text.

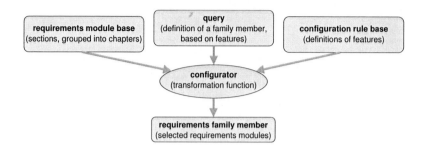

Figure 7.1: The three parts defining a family member in the language Z_F.

A description of a family member in the language Z_F consists of three parts
(Fig. 7.1): the requirements module base, the configuration rule base, and a query.
This is analogous to Conradi's and Westfechtel's framework for intensional versioning in software configuration management (Fig. 3.8 on page 58). The requirements
module base contains all sections that potentially can be part of a family member,
grouped into chapters. The configuration rule base contains the definitions of all
features. A query is a list of those features that are selected for the family member
desired. These three parts may be specified in one document, but they need not. In
particular, we might want to maintain queries separate from the module base and
the rule base. A query is specific to one family member, while the other parts are
common to the entire family.

We therefore define the language Z_F in three independent parts. We leave to the
discretion of the specifiers to maintain these parts. For example, they can keep the
module base in a LaTeX include file, and the rule base in another LaTeX include file.
The specifiers can combine the two files into a family document for printing through
the include mechanism of LaTeX. Any generated family member will contain parts
of the module base, but no parts of the rule base. The latter is not interesting for
the users of the family member document. The rules could even be confusing. The
feature definitions will probably mention excluded sections that are obviously mentioned nowhere else in the family member document. The query can be formulated,
for example, ad-hoc as input on the command line of the configurator tool.

We now define a syntax, a lexis, and two mark-ups for each of the three parts,
and some type rules and a semantics. The semantics is the transformation that maps
the three parts to an individual family member.

Syntax

Requirements module base. We define the syntax by a context-free grammar
in BNF. The grammar is completely separate from the grammar of Z (and of Z_{CI}).
The start symbol is the family. A family consists of chapters and sections that serve

as requirements modules.

$$\text{Family} \; = \; \{\, \text{Chapter} \; | \; \text{Section} \,\} \, ;$$

A chapter and a section are defined similar to the definition in Z_{CI}, with two exceptions. There can be the additional keyword "default". And the body of a section consists of informal text only, with respect to the transformation. We have no rule for a "Paragraph". Any Z_{CI} paragraphs are just informal text. We will associate it to the preceding token. Therefore, any Z_{CI} paragraph will be part of the section whose heading immediately precedes it.

$$
\begin{aligned}
\text{Chapter} \; = \;\; &\text{ZEDCHAR}\,,[\,\text{private}\,,[\,\text{default}\,]\,]\,,\text{chapter}\,,\text{NAME}\,,\text{ENDCHAR}\,, \\
&\{\,\text{Chapter}\;|\;\text{Section}\,\}\,, \\
&\text{ZEDCHAR}\,,\text{endchapter}\,,[\,\text{NAME}\,]\,,\text{ENDCHAR}\,;
\end{aligned}
$$

$$
\begin{aligned}
\text{Section} \; = \;\; &\text{ZEDCHAR}\,,[\,\text{private}\,,\;[\,\text{default}\,]\,]\,,\text{section}\,,\text{NAME}\,, \\
&[\,\text{parents}\,,[\,\text{NAME}\,,\{\,\text{,-tok}\,,\text{NAME}\}\,]\,]\,,\text{ENDCHAR}\,;
\end{aligned}
$$

The keyword "default" serves to specify the parts of the base system. The base system consists of all interface sections/chapters and of all private sections/chapters that are marked as "default".

An alternative in the language definition would have been to specify the base system by a list of sections and chapters, similar to the inclusion list of a feature below. But this would have been less readable. We expect such a list to be usually quite long. And the reader would need to jump back and forth many times to find out what the base system is, even though the base system is a quite important configuration.

Configuration rule base. The BNF start symbol is the list of features. A feature is a list of sections added and a list of sections removed. The list of added sections is differentiated into essential and into changeable sections. A feature has a name.

$$
\begin{aligned}
\text{FeatureList} \; = \;\; &\{\,\text{Feature}\,\}\,; \\
\text{Feature} \; = \;\; &\text{ZEDCHAR}\,,\text{feature}\,,\text{NAME}\,,:\,,\text{ENDCHAR}\,, \\
&\text{ZEDCHAR}\,,\{\,\text{FeatAddEss}\;|\;\text{FeatAddChg}\;|\;\text{FeatRemove}\,\}\,, \\
&\text{ENDCHAR}\,; \\
\text{FeatAddEss} \; = \;\; &+\,,\text{NAME}\,; \\
\text{FeatAddChg} \; = \;\; &\text{(-tok}\,,+\,,\text{)-tok}\,,\text{NAME}\,; \\
\text{FeatRemove} \; = \;\; &-\,,\text{NAME}\,;
\end{aligned}
$$

The add list and the remove list can also refer to entire chapters instead of individual sections. This is an abbreviation. We will define below adding a chapter to be equivalent to adding all its default sections.

Query. A family member is specified by a list of feature names.

$$\texttt{FamilyMember} \; = \; \texttt{ZEDCHAR} \, , \, \{ \, \texttt{NAME} \, \} \, , \texttt{ENDCHAR} \, ;$$

Lexis

The lexical analysis phase groups Z characters to tokens. For each of the three parts of a family member description, the lexis specifies a function that maps sequences of Z characters to sequences of tokens. Furthermore, each lexis is composed of a first step that groups the input using a context-free grammar, and a second step that identifies the keywords.

For the requirements module base, the lexis also specifies a second function. This second function attributes each token with the sub-sequence of input Z characters that were grouped into this token. We will need these sub-sequences to compose the output of the translation to a family member.

We partition the Z characters into DIGITs, LETTERs, BLANKs, and SYMBOLs, similar as in plain Z. But we make the first two sets smaller to simplify tool support. A DIGIT can be only one of the ten ASCII digits (no other UCS characters with, e. g., number property), a LETTER can be only one of the 2×26 LATIN ASCII letters or the underscore "_" (no greek letters and no $\mathbb{A}$, $\mathbb{N}$, $\mathbb{P}$), and a BLANK can be either NLCHAR or SPACE. All remaining Z characters are SYMBOLs. SYMBOLs include, among other characters, ZEDCHAR and ENDCHAR.

The context-free grammar of the lexis is, for all three parts:

$$\texttt{TOKENSTREAM} \; = \; \{ \, \texttt{BLANK} \, \} \, , \, \{ \, \texttt{TOKEN} \, , \{ \, \texttt{BLANK} \, \} \, \} \, ;$$

$$\texttt{TOKEN} \; = \; \texttt{WORD} \mid \texttt{SYMBOL} \, ;$$

$$\texttt{WORD} \; = \; (\, \texttt{LETTER} \mid \texttt{DIGIT} \,) \, , \{ \, \texttt{LETTER} \mid \texttt{DIGIT} \, \} \, ;$$

The second step of the lexis maps each WORD either to a keyword token or to the NAME token. It also strips all BLANKs from the input stream. With respect to the attribution of tokens with sub-sequences of input Z characters, these BLANKs are associated to the preceding token. Any initial BLANKs are associated to an implicit begin-of-input token.

We only have alphabetic keywords. They are:

requirements module base		configuration rule base		query
Spelling	**Token**	**Spelling**	**Token**	(no keywords)
chapter	chapter	feature	feature	
default	default			
endchapter	endchapter			
parents	parents			
private	private			
section	section			

requirements module base		configuration rule base	
LaTeX	Unicode char/string	LaTeX	Unicode char/string
\begin{zchapter}	ZEDCHAR	\begin{zchanges}	ZEDCHAR
\end{zchapter}	ENDCHAR	\end{zchanges}	ENDCHAR
\begin{zsection}	ZEDCHAR	\begin{zfeature}	ZEDCHAR
\end{zsection}	ENDCHAR	\end{zfeature}	ENDCHAR
\CHAPTER	"chapter"	\feature	"feature"
\ENDCHAPTER	"endchapter"	\fAdd	"+"
\SECTION	"section"	\fAddChg	"(+)"
\default	"default"	\fRemove	"−"
\parents	"parents"		
\private	"private"		

query	
LaTeX	Unicode char/string
\begin{familymember}	ZEDCHAR
\end{familymember}	ENDCHAR
\feat[a]	""

---

[a]The mark-up "\feat" maps to nothing; it is intended to start a new line when typesetting the list of features.

Figure 7.2: The non-trivial LaTeX mark-up mappings of Z_F.

LaTeX Mark-Up

The LaTeX mark-up maps the LaTeX input characters to Z characters in Unicode. The LaTeX commands for the formal constructs are mapped to their special Z characters. The informal text between the formal constructs is deleted.

Analogous to the lexis, there is also a second mapping for the requirements module base that attributes each Z character with the sub-sequence of input LaTeX characters that were grouped into this Z character. Any informal text is associated to the preceding formal Z character, again. Except for the formal LaTeX constructs, the mapping is mostly a trivial one-to-one mapping.

Figure 7.2 lists the non-trivial mark-up mappings.

Email Mark-Up

The email mark-up is straightforward. As in Z_{CI}, the input "%%Z" on a line by itself is mapped to ZEDCHAR, starting formal text, and "%%" on a line by itself is mapped to ENDCHAR, ending formal text. As an exception, Z paragraphs shall be treated as informal text, even if they start with "%%Z". This can be detected via the first following keyword. The rest of the formal text is mapped trivially one-to-one. Any informal text is handled as in the LaTeX mark-up.

Type Inference Rules

Some type inference rules provide general consistency and furthermore adherence to our intended restrictions on essential sections and chapters. This enables suitable type checks on the specification of the family and on any query.

Requirements module base. We adapt the applicable type inference rules from Z_{CI} on chapters and sections (omitting the rules on parents). Additionally, we demand that multiple appearances of a chapter name are marked consistently as "default". This gives us some general consistency.

Formally, this means that

- All section names are different.

- The name of a chapter is different from that of any section.

- For all chapters c, their extended chapter interface environment $\Upsilon_c^{l,d}$ is uniquely defined.

  The extended chapter interface environment $\Upsilon_c^{l,d}$ is like the chapter interface environment Υ_c^{l} defined in Sect. 6.3.4, but additionally allows "default" chapters.

The formal type inference rule is presented in Fig. 7.3. In this rule, p is a phrase that is either the token "private", the tokens "private default", or empty. $\Upsilon_s^{l,d}$ is the extended chapter interface environment for sections; we will need it below.

Configuration rule base. We define four obvious consistency rules:

- All features must have distinct names.

- Feature names are in the same name space as section and chapter names; hence they all must be different.

- Each section and chapter name may appear only once in the list of a feature.

- All section and chapter names that appear in the list of a feature must be defined in the requirements module base.

Additionally, we define the following consistency rule:

- No feature may remove a section or chapter which is an interface.

This means that interfaces can never be changed by a feature. As a consequence, any feature can rely on the interface of a module to be always present. However, if the module is not an interface itself, the entire module may be removed. This implicitly

$$\vdash^{\mathcal{FM}}$$

ZED $p_{1,1}$ chapter $c_{1,1}$ END

    ... ZED $p_{1,l}$ chapter $c_{1,l}$ END

ZED p_1 section i_1

parents $i_{1,1}, \ldots i_{1,q}$ END

ZED endchapter END

    ... ZED endchapter END

...

ZED $p_{n,1}$ chapter $c_{n,1}$ END

    ... ZED $p_{n,m}$ chapter $c_{n,m}$ END

ZED p_n section i_n

parents $i_{n,1}, \ldots i_{n,s}$ END

ZED endchapter END

    ... ZED endchapter END

$$
\left(
\begin{aligned}
&\Upsilon^{I,d}_{c_{1,1}} = c_{1,1} \mapsto \langle c_{1,1} \mapsto p_{1,1} \rangle \\
&\Upsilon^{I,d}_{c_{1,2}} = c_{1,2} \mapsto \langle c_{1,1} \mapsto p_{1,1}, c_{1,2} \mapsto p_{1,2} \rangle \\
&\qquad\qquad \vdots \\
&\Upsilon^{I,d}_{c_{n,m-1}} = c_{n,m-1} \mapsto \langle c_{n,1} \mapsto p_{n,1}, \quad \ldots, \\
&\qquad\qquad\qquad\qquad c_{n,m-1} \mapsto p_{n,m-1} \rangle \\
&\Upsilon^{I,d}_{c_{n,m}} = c_{n,m} \mapsto \langle c_{n,1} \mapsto p_{n,1}, \quad \ldots, \\
&\qquad\qquad\qquad\qquad c_{n,m} \mapsto p_{n,m} \rangle \\
&\Psi^{I,d}_c = \{\Upsilon^{I,d}_{c_{1,1}}\} \cup \{\Upsilon^{I,d}_{c_{1,2}}\} \cup \ldots \cup \\
&\qquad\qquad \{\Upsilon^{I,d}_{c_{n,m-1}}\} \cup \{\Upsilon^{I,d}_{c_{n,m}}\} \\
&\Psi^{I,d}_c \subseteq (\operatorname{dom} \Psi^{I,d}_c \nrightarrow \operatorname{ran} \Psi^{I,d}_c) \\
&\Upsilon^{I,d}_{s_1} = i_1 \mapsto \langle c_{1,1} \mapsto p_{1,1}, \quad \ldots, \\
&\qquad\qquad\qquad c_{1,l} \mapsto p_{1,l}, \quad i_1 \mapsto p_1 \rangle \\
&\qquad\qquad \vdots \\
&\Upsilon^{I,d}_{s_n} = i_n \mapsto \langle c_{n,1} \mapsto p_{n,1}, \quad \ldots, \\
&\qquad\qquad\qquad c_{n,m} \mapsto p_{n,m}, \quad i_n \mapsto p_n \rangle \\
&\Psi^{I,d}_s = \{\Upsilon^{I,d}_{s_1}\} \cup \ldots \cup \{\Upsilon^{I,d}_{s_n}\} \\
&\# \operatorname{dom} \Psi^{I,d}_s = n \\
&\operatorname{dom} \Psi^{I,d}_c \cap \operatorname{dom} \Psi^{I,d}_s = \varnothing
\end{aligned}
\right)
$$

Figure 7.3: The type inference rule of Z_F for the requirements module base.

also removes the module's interface. Forbidden are only explicit modifications of an interface.

Formally, we define three feature relations F^{ess}, F^{chg}, and F^{rem} that each associate feature names to sets of section and chapter names. These three feature relations denote the essential, the changeable, and the removed sections/chapters of a feature name. We build these feature relations from feature relations for each definition of a feature. The feature relations F_n^{ess}, F_n^{chg}, and F_n^{rem} of a feature f_n are mappings from their own feature name f_n to their own three sets. The feature relations F^{ess}, F^{chg}, and F^{rem} of the entire configuration rule base then are the union of all respective feature relations. Additionally, we construct the set *IF* such that it contains the names of all interface sections/chapters. The formal type inference rule is presented in Fig. 7.4.

In this rule, the operator "$r(\!| X |\!)$" is the relational image from Z's mathematical toolkit, the operator applies the relation r in turn to all elements in the set X and merges the results.

Query.   We define one general consistency rule and one restriction rule:

- All feature names in the query must be defined in the configuration rule base.

- For all feature names in the query, no feature may remove a section or chapter that is listed among the essential sections and chapters of some feature of this query.

The formal type inference rule is presented in Fig. 7.5. In this rule, Q is the set of feature names selected by this query. The operator "$r(\!| X |\!)$" again is the relational image from Z's mathematical toolkit, the operator applies the relation r in turn to all elements in the set X and merges the results.

Note that being essential does *not* propagate from a chapter to all of its sections. A chapter may be marked as essential, but nevertheless some of its default sections can be removed.

Note furthermore that a feature may remove a section that is needed as a parent by another, included section. We leave this consistency check to the definition of Z_{CI}, where it is performed anyway. This simplifies the definition of Z_F. We do not need to check the parents relation at all here. Similarly, we do not check the access restrictions to private sections and chapters here.

Semantics

The semantics is the transformation that maps the three parts to an individual family member. The sets and relations defined for the type inference rules provide us with most of the information we need. For the requirements module base, we get information about the structure of the chapters and sections from the extended chapter interface environment $\Psi_c^{l,d}$ for chapters and from the extended chapter interface environment $\Psi_s^{l,d}$ for sections. For the configuration rule base, we get the relations from feature names to essential/changeable/removed sections and chapters from the

$$\vdash^{\mathcal{F}c} \frac{\begin{array}{l} \text{ZEDCHAR feature } f_1 \text{ ENDCHAR} \\ \text{ZEDCHAR} \\ \quad + s_{1,1}^{ess} \ldots + s_{1,k}^{ess} \\ \text{(-tok +)-tok } s_{1,1}^{chg} \ldots \\ \qquad \text{(-tok +)-tok } s_{1,l}^{chg} \\ \quad - s_{1,1}^{rem} \ldots - s_{1,m}^{rem} \\ \text{ENDCHAR} \\ \quad \ldots \\ \text{ZEDCHAR feature } f_n \text{ ENDCHAR} \\ \text{ZEDCHAR} \\ \quad + s_{n,1}^{ess} \ldots + s_{n,o}^{ess} \\ \text{(-tok +)-tok } s_{n,1}^{chg} \ldots \\ \qquad \text{(-tok +)-tok } s_{n,p}^{chg} \\ \quad - s_{n,1}^{rem} \ldots - s_{n,q}^{rem} \\ \text{ENDCHAR} \end{array}}{\left(\begin{array}{l} F_1^{ess} = \{f_1 \mapsto \{s_{1,1}^{ess}, \ldots, s_{1,k}^{ess}\}\} \\ F_1^{chg} = \{f_1 \mapsto \{s_{1,1}^{chg}, \ldots, s_{1,l}^{chg}\}\} \\ F_1^{rem} = \{f_1 \mapsto \{s_{1,1}^{rem}, \ldots, s_{1,m}^{rem}\}\} \\ \quad \vdots \\ F_n^{ess} = \{f_n \mapsto \{s_{n,1}^{ess}, \ldots, s_{n,o}^{ess}\}\} \\ F_n^{chg} = \{f_n \mapsto \{s_{n,1}^{chg}, \ldots, s_{n,p}^{chg}\}\} \\ F_n^{rem} = \{f_n \mapsto \{s_{n,1}^{rem}, \ldots, s_{n,q}^{rem}\}\} \\ F^{ess} = F_1^{ess} \cup \ldots \cup F_n^{ess} \\ F^{chg} = F_1^{chg} \cup \ldots \cup F_n^{chg} \\ F^{rem} = F_1^{rem} \cup \ldots \cup F_n^{rem} \\ \#\operatorname{dom} F^{ess} = n \\ \operatorname{dom} F^{ess} \cap (\operatorname{dom} \Psi_c^{I,d} \cup \operatorname{dom} \Psi_s^{I,d}) = \varnothing \\ \#\{s_{1,1}^{ess}, \ldots, s_{1,k}^{ess}\} = k \\ \#\{s_{1,1}^{chg}, \ldots, s_{1,l}^{chg}\} = l \\ \#\{s_{1,1}^{rem}, \ldots, s_{1,m}^{rem}\} = m \\ \quad \vdots \\ \#\{s_{n,1}^{ess}, \ldots, s_{n,o}^{ess}\} = o \\ \#\{s_{n,1}^{chg}, \ldots, s_{n,p}^{chg}\} = p \\ \#\{s_{n,1}^{rem}, \ldots, s_{n,q}^{rem}\} = q \\ (\operatorname{ran} F^{ess} \cup \operatorname{ran} F^{chg} \cup \operatorname{ran} F^{rem}) \subseteq \\ \quad (\operatorname{dom} \Psi_c^{I,d} \cup \operatorname{dom} \Psi_s^{I,d}) \\ IF = \operatorname{dom} \big((last(\!| \operatorname{ran}(\Psi_s^{I,d}) \cup \\ \qquad \operatorname{ran}(\Psi_c^{I,d}) |\!)) \rhd \{`` "\} \big) \\ IF \cap \operatorname{ran} F^{rem} = \varnothing \end{array} \right)}$$

Figure 7.4: The type inference rule of Z_F for the configuration rule base.

$$\vdash^{\mathcal{F}Q} \frac{\text{ZEDCHAR } f_1 \ldots f_j \text{ ENDCHAR}}{\left(\begin{array}{l} Q = \{f_1, \ldots, f_j\} \\ Q \subseteq \operatorname{dom} F^{ess} \\ F^{rem}(\!| Q |\!) \cap F^{ess}(\!| Q |\!) = \varnothing \end{array} \right)}$$

Figure 7.5: The type inference rule of Z_F for a query.

feature relations F^{ess}, F^{chg}, and F^{rem}. For the query, we have the set of feature names Q.

Furthermore, we need an association of the syntax grammar non-terminals "Chapter" and "Section" to their corresponding input. In the lexis, we already have defined a function that attributes each token with the sub-sequence of input Z characters that were grouped into this token. In the mark-up, we already have defined a function that attributes each Z character with the sub-sequence of input LaTeX/email characters that were grouped into this Z character. Therefore, we can construct the association easily for any match of the syntax grammar non-terminals. We omit further details here. One implementation idea is to attribute each non-terminal with the position in the input stream where it starts and with the position in the input stream where it ends. We used this technique in the tool GenFam-Mem 2.0 [Bre00c].

We define the result of the transformation by the following steps. We start out with a base system consisting of everything that is either an interface or marked as default. To be more precise, the set of base sections B is the set of all those sections which are not marked as "private", and for which none of its enclosing chapters is marked as "private". (That is, they are marked either not at all, denoting an interface, or they are marked as "private default".)

$$B \;=\; \{\, i : \operatorname{dom} \Psi_s^{I,d} \mid \text{private} \notin \operatorname{ran} \operatorname{ran}(\Psi_s^{I,d}(i)) \,\}$$

We then add to the base system B all the sections that the features in the query demand; and for the chapters that the features in the query demand, we also add all their non-"private" sections. This means adding both the essential and the changeable sections/chapters. The result is an extended set of sections E.

$$
\begin{aligned}
E \;=\; B \;\cup\; & \big((F^{ess}(\!(Q)\!) \cup F^{chg}(\!(Q)\!)) \cap \operatorname{dom} \Psi_s^{I,d} \big) \;\cup\; \\
& \big\{ i : \operatorname{dom} \Psi_s^{I,d}; \; c : \big((F^{ess}(\!(Q)\!) \cup F^{chg}(\!(Q)\!)) \cap \operatorname{dom} \Psi_c^{I,d} \big) \mid \\
& \quad c \in \operatorname{dom} \operatorname{ran}(\Psi_s^{I,d}(i)) \wedge \text{private} \notin \operatorname{ran} \operatorname{ran} cps((\Psi_s^{I,d}(i)), c) \bullet i \big\}
\end{aligned}
$$

(In this formula, we use the chapter path suffix $cps(s, c)$ defined in Sect. 6.3.4 above.)

We next remove from E all the sections that the features in the query demand to be removed; and for the chapters that shall be removed, we remove all their sections. The result is the set of sections S of the family member.

$$
\begin{aligned}
S \;=\; E \setminus F^{rem}(\!(Q)\!) \setminus & \\
\big\{ i : \operatorname{dom} \Psi_s^{I,d}; \; c : (F^{rem}(\!(Q)\!) & \cap \operatorname{dom} \Psi_c^{I,d}) \mid c \in \operatorname{dom} \operatorname{ran}(\Psi_s^{I,d}(i)) \bullet i \big\}
\end{aligned}
$$

Note that our type inference rules ensure that no section is removed which another feature marks as essential.

After having determined the set of sections of the family member, we can define the set of chapter headings C of the family member. We keep only those chapter headings for which at least one section exists.

$$C \;=\; \{\, i : \operatorname{dom} \Psi_s^{I,d}; \; c : \operatorname{dom} \Psi_c^{I,d} \mid c \in \operatorname{dom} \operatorname{ran}(\Psi_s^{I,d}(i)) \bullet c \,\}$$

The final step is the definition of the output sequence of Z characters (and markup). The output is the same as the requirements module base, but with some parts removed. The order of the output characters is otherwise the same as in the requirements module base. We remove all Z characters associated to syntax grammar non-terminals "`Section`", where the corresponding section name is not in S, and we remove all Z characters associated to syntax grammar non-terminals "`Chapter`", where the corresponding chapter name is not in C. Additionally, we remove all Z characters associated to any token "default". Note that all informal text blocks are associated to some formal text; they are also removed suitably where necessary.

Example of a Usage

To illustrate our extension, Fig. 7.6 shows a simplified example of a usage from our family of LAN message services in Appendices A, B, and C. Figure 7.6(a) contains an excerpt of the requirements module base, Figure 7.6(b) some of the feature definitions, and Figure 7.6(c) some queries for family members that are specified using features. The complete requirements module base contains more feature definitions; also not all requirements modules referenced here are shown in Figure 7.6(a).

Note that the feature deskPhoneXY_hardware means that the system uses the hardware of the office desk phones of brand XY instead of computer terminals. These phones only have a small text display with two lines. The associacted software platform is restricted to the language Pascal.

Graphical Illustration of Configuring a System Using Features

Figures 7.7, 7.8, and 7.9 illustrate how we configure a system using features. We take our LAN message service family, again. Figure 6.7 on page 113 presented its requirements module hierarchy. The first two figures here contain scaled-down versions; please refer to the original figure for the text labels.

A consistent configuration. In Figure 7.7, the four sub-figures show the base system, two features, and the resulting complete system. The base system of our family is in Figure 7.7(a). The black boxes mark those sections which are part of the "plain" family member that has no features.

The changes by the feature lunch_alarm are in Figure 7.7(b). An automated alarm clock informs everybody when it is time for the lunch break. By default, the alarm is a short text message. A bold frame marks those sections and chapters which the feature adds on top of the base system. A dashed frame means that this addition is not essential and could be overruled by another feature.

Two remarks may help to understand some of the changes better: The left, bold frame is around the default section broadcast_message_delivery which is already part of the base system. This makes the section essential such that it must not be removed by another feature. The non-essential section addition drawn as a dashed frame does not actually change anything, because the section is a default in the base system anyway. This is due to our wish to express our intention behind the feature lunch_alarm better.

1. chapter environment

1.1 chapter computing_platform

1.1.1 chapter data_types

...

1.1.1.2 chapter text_strings

1.1.1.2.1 section text_string_base

...

1.1.1.2.2 private default section c_text_string

...

endchapter text_strings

1.1.1.3 chapter graph_images

1.1.1.3.1 section graph_image_base

...

endchapter graph_images

endchapter data_types

...

endchapter computing_platform

1.2 chapter device_interfaces

...

1.2.2 chapter communicating_entities

1.2.2.1 chapter messages

...

endchapter messages

...

1.2.2.8 private default chapter user_interface

1.2.2.8.1 section user_base

...

1.2.2.8.2 private default chapter graphical_user_interface

1.2.2.8.2.1 section gui_comm_base

...

1.2.2.8.2.2 private default section gui_io_base

...

endchapter graphical_user_interface

1.2.2.8.3 private chapter textual_user_interface

...

endchapter textual_user_interface

endchapter user_interface

...

endchapter communicating_entities

endchapter device_interfaces

endchapter environment

2. chapter system_behaviour

2.1 chapter function_drivers

2.1.1 chapter message_delivery

...

2.1.1.2 private default section timely_message_delivery

...

2.1.1.3 private default section correct_message_delivery

...

2.1.1.4 private default section broadcast_message_delivery

...

endchapter message_delivery

endchapter function_drivers

...

endchapter system_behaviour

(a) Some of the formal chapter and section headings in the requirements module base. We omitted the "parents" construct and all of the actual contents of the sections.

---

feature note_to_all:
+   broadcast_message_delivery
+   text_message_base
(+) one_line_message

feature scroll_text_message:
+   multi_line_message
−   one_line_message
+   graphical_user_interface
−   textual_user_interface

feature birthday_cake_picture:
+   broadcast_message_delivery
+   graphical_message_base
−   text_message_only
+   graphical_user_interface

feature lunch_alarm:
+   automated_agent_interface
+   broadcast_message_delivery
(+) text_message_base

feature deskPhoneXY_hardware:
−   graphical_user_interface
+   textual_user_interface
+   max_lines2_message
+   pascal_text_string
−   c_text_string

...

(b) Some of the feature definitions in the configuration rule base.

The "Lunch Phone" system:

    lunch_alarm

    deskPhoneXY_hardware

The "Classic PC" edition:

    note_to_all

    multi_line_text_message

    standardPC_hardware

The "Deluxe PC" edition:

    lunch_alarm

    birthday_cake_picture

    note_to_all

    multi_line_text_message

    scroll_text_message

    standardPC_hardware

(c) Some queries for family members.

Figure 7.6: An example usage of Z_F, our Z extension for families and features, extracted from the specification in Appendices A, B, and C.

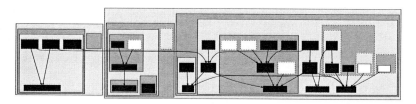

(a) The base system.

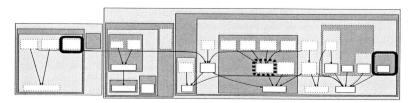

(b) The feature lunch_alarm.

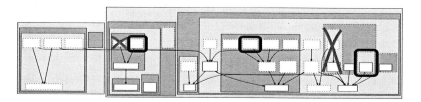

(c) The feature deskphone_hardware.

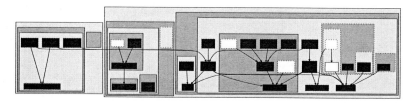

(d) The complete "Lunch Phone" system.

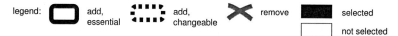

Figure 7.7: Configuring a system using features in the LAN message service family. (See Figure 6.7 on page 113 for the text labels of the boxes.)

The changes by the feature deskPhoneXY_hardware are in Figure 7.7(c). A bold cross marks those sections and chapters which the feature explicitly removes.

The final configuration of the "Lunch Phone" system is in Figure 7.7(d). It consists of the above two features. Compare also the formal descriptions of the features and of the "Lunch Phone" system in Figure 7.6, and in Appendices B and C.

An inconsistent configuration.   Figure 7.8 shows an inconsistent configuration. The base system of our family is repeated in Figure 7.8(a). We also request again the feature deskPhoneXY_hardware. Its changes are repeated in Figure 7.8(c).

We request the feature birthday_cake_picture now, instead of the feature lunch_alarm. The changes by the feature birthday_cake_picture are in Figure 7.8(b).

This combination of features causes an inconsistency. The module graphical_user_interface is essential for the feature birthday_cake_picture, but the feature deskPhoneXY_hardware excludes it. This particular kind of hardware does not support a graphical user interface, even though it is required for displaying birthday cake pictures.

The type rules of Z_F flag this inconsistency as a type error. We are not allowed to generate the corresponding family member.

More examples.   Figure 7.9 presents more examples for the type rules and semantics of Z_F. These examples are small toy examples in order to show many different cases in limited space.

Outlook: Adding More Complex Configuration Rules And Parameters

We can see use for more complex configuration rules beyond simple feature definitions. Our separation of requirements modules and configuration rules opens ways for documenting further kinds of configuration constraints in the configuration rule base, and for analyzing them by tools. Also, generic parameters for modules and for features can be a notational convenience for a recurring kind of configuration task. We will come back to these issues in the outlook in Section 7.10.

7.5   Composing the Properties of a Family Member in the Formalism Z

We describe how we can compose the properties in the requirements to a complete system description; we do this in a way that works together with the configuration transformation. We briefly recapitulate the parts of Chap. 2 on how we can specify an event-oriented, embedded software system in Z using the inverted four-variable model. Z allows to specify requirements incrementally in a constraint-oriented way; we describe how this can be done. Building on this, we present conventions for composing the meaning of a family member from requirements modules in Z_F. Finally, we show that our formalism is sufficiently general such that we can express arbitrary constraints on dynamically changing values of variables.

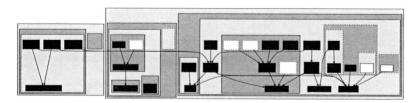

(a) The base system.

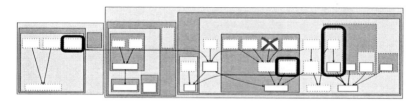

(b) The feature birthday_cake_picture.

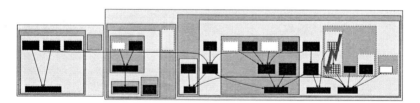

(c) The feature deskphone_hardware.

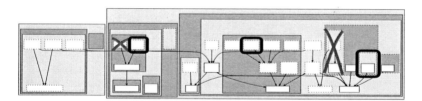

(d) Resulting inconsistent configuration.

Figure 7.8: An inconsistent configuration which is a type error in Z_F. (See Figure 6.7 on page 113 for the text labels of the boxes.)

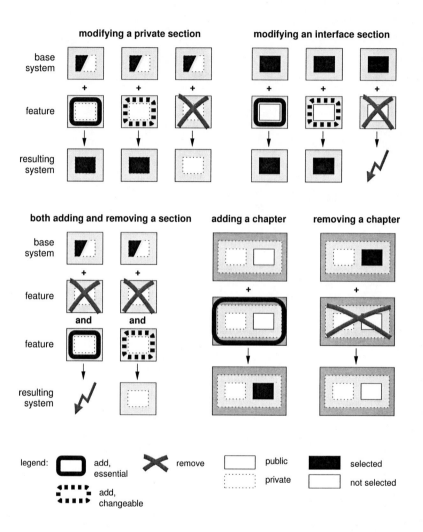

Figure 7.9: More examples for the type rules and semantics of Z_F.

7.5.1   Again: Using the Inverted Four-Variable Model for Specifying in Z

We briefly recapitulate the parts of Chap. 2 on how we can specify an event-oriented, embedded software system in Z using the inverted four-variable model.

The inverted four-variable model allows to specify the required behaviour over a set of variables that describe values of entities in the real world. The requirements are separated into requirements on the system, REQ, and requirements on the environment of the system, NAT. The variables are separated into a vector of monitored variables $\underline{m}^t$ and a vector of controlled variables $\underline{c}^t$.

A first design step separates the software requirements from the requirements on the input devices (sensors) and on the output devices (actuators). The input devices set the software's input variables $\underline{i}^t$ according to the monitored variables, and the output devices set the controlled variables according to the software's output variables $\underline{o}^t$.

We structure the software requirements in a particular way in order to ease maintenance. We introduce estimates $\overline{\underline{m}}^t$ and $\overline{\underline{c}}^t$ for the monitored and controlled variables $\underline{m}^t$ and $\underline{c}^t$. The software requirements specification SoRS consists of the relations D_IN, D_OUT, and $\overline{\text{REQ}}$. D_IN relates the input variables $\underline{i}^t$ to $\overline{\underline{m}}^t$, and D_OUT relates $\overline{\underline{c}}^t$ to the output variables $\underline{o}^t$. Accordingly, the input and output devices are specified by the inverse relations of D_IN and D_OUT. The relation $\overline{\text{REQ}}$ is quite similar to REQ. Usually, $\overline{\text{REQ}}$ is just an extension of REQ. REQ describes only "ideal" behaviour. $\overline{\text{REQ}}$ also must specify how to deal with failures of input and output devices. Furthermore, $\overline{\text{REQ}}$ may need to take care of the inaccuracies of the input and output devices.

We can specify discrete behaviour if we define events. An event occurs when a predicate over some variables changes its boolean value. We can use a state transition system based on such events to specify the discrete part of the behaviour of the controlled variables.

There are common conventions for specifying a state transition system using the general mathematics of Z. We describe the state space of the transition system by the set of values that a Z schema may take. We describe the state transition relation by other, special Z schemas called operations. And we describe the set of initial states by one more Z schema. Informal text must make clear which Z schema takes which of these purposes. Operations are special Z schemas since they refer to the pre- and post-state through a naming convention. Another naming convention allows to specify input and output values for state transitions.

We interpret transitions such that the system evolves by events that happen. An event is specified by a transition, then. The event has a name and is distinguishable from other events. The effect of the event is specified by the post-states of the transition. The event may happen only if the current state is in the set of pre-states. Additionally, an event belonging to the environment may happen only if the environment agrees, and the system must not refuse it. We call this an input event. This interpretation allows for systems without any externally visible state space. In this case, any definition of a state variable is just an auxiliary definition.

We use the naming convention that all schemas whose names start with "*in_*" shall describe the transitions of the software's environment that are linked to events denoting changes of the input variables. The name of an input variable starts with "*vin_*" and that the name of an estimated monitored variable starts with "*vmon_*".

We can abstract the changes to the (auxiliary) estimated monitored variables by introducing monitored events. Our naming convention is "*mon_*" for such monitored events. These monitored events are caused by the software; to be more precise, they belong to D_IN. These events occur when the software has computed the estimates of the monitored variables.

We will use implicit output variables here. An output event is an abstraction of a change to the output variables. We can specify the values of the output variables indirectly by stating constraints on output events. We describe the state changes that are abstracted to an output event by an output transition. Our naming convention is that the names of the schemas of output transition start with "*out_*". The parameters of the output event specify the details of the change to the (implicit) output variables. Accordingly, output transitions are system transitions. To be more precise, they belong to D_OUT.

We complete the separation of D_IN, $\overline{\text{REQ}}$, and D_OUT by introducing (auxiliary) estimated controlled variables and the corresponding controlled events and controlled transitions. Our naming convention is "*ctrl_*". This is analogous to the distinction between input variables and monitored variables. The controlled events belong to $\overline{\text{REQ}}$.

We also introduce another kind of event, the operation. An operation roughly is an output event followed by an input event. An important example where operations are suitable are function calls in programming languages. The underlying software platform of a system is part of its environment, and we must be able to specify the interface between the system and this part of the environment, too. The input parameters of the operation specify the changes to the output variables of the system, and the output parameters specify the changes to the input variables of the system. An operation is part of the specification of the environment NAT of the system; we assume that the environment always performs suitable changes to the input variables. We identify operations by the convention that operation names start with "*op_*".

7.5.2 Incremental Constraint-Oriented Specification in Z

Z allows to specify requirements incrementally in a constraint-oriented way; we describe how this can be done. A constraint-oriented specification helps to specify the individual requirements separately and to then compose them in different ways as needed. We can use the section construct, in particular. Each section has a self-contained formal meaning (compare Sect. 5.6.1). Any initial sequence of sections can be taken as the set of requirements for a variant of the specified system. Each further section adds more constraints on the system (and new declarations).

At the level of Z schemas, we can compose by conjunction. A schema can be defined to be the logical conjunction of other schemas. And a schema can include other schemas, conjoining their definitions and predicates. For example, we can write

$$init\_All == myInit\_Left \land myInit\_Middle \land myInit\_Right$$

and we can write

```
┌─ init_All2 ──────────────────────────────────────────────┐
│  myInit_Left                                              │
│  myInit_Middle                                            │
│  myInit_Right                                             │
├──────────────────────────────────────────────────────────
│  . . .                                                    │
└──────────────────────────────────────────────────────────┘
```

We can also compose Z schemas by disjunction (and by arbitrary combinations of logical operators). These composition facilities allow us to define a transition system out of schemas by a convention as described above, and in turn compose these schemas out of many "small" schemas as needed.

In a constraint-oriented, event-based specification, we have no convention for a visible state space; therefore it helps to have a convention for an explicit state invariant. We could specify constraints on the auxiliary state space in the pre- and postconditions of the transitions and in the specification of the initial state. But they are easier to enforce during incremental specification if we can specify each of them in a single place. The meaning of such an explicit state invariant is, of course, that it is added to all pre- and postconditions and to the specification of the initial state. We will present a concrete convention for this in the next subsection.

We discuss practical examples of incremental constraint-oriented specification in Section 6.5.6 on our family of LAN message services. We demonstrate the general expressiveness of constraints in Z_F in another, pedagogical example in Section 7.5.4 below.

7.5.3 Conventions in Z_F for Composing the Meaning of a Family Member

We present conventions for composing the meaning of a family member from requirements modules in Z_F. In this, we concentrate on specifications of event-based state transition systems. Embedded communication systems are often such systems. The example LAN message service system in Appendices A, B, and C is such a system. Of course, similar conventions for other kinds of systems are possible, too.

The meaning of a family member shall be an event-based state transition system. Then, we must link the parts of the state transition system further to the real world, in a way specific to the family. We describe the state transition system by

- sets of different kinds of transitions, as discussed in Sect. 7.5.1 above (*"in_"*, *"mon_"*, *"ctrl_"*, *"out_"*, and *"op_"*),

- an initial state (maybe internal only),

- a state invariant (maybe internal only), and

- auxiliary definitions.

Sets of Z schemas with special names describe the transitions, the initial state, and the state invariant, respectively. All other Z schemas are auxiliary definitions. The initial state is the conjunction of all schemas whose name begins with "*init_*". The state invariant is the conjunction of all schemas whose name begins with "*inv_*".

We use sets of schemas instead of a single schemas for the initial state and for the state invariant in order to facilitate the flexible composition of requirements modules. The members of such a set together specify the corresponding part.

An example is in Appendix A. Some of the state invariants are specified by the schemas *inv_timely_msg_delivery*, *inv_hist_correct_msg*, and *inv_hist_broadcast_msg* on page 259 and following. These schemas describe state invariants because their name starts with "*inv_*". Those schemas which are selected for a specific family member are composed implicitly by logical conjunction.

We do not explicitly write down these conjunctions. This makes the specification more compact. We do not have to specify a large number of explicit conjunctions for all possible family members. Nevertheless, the specification remains rigorous as long as the composition convention is precise.

Note that our access restrictions on "private" sections do not apply for the composition of the state transition system. Any section can contribute to this last composition step. The access restrictions only prevent dependencies that could obstruct consistent configurations of sections.

Not every formal section must contain the special schemas that define the transition system. A section without them can provide definitions that serve as a base for another section that contains such schemas. Also, a section without them can contain axiomatic definitions that restrict the possible set of values for constants defined in an axiomatic definition of another section.

7.5.4   Expressiveness of Z_F: Arbitrary Constraints on Dynamically Changing Variables

Our formalism is sufficiently general such that we can express arbitrary constraints on dynamically changing values of variables. The LAN message service family example discussed in Sections 6.5.6 and 7.6 does not exploit the full potential of Z, and thus of Z_F. Therefore, we additionally demonstrate the expressiveness at a pedagogical example here.

The specification in Figures 7.10 and 7.11 is concerned with system memory consumption. The constraints depend both on which system functionality is configured and on the dynamic behaviour of these components.

Section system_resources in Figure 7.10 specifies the system memory available. The current value is in the (auxiliary) variable avail_mem. It must be between 0 and 65536. The initial value is the maximum value. This section is an interface section (no keyword "private"). It is therefore present in all members of the family.

Section audio_resources in Figure 7.10 specifies the system memory consumption by an optional audio subsystem. The audio subsystem may be absent in some family members. The variable au_mem describes the current memory use of the audio

1. section system_resources

parents standard_toolkit

```
┌─ memory ──────────────────┐    ┌─ init_memory ──────────────┐
│ avail_mem : ℕ             │    │ memory                     │
├───────────────────────────┤    ├────────────────────────────┤
│ avail_mem ≤ 65536         │    │ avail_mem = 65536          │
└───────────────────────────┘    └────────────────────────────┘
```

2. private section audio_resources

parents system_resources

```
┌─ audio_memory ────────────┐    ┌─ init_audio_memory ────────┐
│ au_mem : ℕ                │    │ audio_memory               │
├───────────────────────────┤    ├────────────────────────────┤
│ au_mem ≤ 32768           │    │ au_mem = 0                 │
└───────────────────────────┘    └────────────────────────────┘
```

```
┌─ in_track ────────────────┐    ┌─ out_track ────────────────┐
│ fail! : {0, 1}            │    │ Δaudio_memory              │
│ Δaudio_memory             │    │ Δmemory                    │
│ Δmemory                   │    ├────────────────────────────┤
├───────────────────────────┤    │ au_mem′ = au_mem − 1 ∧    │
│ (  au_mem′ = au_mem + 1 ∧ │    │ avail_mem′ = avail_mem + 1 │
│    avail_mem′ = avail_mem − 1 ∧│  └────────────────────────────┘
│    fail! = 0 )  ∨         │
│ (  au_mem′ = au_mem ∧     │
│    avail_mem′ = avail_mem ∧│
│    fail! = 1 )            │
└───────────────────────────┘
```

Figure 7.10: Specification of a family of system memory consumers in Z_F, first part.

subsystem. Initially, it is zero. The audio subsystem will never request more than half of the total system memory. The invariant of schema **audio_memory** ensures this. Input event **in_track** denotes that a sound track enters the system. Accordingly, the memory consumption of the audio subsystem increases, and the memory available decreases. The input of a sound track may fail (for various, unspecified reasons). Then, the memory consumption does not change. In case there is not enough memory left, the input *must* fail. Output event **out_track** denotes that a sound track leaves the system, and that the memory associated is freed again. The output event can occur only when there is at least one track in the system.

In a family member that consists of the base system and of the audio subsystem only, the memory limit is determined by these only. The internal limit by the audio subsystem is lower than the system limit. Therefore, the limit by the audio subsystem governs how much memory the audio subsystem can acquire.

Section **video_resources** in Figure 7.11 specifies the system memory consumption by an optional video subsystem. This section belongs to the same specification

3. private section video_resources

parents system_resources

$$
\begin{array}{|l}
\hline
\;video\_memory \underline{\hspace{2cm}} \\
\hline
vi\_mem : \mathbb{N} \\
\hline
vi\_mem \leq 49152 \\
\hline
\end{array}
$$

$$
\begin{array}{|l}
\hline
\;init\_video\_memory \underline{\hspace{2cm}} \\
\hline
video\_memory \\
\hline
vi\_mem = 0 \\
\hline
\end{array}
$$

$$
\begin{array}{|l}
\hline
\;in\_frame \underline{\hspace{2cm}} \\
\hline
fail! : \{0, 1\} \\
\Delta video\_memory \\
\Delta memory \\
\hline
(\;\; vi\_mem' = vi\_mem + 1 \;\wedge \\
\quad avail\_mem' = avail\_mem - 1 \;\wedge \\
\quad fail! = 0\;)\;\;\vee \\
(\;\; vi\_mem' = vi\_mem \;\wedge \\
\quad avail\_mem' = avail\_mem \;\wedge \\
\quad fail! = 1\;) \\
\hline
\end{array}
$$

$$
\begin{array}{|l}
\hline
\;out\_frame \underline{\hspace{2cm}} \\
\hline
\Delta video\_memory \\
\Delta memory \\
\hline
vi\_mem' = vi\_mem - 1 \;\wedge \\
avail\_mem' = avail\_mem + 1 \\
\hline
\end{array}
$$

Figure 7.11: Specification of a family of system memory consumers in Z_F, second part.

document; we split the specification into two figures for layout reasons only. The specification of the video subsystem is rather similar to that of the audio subsystem. The only differences are the names of variables and schemas, and that the maximum memory consumption is three quarters of the system memory instead of half the system memory.

Any combination of the audio and video subsystems can be configured: none, audio only, video only, and both.

The family member with both audio and video is particularly interesting. Both subsystems must contend dynamically for the system memory. Each subsystem can acquire at most the amount of memory specified in its corresponding section. This is half of the system memory for the audio subsystem, and three quarters for the video subsystem. No subsystem can acquire any more memory when the system limit has been reached. For example, if the video subsystem first demands all the memory it can, then the audio subsystem can only get the remaining quarter of the system memory, instead of the half it could get in a better situation. It should be clear now how we can extend our example by even more consumers and by more complex scheduling strategies.

This example shows how we can express constraints that depend both on which system functionality is configured and on the dynamic behaviour of these components.

We omit the configuration rule base of the specification in Z_F as well as any actual queries for brevity here.

7.6 Example: Some Features and Family Members for the Family of LAN Message Services

We illustrate our approach by presenting some features and family members for our family of LAN message services from Sect. 6.5 above. Appendix B contains the configuration rule base and Appendix C specifies some family members for the requirements module base in Appendix A. Figure 7.6 on page 140 already presented an excerpt of the three appendices.

7.6.1 Features

We now present some features from Appendix B, and we investigate the pair-wise compatibility of all the features. A feature is a list of sections added and a list of sections removed. The list of added sections is differentiated into essential and into changeable sections.

Note how the features are taylored to specific marketing situations, and how they cross-cut the structure of the requirements module base. We could configure systems much less flexibly if we would structure the family along the features instead of the information-hiding requirements modules.

Examples of Features

The feature note_to_all is quite basic for a message service. The users can write a note to everybody. A note is a text message. A note by default is short. That means only one line with at most 40 characters.

The feature lunch_alarm adds a specialty. An (external) automated alarm clock informs everybody that it is time for the lunch break. By default, the alarm is a short text message.

The features deskPhoneXY_hardware and standardPC_hardware allow to select a suitable underlying hardware platform. With the feature deskPhoneXY_hardware, the system uses the hardware of the office desk phones of brand XY instead of computer terminals. These phones only have a small text display with two lines of 20 characters. The associated software platform is restricted to the language Pascal. With the feature standardPC_hardware, the system uses the hardware of standard PCs. These machines have a graphical user interface, and they can display windows with text messages, too. But the associated software platform does not offer the language Pascal anymore. Instead, we can use the language C.

Please find more feature specifications in Appendix B.

Compatibility of Features

We can compute the pair-wise compatibility of the features by the type rules of Z_F. Table 7.1 shows the result.

It turns out that nearly all features are compatible. We attribute this to our well-structured requirements module base. The only exceptions are limitations of resources imposed by deskPhoneXY_hardware, which conflict with resource demands

	standardPC_hardware	deskPhoneXY_hardware	lunch_alarm	birthday_cake_picture	scroll_text_message	multi_line_text_message	note_to_all
note_to_all	√	√	√	√	√	√	
multi_line_text_message	√	√	√	√	√		
scroll_text_message	√	×	√	√			
birthday_cake_picture	√	×	√				
lunch_alarm	√	√					
deskPhoneXY_hardware	×						
standardPC_hardware							

Table 7.1: The pair-wise compatibility of the features of the LAN message service in Appendix B according to the type rules of Z_F.

of two other features. Our type rules let us detect these conflicts already in the configuration rule base. Also, the two different hardware platforms are in conflict; they have no common text string representation.

7.6.2 Family Members

Appendix C contains specifications of some family members. A family member is specified by a list of selected features. Each of the sections of this appendix specifies one complete family member.

The Lunch Phone system is a very minimalistic system, it does not even contain the feature note_to_all. This system informs everybody that it is time for the lunch break, using only the hardware of the office desk phones (of brand XY) instead of computer terminals.

The Classic PC edition is a "plain" version without any particular specialties; it would be sold for a comparably low price. The users can write a note of several lines to everybody, and the system uses the hardware of standard PCs.

The Deluxe PC edition is a "premium" version to be sold at a higher price than the Classic PC edition. This version has many more, attractive-sounding features than the Classic PC edition: lunch alarm, birthday cake picture, and scroll text message.

7.7 Tool Support

Configuring requirements family members needs tool support; some tools already exist, more are planned. We have written a LaTeX style for typesetting specifications in Z_F. We have implemented and used a configurator and a type checker for a predecessor of Z_F; we now plan the same for the current Z_F, following the precise specification in Sect. 7.4.2 and 6.3.4. We can exploit our experience with the tool genFamMem 2.0 [Bre00c] for an extension of CSP-OZ [Fis00, Fis97]. We already use the free tool CADiZ [To⁺02] for general type checking. CADiZ is for plain (ISO-)Z, but we have written a simple transformator from Z_{CI} to plain Z.

7.7.1 Typesetting

We have written a LaTeX style for typesetting specifications in Z_F. The style provides LaTeX environments and macros for the new constructs of Z_F defined in Section 7.4.2. The markup syntax is in Figure 7.2 on page 133 above. An example layout is in Figure 7.6 on page 140 above. The style file can be downloaded free of charge [Bre05a].

The style typesets standard Z constructs by including the style for the CADiZ toolset [To⁺02], which in turn uses the style for Object-Z [Smi00] of the associated tool Wizard [Joh96].

The style itself provides the LaTeX environment `zchapter`, in particular. This environment formats chapter headings in a suitable font and size. The style also redefines the environment `zsection` to match the look. Since chapters may be nested, outer chapter headings are typeset larger than inner chapter and section headings.

The LaTeX environments `zchapter` and `zsection` also provide a suitable automatic, hierarchical chapter and section numbering scheme. This can aid the reader. There is also a command to generate a table of contents specifically for the formal chapters and sections.

To round the typesetting support off, we have also written a syntax highlighting for the LaTeX source of Z specifications in the editor Vim [Oua01]. This add-on to normal syntax highlighting for LaTeX takes care of the additional mathematical LaTeX environments that (plain) Z provides. The new environments and commands are displayed with suitable colours. Of course, our extensions to plain Z are supported, too. The syntax file can be downloaded free of charge [Bre05b].

7.7.2 Configurator

We have implemented and used a configurator for a predecessor of Z_F; we now plan to write a configurator for the current Z_F, following the precise specification of the configurator in Sect. 7.4.2. We can exploit our experience with the tool genFamMem 2.0 [Bre00c]. genFamMem 2.0 takes a specification written in CSP-OZ, enhanced with family constructs, and generates a family member in plain CSP-OZ.

CSP-OZ [Fis00, Fis97] is is a combination of the process algebra CSP (Communicating Sequential Processes) [Ros97] and of Object-Z [Smi00]. Object-Z is an

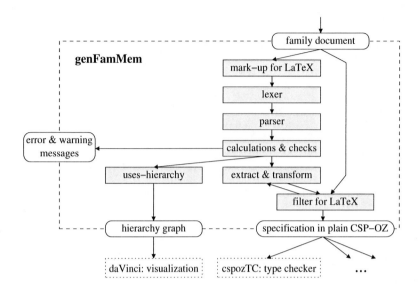

Figure 7.12: Data flow structure of the tool genFamMem 2.0.

object-oriented extension of Z. (We will discuss our experiences with CSP-OZ in Sect. 7.8.4 below.)

The tool contains a lexer/parser for our extension of CSP-OZ which is written using the lex/yacc parser generator [LMB92], and C code. The tool comprises about 8500 lines of commented source code. Figure 7.12 shows its data flow structure. It reflects the well-structured definition of the Z semantics in the ISO standard. The tool is available without charge through its Web home page [Bre00b].

genFamMem 2.0 is more than a configurator tool. The tool also helps to avoid feature interaction problems, and it detects remaining feature interaction problems. genFamMem 2.0 helps to avoid feature interaction problems by generating documentation on the structure of the family. It can generate a dependency graph among sections. This graph then is visualized graphically using the tool "uDraw(Graph)" [Wer05] (formerly known as daVinci). This helps a maintainer of the family to get an overview and thus to avoid mistakes. genFamMem 2.0 detects remaining feature interaction problems by type checking; we will discuss this in the following section.

7.7.3   Type Checker

We have implemented and used a type checker for a predecessor of Z_F; we now plan to write a type checker for the current Z_F, following the precise specification in Sect. 7.4.2 and 6.3.4. Again, we can exploit our experience with the tool genFamMem 2.0.

Type checking a specification in Z_F should happen in three stages, due to the layered definition of Z_F:

1. A configurator tool should also check the type rules that are specific to Z_F (in contrast to the rules for Z_{CI}). This is because Z_F is defined as a transformation to Z_{CI}. For example, the tool should check whether all section and chapter names that appear in the list of a feature are defined in the requirements module base.

   If this check passes, the configurator generates a family member in Z_{CI}.

2. There should be another type checker for the type rules specific to Z_{CI}, as specified in Sect. 6.3.4. For example, an interface module must never depend on a secret module. This type checker can be small, since it can ignore the contents of the formal paragraphs of plain Z.

   If this check passes, a small transformator tool can convert the specification from Z_{CI} to plain Z. The transformation simply consists in removing the keyword "private". We have written such a tool. It is a small script that performs the corresponding text substitution.

3. The other type rules of Z_{CI} can be checked using a type checker for plain Z. Such tools already exist. On example is the free toolset CADiℤ [To$^+$02]. We can use a type checker for plain Z because all of Z_{CI}'s extensions to plain Z appear as informal text to such tools, except the keyword "private". For example, there is no markup in plain Z for chapter headings. Accordingly, the markup phase of the Z type checker will remove any Z_{CI} chapter headings.

The toolset CADiℤ comprises more than a type checker. For example, there is also a theorem prover. However, we have practical experience with the type checker only.

We have implemented and used the tool genFamMem 2.0 as a type checker for a predecessor of Z_F, that is, for an extension of CSP-OZ (see above). We also used a staged approach to type checking. First, genFamMem 2.0 checks for those type rules that are an extension of CSP-OZ. In a second stage, von Garrel's type checker cspozTC [vG99] checks the generated family member in plain CSP-OZ.

This type checking detects feature interaction problems. Our extension of CSP-OZ imposes certain type rules, similar to the rules on the parents relation and to the rules on private modules in Z_F. Some kinds of feature interaction problems therefore become type errors. The tool detects these errors. The tool also checks further, heuristic rules that indicate probable feature interaction problems. We will report on practical experiences in the following section.

7.8 Application: Organizing the Requirements of a Telephone Switching System

We already collected considerable experience with the requirements for a telephone switching system in a predecessor version of our formalism.

Wie applied many of the ideas in this book, but we developed two important ideas only after this work, such that we did not use them for it. There is no distinction between a feature and a requirements module (Sect. 7.2). And there is no multi-level hierarchy for the requirements modules (Sect. 5.3), there is only the dependency hierarchy (Sect. 6.1.1).

7.8.1   The Telephone Switching System and Its Specification

We specified how humans can converse using a system of connected telephone devices [Bre01, Bre00a, Bre99]. The specification is quite large. The current version comprises about 40 pages of commented formal specification, with about 50 sections in nine features/modules, including the base system.

We wanted to investigate a desirable structure for requirements, therefore we did not re-specify a currently existing system. For example, one of the biggest conceptual problems in current telephone systems is the notion of a "call", which has become fuzzy since long (compare, e.g., [Zav97]). Accordingly, we introduced and used the notion of a "connection" instead. A connection always is a relation between exactly two users. It is yet independent of any communication medium. In comparison, a call usually consists of a half-call for the originating device and another half-call for the terminating device. A call already implies a voice channel. If more devices or more users become involved in a call, or other media than a voice channel, things become complicated (see Sect. 1.2).

We used the four-variable model (Sect. 2.1) for distinguishing between the system and its environment. In this, we drew the boundary of the system very close to the users; in fact, we draw it even a little inside their heads. The monitored and controlled variables are the users' decisions and perceptions, respectively. This follows our approach for encapsulating the user interface requirements in Chapter 8 below. The shape of the physical user interface becomes a question of the system design, not of the requirements on the system behaviour.

We introduced important abstractions explicitly and early. Besides the notions of a connection and of the users' decisions and perceptions, we also introduced the three notions of "telephone device", "human", and "user role" explicitly and early. As a consequence, the feature interaction problems between call screening and call forwarding (Sect. 1.2.1 and 1.2.4) vanish. Call screening now appears as two different features: device screening and user screening. Similarly, call forwarding is differentiated into a re-routing when a human moves to another device, and into the transfer of a user role to another human. All combinations of screening and forwarding now work without adverse interactions. For each combination it is clear whether the phone should ring. A subscriber of user screening will be protected against a connection from a screened user from all devices, at the device where she is registered currently. A subscriber of device screening will not expect to be protected from humans that are able to use different devices. We just don't have the ambiguous notion of a "caller" anymore.

We specified the requirements in the formalism CSP-OZ [Fis00, Fis97] (see Sect. 7.7.2), which we extended by means to specify a family of requirements. All family members are specified in one document. A family member is composed of a list of features. A feature consists of a set of modules and of a list of modules "to remove". A module is represented in CSP-OZ by the formal construct of a section. Each module, i.e., section, holds one abstract requirement. There is a formal semantics both for CSP-OZ [Fis00] and for our additional family construct [Bre00c].

The formalism forces to make certain information explicit. It forces the original specifier of a feature to state whether a property is essential for the feature or not. A feature's changeable properties can be removed from the system by another feature through a suitable operator. This allows for non-monotonous changes. But only entire properties, i.e., sections, can be removed and added. This is very similar to the essential and changeable sections of features in Z_F (Sect. 7.4.2) that allow to express configuration priorities (Sect. 7.3.2). The formalism also forces the specifier of any section to state on which other sections it depends. There can be a dependency because the section uses a definition from the other section.

7.8.2   Adding Features

Besides features describing the base system, there are features for different kinds of screening and for different kinds of forwarding.

Again, we introduced important abstractions explicitly and early. The base system has no notion of screening. It only has the general notion that resources may or may not be available. Therefore, first the feature ScreeningBase introduces the abstraction of a relation about whether a user A is available for a user B or not. This feature does not change the behaviour of the system yet. But based on this feature, we introduce real screening features which build on the new abstraction. Due to this explicit abstraction, they do this in a coordinated way.

A constraint-oriented specification style helped to specify the individual requirements separately. Each formal section contains one property, that is, one constraint. We made each property as small as usefully possible. The properties are then composed by logical conjunction.

Some of the features are non-monotonous, that is, they change the behaviour of another feature. For example, the feature BlackListOfDevices removes the property ConNoScreen of the feature ScreeningBase. This property states that a connection is never blocked due to screening.

7.8.3   Example of a Feature Interaction Detected and Resolved

We cannot demonstrate the detection of a feature interaction at the standard example of the interaction between Terminating Call Screening and Call Forwarding. We avoided this kind of adverse interaction completely, as shown above.

Nevertheless, the type rules for our extension of CSP-OZ pointed us to some remaining problems. For example, both screening features "remove" the same changeable section ConNoScreen of the feature ScreeningBase. Each of the two features then states in one new, essential section the conditions where no connection is allowed.

Our type rules flag this double removal as a warning. A manual analysis shows immediately that the two replacing, simple sections are not contradictory. But a further look reveals that both features also have a changeable section each that states that its respective feature is the only screening feature, such that otherwise no screening happens. This of course is a contradiction in the general case.

We needed to resolve the feature interaction problem. As in most cases, the harder part was to detect the problem before a customer notices it, and the relatively easy part was to find a specific remedy. We specified this remedy as just another feature which we select whenever both of the above features are included. It contains a section that states that screening happens exactly when either of the two screening features demands it. Furthermore, it removes both conflicting sections. We are explicitly allowed to do this since both sections are marked as changeable.

7.8.4 More Experiences

The previous section proves that our extension of CSP-OZ helped to maintain the requirements and to tackle feature interaction problems; but we also had experiences with this formalism that lead us to improve our approach.

Requirements Modules vs. Features

We did not yet distinguish between a requirements module and a feature in our extension of CSP-OZ. This had the disadvantages already discussed in Sect. 7.2 above. Our formalism Z_F (Sect. 7.4.2) now makes the distinction and solves the problem.

Two Overlapping Requirements Grouping Constructs in Plain CSP-OZ

Plain CSP-OZ provides two independent constructs for grouping requirements; this complicated our extension. Plain CSP-OZ has the class construct from object orientation. But CSP-OZ also has the section construct from ISO Z. The latter was adopted together with the detailed definition of the syntax and semantics of Z which only the ISO standard provides. Consequently, our extension ended up having two similar, but nevertheless different means for grouping requirements, too.

We based our extension on the section construct of CSP-OZ and not on the class construct, because the latter cannot group together certain parts of a specification, as discussed in Sect. 5.6.2 above. The class construct construct comes from Object-Z [Smi00]. Object-Z, and thus CSP-OZ, allows all the different kinds of paragraphs of Z to be used, outside of any class. A paragraph can be, for example, one type definition, one axiomatic description, or one schema definition.

The class construct did not interwork too well with the section construct. There were many sections that contained exactly one class. This turned out to be syntactic clutter. We removed it by defining a shorthand notation in our extension of CSP-OZ. The shorthand allows to use a class in the places where a section can occur, too. A syntactic transformation then implicitly adds a suitable section heading for such a class [Bre01, Bre00c]. This shorthand fixed the problem at the surface, but conceptually it is not entirely satisfactory. Our current formalism Z_F (Sect. 7.4.2) does not have this problem anymore. Z_F does not build on Object-Z, only on ISO Z.

Multi-Level Hierarchy of Modules

CSP-OZ offers no formal way to express a multi-level hierarchy of modules; and our extension of CSP-OZ did not add such a mean. In Object-Z, and thus CSP-OZ, class definitions may not be nested. The mechanism of inheritance is a rather different thing. Inheritance allows to delegate the processing of a message to a superclass and it allows to reuse the syntactic interface of a superclass, but it does not group classes together, as we already argued in Sect. 5.6.2 above. And the mechanism of the package is missing in Object-Z entirely.

CSP-OZ allows to express the dependency relation among modules through its parents construct, but this is something quite different than a module hierarchy, as discussed in Sect. 6.1.1 above. In general, there is not necessarily a correlation between two requirements depending on each other, and being likely to change together. Our current formalism Z_F (Sect. 7.4.2) now makes this distinction.

7.9 Application: Maintaining a Set of Communication Protocol Test Specifications

We applied our notion of requirements modules in an industry project where we had to maintain a set of communication protocol test specifications. The application domain is the wireless telecommunication standard UMTS, and its radio link control (RLC) layer in particular. Our customer was Siemens AG, Salzgitter. Our testing task demanded that we maintained an entire family of requirements; the causes are not particular to this application. We executed the specified tests using an automated, flexible testing environment. However, we had to apply our approach to a different formalism than to the one in this book because of the testing tool used. Nevertheless, we applied our ideas on requirements structuring to ease the maintenance of the family of requirements.

7.9.1 The UMTS Protocol Stack and Its RLC Layer

The application domain is the wireless telecommunication standard UMTS, and its radio link control (RLC) layer in particular. UMTS (Universal Mobile Telecommunications System) is a new international wireless telecommunications standard developed by the 3GPP consortium [3GP]. The standard comprises a layered communication architecture. Each layer relies on primitive services of the layer below and provides complex services to the layer above. Conceptually, each layer in the user equipment communicates with the same layer in the UMTS terrestrial radio access network.

There are several communication layers. Layer 1 is the physical layer of hardware services provided by the chip set. Layer 2 is the data link layer. It provides the concept of a point-to-point connection to the network layer above. Layer 3, the

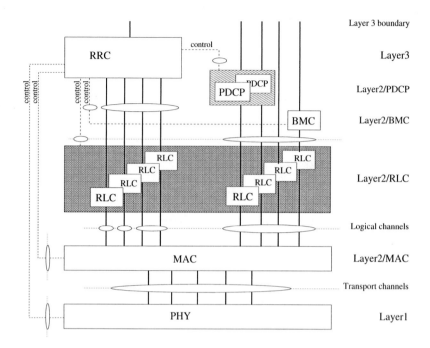

Figure 7.13: Overall architecture of the UMTS radio interface protocol stack.

network layer, provides network services such as establishment / release of a connection, hand-over, broadcast of messages to all users in a certain geographical area, and notification of information to specific users. It includes the Radio Resource Control (RRC), which assigns, configures and releases wireless bandwidth (codes, frequencies etc.). Above layer 3 there are application layers containing functionality such as Call Control (CC) and Mobility Management (MM).

Layer 2 consists of several sub-layers: Medium Access Control (MAC), Radio Link Control (RLC), Packet Data Convergence Protocol (PDCP), and Broadcast and Multicast Control (BMC) layer. The MAC provides unacknowledged transfer of service data units, reallocation of parameters such as user identity number and transport format. It furthermore reports local measurements such as traffic volume and quality of service indication to the RRC. The main task of the RLC is segmentation and reassembly of long data packets from higher layers into fixed width protocol data units, respectively. This includes flow control, error detection, retransmission, duplicate removal, and similar tasks. An overview of this architecture is given in Fig. 7.13, which is from the 3GPP standard.

The RLC layer of the UMTS protocol stack [RLC01] provides three modes of data transfer: acknowledged (error-free), unacknowledged (immediate), and transparent (unchanged) mode. In acknowledged mode, the correct transmission of data is guaranteed to the upper layer; if unrecoverable errors occur, a notification is sent. In unacknowledged mode, erroneous and duplicate packets are deleted, but there is no retransmission or error correction: messages are delivered as soon as a complete set of packets is received. In transparent mode, higher layer data is forwarded without adding any protocol information; thus no error correction or duplicate removal can be done.

Segmentation and reassembly is necessary in all of the RLC layer's modes. The variable-length data packets received from the upper layer must be segmented into fixed-length RLC protocol data units (PDUs). Vice versa, received PDUs have to be reassembled according to the attached sequence numbers for delivery to the higher layer. The RLC layer also offers a cipher mechanism. It prevents unauthorized access to message data.

Transmission of data works as follows. The RLC layer reads messages from the upper layer service access points (SAPs), performs segmentation and concatenation with other packets as needed, optionally encrypts the data, adds header information such as sequence numbers, and puts the packets into the transmission buffer. From there, the MAC assigns a channel for the packet and transmits it via layer 1 and radio waves. On the opposite side, packets arriving from the MAC in the receiver buffer are investigated for retransmissions, stripped from the RLC header information, decrypted if necessary and then reassembled according to the sequence numbering, before they are made accessible to the upper layers via the corresponding SAP.

There may be several instances of the RLC protocol machine coexisting at the same time. This is necessary since the services to the upper layers provide a variable number of connections, whereas the service of the lower layer provides a fixed number of logical channels. However, the maximum number of parallel instances is statically fixed in the system. This is for efficiency reasons. We will come back to the concurrent protocol instances below when we discuss how to test them.

7.9.2   The Customer

Our customer was Siemens AG, Salzgitter. Siemens provided an implementation of the RLC layer. We tested this implementation. This cooperation was conducted in the context of Siemens' efforts to develop a UMTS mobile phone. Several sites of Siemens took part in the entire development. The Salzgitter site was responsible for the RLC layer. They generated the implementation directly from a specification that they have written in the Specification and Description Language SDL [EHS97, ITU99].

7.9.3   Families of Requirements in Testing

Our testing task demanded that we maintained an entire family of requirements; the causes are not particular to this application. We used an explicit specification of the required behaviour for testing. We had to manage many variants and versions of this requirements specification.

Testing and Requirements

We used an explicit specification of the required behaviour of the RLC layer for testing this layer. This means that we used black-box testing, not structural testing. Black-box testing is better to ensure inter-operability between devices from different providers. In the case of UMTS, user equipment and base stations are developed by different companies. Moreover, even the development of the software for different layers of the protocol was distributed between different sites within our cooperation partner.

Black-box, specification-based testing has significant advantages over structural testing even when inter-operability is not an issue: the testing process concentrates on the user requirements and functionality aspects rather than on implementation details, ambiguities and misinterpretations of the tasks are exhibited, and errors arising from omissions and missing cases can be found.

Testing and Configuration Management

We had to manage many variants and versions of the requirements specification of the behaviour to test. This could have led easily to inconsistencies or to large amounts of maintenance effort. The causes are not particular to this application.

Many versions. We had many versions of the requirements. The standard describing the requirements for UMTS was still subject to considerable change during the development of the test suites. The "December 1999" release was available shortly after the start of our specification work. This release was supposed to be stable. But even after it, a large number of changes were made, and more had to be expected. This concerns, for example, the parameters of the service primitives and the details of the data at the interfaces, such as the structure of the protocol data units. Even the behaviour of the protocol machines was still expected to change, in particular for error handling.

Many variants. We also have many variants of the test suites. They result from three orthogonal sources of variation: adjustments of the test coverage, stepping from component tests to integration tests, and stepping from active testing to passive testing.

We must adjust the test coverage in different variants of a test suite for the same requirements. This is for the following reasons: we have to test the system under test (SUT) with selected, interesting sets of signal parameters, while using the same behaviour description. Furthermore, we want to test the SUT with different choices of its possible behaviour, which are either completely random, or which have a selectively increased probability for certain choices, or which are manually selected, fixed and deterministic test traces. All these test cases use the same description of admissible behaviour.

Integration tests need to be prepared already during the specification of component tests. The component tests check an individual layer of the UMTS protocol stack. The integration tests check several layers together. These tests should re-use the same description of admissible behaviour of the individual layers. Furthermore, already the RLC layer allows for multiple parallel instances of the same protocol machine. These run independently, at least at the black box behaviour level. But the implementation in SDL has a different, less decoupled structure. Therefore, integration tests for the protocol machine instances of this protocol layer were necessary.

Similarly, passive tests need to be prepared during the specification of active tests. In active tests, the test specification generates the test stimuli. In passive tests, real UMTS air interfaces and upper protocol layers provide the stimuli to the SUT. The testing system then cannot monitor internal signals, but only external stimuli and reactions. Again, these tests should re-use the same description of admissible behaviour.

Common causes. All of these sources for multiple versions and variants appear often in testing. Unstable requirements are common in software development. Fine-tuning the test coverage is always advisable to improve the quality of the tests. Integration tests are a must. Passive testing is often a consequence of an embedding of the software into an even larger system.

7.9.4 The Automated Testing Environment

We executed the specified tests using an automated, flexible testing environment. The specification-based test suites were executed automatically by a tool. We developed a generator tool that produces automatically all necessary interface code.

The Testing Tool

The specification-based test suites were executed automatically by a tool. The tool RT-Tester [Ver] reads the specification and generates a transition graph. In a separate stage, RT-Tester generates test scripts from the transition graph. They are executed on a separate testing machine automatically and in real time. They may run over long periods of time: hours, days, weeks and more – without the necessity of manually writing test scripts of an according length. The testing machine and the system under test (SUT) communicate via TCP/IP sockets, and test results are evaluated on the fly in real time during the run of the SUT, by using the compiled specification as a test oracle. To ensure that the tests cover the whole bandwidth of all possible system situations, a mathematically proven testing strategy is used [Pel96].

The test specification language is CSP. CSP (Communicating Sequential Processes, see [Ros97]) is a specification language for the black-box behaviour of a system. The structure of the requirements is reflected by particular operators such as sequential or parallel composition, choice, iteration and hiding. Communication between the processes and with the outside is by the exchange of events. We use a timed version of CSP, where it is possible to set timers which generate events upon elapse. This way, it is possible to test real-time behaviour of applications, which is especially important for embedded systems. Since CSP arose from theoretical considerations, it has a well-defined formal semantics and a rich theory. The example in Fig. 7.14 introduces a few basic operators of CSP, in particular the event prefix, the external choice, and one of the parallel composition operators.

The test specification language CSP is different from the implementation specification language SDL. This is because the test specification is developed independently of the implementation by different people. For each of both tasks, the language most suitable is used. Our experience is that most specification errors are made by one of the teams only, such that they show up in the tests.

The automated tests require interface code between the test system and the implementation. This code must translate between the test system's representation of the abstract CSP events and the interface of the implementation written in C. the code must be rewritten every time the specification or the implementation is changed.

The Testing Environment

We developed a generator tool that produces automatically all necessary interface code. Since the generation is completely automated, consistency between the interfaces is guaranteed. It would have been extremely tedious and error-prone to adapt the rather complex interface code manually. We do not describe the generator tool itself further in this book. Two conference papers provide more details [BrSc01, BrSc02]. Instead, we concentrate on the requirements structuring aspects here.

7.9.5   Applying our Approach to the Tool's Language CSP

We had to apply our approach to a different formalism than to the one in this book because of the testing tool used. We could use our method for structuring the specification. But we had less syntactic support. We often had to rely on stylistic conventions instead. There was no tool support for checking these conventions. And there was no supporting tool like genFamMem for generating documentation automatically. Nevertheless, our experience was that even this light-weight approach was a considerable help for managing all the versions and variants.

We had to map our structuring means and configuration means onto the tool's language CSP. These means are, in particular,

- requirements modules (Sect. 5.2),

- a hierarchy of requirements modules (Sect. 5.3),

- an explicit dependency relation (Sect. 6.1),

- explicit interfaces between requirements modules (Sect. 6.3),

- abstract interfaces between requirements modules (Sect. 6.4),

- configuration management for requirements in general (Sect. 7.1),

- the distinction of features and requirements modules (Sect. 7.2), and

```
include "timers.csp"
pragma AM_INPUT
channel coin, buttonCoffee, buttonTea
nametype MonEv = { coin, buttonCoffee, buttonTea }
pragma AM_OUTPUT
channel coffee, tea
nametype CtrlEv = { coffee, tea }

OBSERVER = (   (coin -> HAVE_COIN)
            [] (buttonCoffee -> OBSERVER)
            [] (buttonTea -> OBSERVER))
HAVE_COIN = (   (coin -> HAVE_COIN))
            [] (buttonTea -> AWAIT({tea}) ; OBSERVER)
            [] (buttonCoffee -> AWAIT({coffee}); OBSERVER)

RANDOM_STIMULI = (|~| x: MonEv @ x -> PAUSE; RANDOM_STIMULI)

TEST_SPEC = RANDOM_STIMULI [| MonEv |] OBSERVER
```

Explanation: A system described by the process OBSERVER accepts either
of the three inputs listed (external choice "[]"). If the input is a coin, then
the system behaves like the process HAVE_COIN (event prefix "->"). A system
described by the process HAVE_COIN outputs the desired drink after the corresponding button press. In this, the sub-process AWAIT waits for any of the
outputs specified (sequential process composition ";"). The definition of this
process is listed in the example in Fig. 7.15 below. The process RANDOM_STIMULI
non-deterministically selects one event from the set MonEv (replicated internal
choice "|~| x : S @ P(x)"), waits a short time, and starts all over (recur-
sion). The process TEST_SPEC describes the complete test suite: the process
RANDOM_STIMULI provides all the test inputs, which are also tracked by the
process OBSERVER. The latter additionally tracks the test outputs. They are
combined by sharing ("P [| S |] Q") the input events in the set MonEv.

Figure 7.14: A vending machine specification featuring a few basic CSP operators.

- configuration priorities (Sect. 7.3).

We realized *requirements modules* by a set of files. The dialect of CSP which we used allows to partition specifications into several files and to compose the parts by an `include` statement. The example in Fig. 7.14 uses such an `include` statement in its first line to compose the example in Fig. 7.15 into the specification.

We realized *a hierarchy of requirements modules* by a hierarchical directory structure for the files. For example, in our UMTS application there is a sub-directory for each protocol layer. And there is a sub-directory for the tester specific issues, which contains a further sub-directory for timer specific issues. All of these directories typically contain several variants of a specification part.

We realized *an explicit dependency relation* by a convention. In the beginning of each CSP file, there is a text comment with a list of the parents files. Of course, this demanded manual work and considerable care to keep the lists up-to-date. Tool support would have been very welcome here. Nevertheless, the information helped in selecting consistent configurations.

We realized *explicit interfaces between requirements modules* by a similar convention. There was an additional text file for each chapter/directory.

We realized *abstract interfaces between requirements modules* by specifying suitable interface modules. However, CSP makes it harder than Z to specify arbitrary constraints. But it is at least easy to specify interface events.

We realized *configuration management for requirements in general* by CSP's file inclusion mechanism and by a convention. We have separate directory trees for the requirements module base and for the queries. (The configuration rule base was separated from the requirements module base by text comments only. This is because we did not yet distinguish clearly between features and requirements modules.) For each family member, there is a top-level CSP source file which textually includes the top-level files of each module used. This text inclusion then continues recursively. This mechanism worked; but explicit configuration rules and feature lists together with an implicit actual composition operator, as presented in this book, would have been much easier and safer to use.

The distinction of features and requirements modules was not yet clearly present in the approach. We developed it only later.

Configuration priorities are also missing. They cannot be realized with CSP's file inclusion mechanism. Therefore, we had to take greater care to keep the specifications consistent.

7.9.6 Structuring the Family of Requirements for Maintainability

We applied our ideas on requirements structuring to ease the maintenance of the family of requirements. We designed the testing requirements as a family of test suites, with a modular structure. An analysis of the commonalities and variabilities of the family lead us to specific rules for modularizing the requirements.

```
pragma AM_SET_TIMER
channel setTimer : { 0, 1 }
pragma AM_ELAPSED_TIMER
channel elapsedTimer : { 0, 1 }
pragma AM_ERROR
channel wrong_reaction, stimulus_overrun
pragma AM_WARNING
channel no_reaction

PAUSE = setTimer!0 -> elapsedTimer.0 -> SKIP

AWAIT(ExpectedEvSet) =
(   -- start timer and wait for things to come:
    setTimer!1 ->
    (   -- Accept correct reaction:
        ([] x: ExpectedEvSet @ x -> SKIP)
    [] -- Flag wrong reaction:
        ([] x: diff(CtrlEv, ExpectedEvSet) @
            x -> wrong_reaction -> SKIP)
    [] -- Flag overrun by next monitored event:
        ([] x: MonEv @ x -> stimulus_overrun -> SKIP)
    [] -- Flag no reaction (timeout):
        elapsedTimer.1 -> no_reaction -> SKIP))
```

Explanation: The process PAUSE sets a timer and waits until it elapses. Then
it terminates and thereby returns to its calling process.
The process AWAIT assures that one of the specified set of legal outputs occurs in
due time. If not, it performs one of the events wrong_reaction, no_reaction,
... which go into the test log. This process also terminates and thereby returns
to its calling process.

Figure 7.15: The timer-related CSP processes for the example in Fig. 7.14.

Analysis of Commonalities and Variabilities

We analyzed the commonalities and variabilities of the family. The aspects of the requirements for UMTS expected to be stable were:

- the layers in the general structure (RRC, RLC, MAC, ...),

- the functionalities of these layers,

- the service primitives, their names, and their general meaning, and

- the service access points.

The expected changes were, as discussed in Sect. 7.9.3 above:

- Details of the requirements for UMTS, in particular:

  - the parameters of the service primitives,

  - the details of the data structures, such as the protocol data units, and

  - the behaviour of the protocol machines, in particular for error handling.

- Variants of the test suites, because of:

  - adjustments of the test coverage,

  - stepping from component tests to integration tests, and

  - stepping from active testing to passive testing.

Rules for Modularizing

Our analysis lead us to two basic rules for modularizing the requirements, which we in turn differentiated into further, more specific rules:

- separate the description of the signature of a module from the description of the properties of its behaviour, and

- identify which requirements will likely change together, and to put them into one requirements module.

For the first of these rules, we discuss the case of the language CSP. A CSP signature consists of a set of channels with their parameters, and the behaviour is described by a composition of CSP processes over these channels. This separation allows to change the description of the behaviour of a module without changing the description of other modules that communicate with this module. The properties of the behaviour are hidden within the behaviour module. For example, with this strategy we can change the level of test coverage without changing the interfaces. Similarly, this separation enables to step from active to passive testing and from component tests to integration tests.

The second rule was instantiated into the following more specific rules:

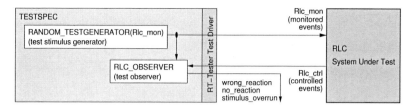

Figure 7.16: Separation of test stimulus generator and test observer.

- separate test stimulus generation from test observation;

- separate application specific and tester specific issues;

- for real-time testing, separate timer handling from application description; and

- for protocol testing, separate protocol layer specifications.

The modularization of requirements can be applied recursively. One example is the sub-structuring of a module into its signature and its behaviour.

In the remainder of this subsection, we discuss these specific rules.

The separation of test stimulus generation from test observation was demonstrated in the vending machine example in Fig. 7.14 on page 165, where RANDOM_STIMULI and OBSERVER are separate CSP processes. We used the same structure for the UMTS protocol layers (see Fig. 7.16).

In this modelling, a test stimulus generator, written in CSP, generates an input to the implementation under test and waits some defined amount of time, then it loops and generates the next input. Concurrently, a test observer process, also written in CSP, observes both the input stimuli and the output reactions of the system under test. If the behaviour of the system under test is incorrect, an error is flagged.

The choice of test coverage is private to the test stimulus generator, and the definition of the correct behaviour is private to the test observer. Therefore, this separation allows for several test suites which concentrate their coverage on a specific issue each but which use the same behaviour description. The separation also allows for additional passive test suites which use only the behaviour description, but not the test stimulus generator at all.

The separation of application specific and of tester specific issues is a consequence of the fact that the testing tool usually is much more stable than the application requirements. Therefore, these should be put into a separate module. For our testing tool, tester specific events include wrong_reaction and no_reaction, which go into the test log, and the timer events.

We have a separate directory tree which contains the actual test suites. Each sub-directory contains a file which composes the particular test specification from the requirements modules, and which contains further test-related data such as test result reports.

The separation of timer handling from application description, which should be done for real-time testing, is a particular instance of the previous rule. The realization of high-level timing processes by primitive set/elapse events of timers is completely internal to the timer handling module. The example in Figure 7.15 above shows the definition of the CSP process AWAIT from the example in Fig. 7.14 which assures that one of the specified set of legal outputs occurs in due time.

The separation of protocol layer specifications, when testing protocols, encapsulates the behaviour of each layer into a separate module. Together with the separation of signatures and behaviours, this facilitates the generation of integration test suites from test suites for the components. If the rule is being followed, then specifications of admissible behaviour for the components can be re-used to get a description of the admissible system behaviour.

There is a sub-directory for each protocol layer. The sub-directory for the tester specific issues contains a further sub-directory for timer specific issues. All of these directories typically contain several variants of a specification part.

During integration testing, several protocol layer instances must be executed at the same time. This can be implemented by the parallel composition operator of CSP. In this composition, CSP process instances are parameterized with an instance number. These processes then run concurrently in parallel. Each process generates test stimuli for one of the protocol instances, and checks the corresponding reactions separately. The RT-Tester tool allows to run several CSP specifications in parallel, with different interleaving strategies for the processes.

7.10 Outlook

This chapter ends with an outlook on several ideas for further research. 1) The systematic reuse of requirements could be complemented by also reusing associated code fragments and, if necessary, associated correctness proof fragments. 2) We can see use for more complex configuration rules beyond simple feature definitions. 3) Generic parameters for modules and for features can be a notational convenience for a recurring kind of configuration task. 4) Our approach is not restricted to the formalism Z; it is applicable to other formalisms, too. 5) The related notion of a policy is worth an investigation with respect to families. 6) The automotive domain starts to experience substantial problems with feature interactions; the application of our results to the automotive domain therefore is promising.

7.10.1 Code Reuse and Proof Reuse Together With Requirements Reuse

The systematic reuse of requirements could be complemented by also reusing associated code fragments and, if necessary, associated correctness proof fragments.

Code Reuse Together With Requirements Reuse

An interesting question for further research is how we can associate code fragments to requirements written in a constraint-oriented style, such that we can also configure all or a part of the implementation automatically from a code base, using features.

The challenge lies in the constraint-oriented specification style. The specification of a property usually leaves many choices for an implementation. We need to choose one for an implementation. Adding another, arbitrary constraint later might invalidate this choice. However, our requirements modules exactly aim at avoiding that arbitrary constraints are added later. A change to the requirements should be local to a single requirements module only. The code then must be structured into a hierarchical design module structure that follows the hierarchical requirements module structure closely. In such a setting, we can expect that the change to the code will be local to a design module, too. However, this still needs to be tried out in experiments.

There is an interesting parallel to domain-specific specification languages (Sect. 3.2). Here, the variability is well-defined, and there are typically many aspects with no variability at all. Accordingly, we can have fixed code for this, and additionally a code base of limited size for the variabilities. In our approach, we do not assume that certain requirements are entirely fixed (Sect. 3.1). Instead, we structure the requirements by their likeliness of change. This is similar to domain-specific languages, but more differentiated. Nevertheless, it should be possible to confine likely code changes to leaf nodes of the design module hierarchy, while only the more and more unlikely changes demand larger and larger design modules to be revised.

Proof Reuse Together With Requirements Reuse

Proof reuse could save even more effort when we already reuse requirements and code for a safety-critical system. When a system is so safety-critical that we need a formal proof of the system's correctness, then the effort for the proof will constitute a large share of the total development effort. Consequently, we can save a part of this effort in a family of such safety-critical systems, if we can reuse parts of such proofs over the family.

Autexier, Hutter, Mossakowski, and Schairer [AHMS02] provide support for reuse of proof steps with their tool Maya. The tool translates a specification of a formal development into the tool's internal development graph representation language. Such a graph allows to determine the dependencies among the proof steps. When the specification is changed, the tool computes a set of minimal changes to the graph. The unchanged parts of the graph can be reused directly. The tool supports several different formalisms and theorem provers.

Broch Johnsen and Lüth [BJBJ04] investigate proof reuse by abstracting the development process. They propose an approach where theorems are generalized by abstracting their proofs from the original setting. The approach is based on a representation of proofs as logical framework proof terms, using the theorem prover Isabelle [NPW02]. The authors use transformational proofs. This means that the development of a program from a specification is technically the same as the proof that the program meets the specification.

Research on relating proof reuse to our families of requirements would be interesting. The above work creates a family of requirements and proofs implicitly by repeated modification. But there is no planning for change during the writing of the proofs. It would be interesting to apply an analysis of commonality and variability in the family before using these approaches. In this way, important abstractions of proof steps could be identified systematically and early.

7.10.2   More Complex Configuration Rules

We can see use for more complex configuration rules beyond simple feature definitions. Our separation of requirements modules and configuration rules opens ways for documenting further kinds of configuration constraints in the configuration rule base, and for analyzing them by tools.

However in this book, we are content with specifying features explicitly. Before we investigate more advanced constructs, we would like to collect more experience with configuring requirements modules first. Then, we will be able to judge whether a more advanced construct is worth its price.

More Complex Rules

More complex rules could range from merely adding an incompatibility relation up to arbitrary configuration constraints, and to using the dependency relation among requirements modules.

Incompatibility relations.   An obvious kind of additional constraint is the incompatibility between an arbitrary pair of requirements modules. If such incompatibilities are documented, the generator tool can automatically exclude the second module if the first is included, and vice versa. If both are demanded to be included, with the same priority, the tool can report an inconsistent configuration without further requirements analysis.

Arbitrary configuration constraints.   In the most general case, we could express arbitrary constraints in the configuration rule base. The feature logic of Zeller and Snelting [Zel96, ZeSn95] appears as one good base for such a language (see the end of Sect. 3.4.4).

Feature models, as the ones by Riebisch *et al.* [Rie03], also provide interesting configuration operators (see Sect. 3.3.3). These operators are more restricted than Zeller's and Snelting's feature logic, but might be sufficient in many cases.

More expressivity is easily possible, but it is not yet clear how much will really be needed.

Use the dependency relation.   Another source of configuration information is the dependency relation among requirements modules. In Z, the parents construct provides us with information about implications between demands for module inclusion. We could use this information for configuration purposes, too. At the moment, this happens only indirectly. After the transformation from Z_F to Z_{CI}, the type rules of Z_{CI} demand that the parents relation is honoured. A type checking tool like CADiℤ can check this. (See Section 7.7 on tool support.)

Configuring With Complex Rules

If the requirements family is particularly complex, then advanced, knowledge-based techniques could support the configuration process. We discussed an approach for knowledge-based configuration of software (but not yet of software requirements) in Section 3.5 above. It should be possible to apply knowledge-based configuration to a family of software requirements, too. This might be helpful if the family is so complex that simple configuration approaches do not suffice anymore.

7.10.3 Generic Parameters for Modules and for Features

Generic parameters for modules and for features can be a notational convenience for a recurring kind of configuration task. We could add such parameters to our formalism Z_F. However, this would need care, because such parameters can also entail serious problems for the language definition.

Some domains have variabilities along certain data types, in particular along enumerations. For example, a family of internationalized software will vary along the user interface language of the software. The choice of the user interface language is from an explicit, finite enumeration of languages.

We can already express such a choice in Z_F; but not always absolutely elegantly. For such a user interface language choice, we specify an abstract interface requirements module that declares a constant with the name of the language to use. And we specify a set of private requirements modules that each define one specific value for this declared constant. These requirements modules will be small since they define one value only. But the number of the configurable language modules can become large, if there are many languages to choose from. Furthermore, consistency demands that exactly one of the modules is selected. (Here, we could use an incompatibility relation to make this configuration rule explicit.)

We could express such a choice more elegantly by allowing a parameter of an enumeration type for requirements modules, and by allowing a similar parameter for a feature. Then, we could have an "internationalization" feature, and the parameter would specify the language of the family member.

Such parameters can entail serious problems for the language definition, however. The type definition for a parameter can cause such problems, in particular. Each parameter needs a type, but the type definition of a parameter cannot be part of an ordinary requirements module.

Type definitions outside any requirements module undermine our goal to organize the *entire* requirements into modules to make them maintainable. As soon as we have a substantial body of definitions of types for parameters, we also have a substantial part of the requirements specification which is not under configuration control.

Putting such type definitions into requirements modules can result in a circular definition of the semantics. Currently, we have a "preprocessor semantics" for Z_F: the configuration takes place before the semantics of the formal Z paragraphs is determined. Letting the semantics of the configuration step depend on the semantics of the configured items can easily lead to a circular definition.

The formalism CSP-OZ [Fis00] appears to be an example of a language that suffers from such a circular definition. Sühl [Süh02, pp. 172] investigated these problems. The definition of CSP-OZ is based on the intermediate language CSP_Z. In CSP_Z, CSP-style process definitions can be parameterized by arbitrary Z expressions. The meaning of a parameterized process definition is given by syntactic translation rules into Z. The result is a Z expression which can also contain terminal symbols of the CSP syntax. However, the semantic function of Z is not defined for CSP-style process expressions.

We conclude that a sound definition of parameters for our Z_F needs a non-trivial effort.

We sketch a feasible extension of Z_F by parameters which imposes suitable restrictions. We only allow parameter types that are finite ranges of integers or that are explicit enumerations of Z words. This already helps in cases such as the internationalization example above, without causing semantic problems.

The meaning of a section with a parameter with n values is the syntactic expansion to n simple sections. Additionally, we might add a mutual exclusion configuration rule for the n sections. The meaning of a feature with a parameter is an analogous syntactic expansion. The syntactic expansion takes place in a new syntactic transformation phase directly before the type inference phase of Z_F. This is analogous to how generic schemas are defined in plain Z.

The syntactic transformation for parameters inflates the syntax grammar of Z_F considerably, however. Up to now, the actual formal Z paragraphs are treated as informal text in Z_F. This is not possible anymore with parameters. The substitution of the formal parameters by the actual parameters demands that the grammar of Z_F parses all formal Z paragraphs.

We also need some additional type rules. For example, there must not be two formal parameters with the same name. Also, the number of the formal parameters and of the actual parameters must match.

7.10.4   Application to Other Formalisms

Our approach is not restricted to the formalism Z; it is applicable to other formalisms, too. Not by chance, the formal definition of the language Z_F is entirely oblivious of the actual Z paragraphs. As far as the transformation to Z_{CI} is concerned, the actual Z paragraphs are comments only (Sect. 7.4.2).

However, the underlying formalism must support a constraint-oriented specification style. This allows to split the requirements into small, independent properties.

In Section 7.8 above, we already reported in detail on a previous application of our approach to the formalism CSP-OZ. And in Section 7.9, we reported on another, more light-weight, application to the formalism CSP.

Our approach is applicable to languages which are more domain-specific, too. Our current base language Z is a rather domain-*un*specific language. The advantage is that our extension Z_F can be used in many different domains. This shows the generality of our approach. The downside of any wide-spectrum formal specification technique is that each specifier must tailor it to the domain himself/herself. For example in our LAN message service example (see Sect. 6.5 and 7.6), we had to define suitable communication primitives ourselves. A base language which already provides such primitives would have saved some work. Of course, such a base language could not be used well in other domains.

Making a specification language more domain-specific means to move a part of the specifications into the language itself. The extreme is domain engineering (see Sect. 3.2). There, we have a clearly defined boundary of the domain; all commonalities are in the language itself; and only the variabilities are specified.

Many specification languages are between these two extremes. They provide some domain-specific constructs. But the domain is not defined precisely, and the boundaries of the applicability of the language are somewhat fuzzy. For example, the language CSP [Hoa85, Ros94] is clearly geared towards the specification of communicating sequential systems. But we can use it also to investigate combinatorial systems like the game "peg solitaire", as done in [Ros94, Sect. 15.1].

Our approach for organizing requirements specifications is applicable to such intermediate languages, too. Only, the more domain-specific a language is, the more this language will already have custom-tailored constructs built in. In a completely engineered domain, the commonality and variability analysis has already rendered a suitable organization of the requirements into requirements modules. And all the important abstractions have been defined explicitly, such that there is no need anymore to specify them for individual family members.

7.10.5 Policies and Families

The related notion of a policy is worth an investigation with respect to families. A *policy* is very similar to a feature in the sense that it is a kind of configuration rule (see, e.g., Reiff-Marganiec [RM04]). The difference is that a feature typically is provisioned statically by a service provider, while a policy is intended to be defined dynamically by a user at run-time. Reiff-Marganiec does not elaborate on the structure of the underlying communications layer of his policy architecture. It would be interesting to extend our work to dynamically configured policies. One idea is to draw on the fact that a policy configuration language can be considered as a kind of a domain-specific language.

7.10.6   Feature Interaction Problems in the Automotive Domain

The automotive domain starts to experience substantial problems with feature interactions; the application of our results to the automotive domain therefore is promising. Car drivers increasingly get support from automated electronic assistants, and more and more car components contain an embedded computer.

Computerized car components increase the complexity of a car. High-end cars today already contain dozens of embedded computers. An ever growing number of features/modules can be configured. In contrast to telephone switching systems, however, the features/modules in a car are much more decoupled. There is no central "basic call process". The features/modules therefore interact less, and there are less feature interaction problems today. However, we expect that the rapidly increasing number of components and of features/modules will also increase the chances for undesired feature interactions. A suitable global view on the family of software systems will be needed. Our approach for families can be useful here.

Part II

The User Interface Module

Chapter 8

Encapsulating the User Interface Requirements

We can and should encapsulate the requirements for the user interface into a dedicated requirements module. For example in telephone switching systems, spread-out user interface concerns cause an entire class of feature interaction problems. The details of the interface's syntax should be hidden in such a module. They change frequently. Instead, the module should provide semantic variables which are much more stable. This moves the syntactic details from requirements to design. We propose a suitable design structure. The approach can be applied to telephone switching systems. It then eliminates the corresponding class of feature interaction problems. We show how the approach can be applied to a legacy telephone switching architecture and in a new communication system. Our design structure also enables a formal verification of two aspects of the user interface.

8.1 User Interface Related Feature Interaction Problems in Telephone Switching

We choose the telephone switching domain to demonstrate the problems due to a missing encapsulation of the user interface requirements. Here, spread-out user interface concerns cause an entire class of feature interaction problems. The widely used Intelligent Network architecture [DuVi92, ITU01] is intended to facilitate the introduction of new features. But it does not provide sufficient support with respect to the user interface.

8.1.1 Some Feature Interaction Problems and Their Causes

The following feature interaction is caused by the way the user interface often is expressed. It can occur between a *Credit Card Calling* (CCC) feature and a *Voice Mail* feature. The example is taken from the feature interaction benchmark by Cameron et. al. [CGL+94]. Credit Card Calling includes an authorization phase where the card's number and PIN must be entered. For convenience, this feature often allows placing another call without re-entering, by just pressing the "#" button at the end of the first call. On the other hand, to access voice mail messages from phones other than his own, a subscriber of some voice mail service can call his own phone number (maybe using the CCC feature) and then press the "#" button followed by some identification to indicate that he is the subscriber. These features can't work together properly since the telephone system has no way to determine whether pressing the "#" button means that the caller just doesn't want to leave a message, or whether he is the subscriber.[1]

The problem in the example is that two features are active concurrently, but they are defined in a way that assumes that each of them is the only feature communicating via the associated user interface. There is no general provision that controls the access to this resource by different features. Today, hundreds of features have been conceived, with many of them requiring user interaction. Nevertheless, many features could be used concurrently and independently, if the user interface resource, and in particular, the signals that a user can generate (or receive) on a standard phone, were not so limited.

There are some more examples of feature interactions in the benchmark [CGL+94] that are caused in this way: *Call Waiting* and *Three-Way Calling* (ambiguous flash hook), *Multi-location Business Service-Extension Dialling* and *CENTREX* (ambiguous numbering plan), *Call Waiting (CW)* and *Personal Communication Services (PCS)* (definition of CW for PCS user X ignores that a phone may be shared with PCS user Y not subscribing to CW), *Call Waiting* and *Call Waiting* (a user may take part in two concurrent CW contexts; hanging up can be ambiguous with respect to ringing back for held parties, if both contexts are in different modes), and *Call Waiting* and *Three-Way Calling* (ambiguous hang up in a complex context).

Still, features are often described as if each of them had exclusive control of the user interface. Notably, the Feature Interaction Detection Contest instructions [GBGO98] take exactly this approach. They specify features in terms of "Flash", "Off-hook", "DialTone", "StartRinging" etc. Many of the case study specifications in the proceedings of previous feature interaction workshops [AmLo03, CaMa00, KiBo98, DBL97, ChOh95, BoVe94] are expressed similarly. Even though they aggregate individual digits to a "dialled number", in general these requirement specifications of features make assumptions about details of the user interface hardware.

There are some exceptions in the literature, for example Blom et al. [BBK95] assume a "parser" that receives signals from the outside (e.g., flash hook), and delivers abstract events, such as "Transfer", "Switch", and "3Way", depending on the state of the system. Other exceptions are Gibson [Gib97] who recommends to distinguish clearly between abstract actions/signals in the requirements model and concrete actions/signals in the implementation model, and Zibman et. al. [ZWO+96] who propose to use "logical names" instead of "specific signals". Even though Cattrall et. al. [CHJB95] do not address low-level signals, they work with abstract signals entirely. Griffeth and Velthuijsen [GrVe94] attempt to derive the intentions behind

---

[1]This feature interaction is resolved in the calling card feature to which the author once subscribed: the "#" button must be pressed at least 2 seconds to take effect. Thus, we have two distinguishable signals.

low-level signals by a goal profile stored in an automated negotiating agent.

8.1.2   Limitations of the Intelligent Network Architecture

The Intelligent Network (IN) standard [DuVi92, ITU01] is intended to facilitate the introduction of new features. Nevertheless, it prescribes only partially how user interactions with these features are processed, and thus there is no general, coordinated way for user interaction processing beyond the provisions for basic call processing. Partially, this is alleviated by imposing restrictions on a concurrent activation of features, but this prevents many useful features from being specified. These restrictions have been reduced in the IN capability set 2 (CS-2) [ITU97c], but in the IN CS-2 architecture there is still no mandatory synchronization protocol among the features concerning user interaction.

8.2   Encapsulating the User's Interface

We can encapsulate the requirements for the user interface into a dedicated requirements module. The details of the interface's syntax should be hidden in such a module. They change frequently. Instead, the module should provide semantic variables which are much more stable. This moves the syntactic details from requirements to design. We propose a suitable design structure. The approach can be applied to telephone switching systems. It then eliminates the corresponding class of feature interaction problems.

8.2.1   A Requirements Module for the User's Interface

A human-computer interface allows a human and a machine to interact; for this, they must use a language. As in other areas concerned with languages, one can distinguish the syntax and the semantics. The model of Foley and Wallace [FvDFH90, FoWa74] (compare also [Shn97]) is often used for (graphical) human-computer interfaces. They distinguish two major components: the form and the meaning. For their kinds of interfaces, they continue and differentiate more levels. For the purposes of this book, we only need the distinction between the specific form of an interaction, i.e., the syntax, and its meaning, i.e., the semantics.

The lessons learned with the human-computer interface can and should be applied to the user-telephone interface, too. We propose to specify the requirements for a telephone switching system, including any additional features, on the semantic level. For the moment, we assume that we are interested in the requirements of an entire such system, and not only a part of it. If we specify the behaviour of the system solely on the semantic level, then all the feature interaction problems listed in Section 8.1 simply disappear from the requirements document, since they have become a design problem.

In the example of Credit Card Calling (CCC) and Voice Mail (VM), we now have separate sets of semantic signals from the user to the system for each of the features. The CCC feature adds something like a *ReleaseAndReconnect* semantic signal to the system, and the VM feature adds something like a *VMlogin* semantic signal. If the functionality of two features is not related, they should always have separate sets of semantic signals.

We propose that a semantic signal should reflect (a) a *user's decision* to perform some action, for example to request a communication connection to some other user, (b) or a *user's perception* that some other user (or the system) has decided to perform some action, for example to request a communication connection with him.

But this move has not yet solved the problem. Eventually, all of the semantic signals must still be mapped onto the few syntactic signals, and back. The exact mapping is a concern of the user interface, and it has little to do with the functionality of the telephone switching system and its features. According to the information-hiding principle (Sect. 5.1), it should therefore be encapsulated as a secret of only one design module, which we call the *user interface module* (UIF). It will still be difficult to find a satisfactory mapping. But if all aspects of this problem are separated and concentrated into a single module, it will be easier to understand its semantics, and thus to conceive a solution, and the module will be easier to change later. The latter is of particular importance to the feature interaction problem. Furthermore, it will be easier to verify and validate a solution, as we will see in Section 8.4 below.

We have to stress that an information-hiding module such as the UIF module is *not* necessarily implemented by some centralized software program or in a single hardware component [Par72]. The different access functions, for example the mapping routines, may be distributed over many software packages and to many physical locations. But the module must be *maintained* as a single unit, with any changes distributed in a consistent manner. We will discuss this issue further in Section 8.3.1.

8.2.2 A Design Structure for the Requirements Module

We propose a design structure for the user interface requirements module. It relates the semantic signals to the pre-existing entities of the user interface. We present the basic structure, and then we show how the user interface can be extensible. But first, we need to extend the relations of the four-variable model from Section 2.1 in order to be able to describe a design.

Our approach is different from the four-variable model with one respect: there is no clear distinction between input devices and output devices. This distinction is appropriate in the classical application domains of the four-variable model. But it does not fit well for complex user interfaces. In these, input and output depend on each other even without considering the system's functionality. Therefore, we do not use input and output variables here. Instead, we introduce more general *design variables*. However, the monitored and controlled variables are the same.

Requirements Specification in the Four-Variable Model

We summarize how we can specify requirements using the four-variable model from Section 2.1, in this paragraph. The four-variable model describes the binary relation between monitored and controlled variables, denoted by two vectors of time-functions $\underline{m}^t$ and $\underline{c}^t$, respectively. The environment to be assumed is specified as a relation

NAT. NAT describes how the relevant part of the world may behave over time without or despite the system to construct: domain(NAT) exactly contains the instances of $\underline{m}^t$ allowed by the environmental constraints, and range(NAT) exactly contains the instances of $\underline{c}^t$ allowed by the environmental constraints. $(\underline{m}^t, \underline{c}^t) \in$ NAT if and only if the environmental constraints allow the controlled quantities to take on the values described by $\underline{c}^t$, if the values of the monitored quantities are described by $\underline{m}^t$. The world, as it may behave with the system present, is described by the intersection NAT $\cap$ REQ. The relation *REQ* may restrict the behaviour of controlled variables only, but not of monitored variables: domain(REQ) exactly contains the instances of $\underline{m}^t$ allowed by the environmental constraints, and range(REQ) exactly contains the instances of $\underline{c}^t$ allowed by a correct system. $(\underline{m}^t, \underline{c}^t) \in$ REQ if and only if the system should permit the controlled quantities to take on the values described by $\underline{c}^t$ when the values of the monitored quantities are described by $\underline{m}^t$.

Extending the Four-Variable Model Relations by Design Variables

In this chapter, we will also employ relations over subvectors of $\underline{m}^t$ and $\underline{c}^t$, and over vectors of variables $\underline{v}^t$ introduced during design. Thus, relations become ternary, with REQ and NAT having an empty vector of design variables $\underline{v}^t$ as a special case. For a relation R, we generalize domain(R) to mon(R), range(R) to ctrl(R), and we add des(R) to designate the third design variable vector. We assume some total ordering over each kind of variables, and further we assume that all vectors of variables have their components sorted. We denote the restriction of a triple of variable vectors $r = (\underline{m}^t, \underline{c}^t, \underline{v}^t)$ to the variables of a relation R as $r{\downarrow}_R$ (R must comprise no other variables than those of the vector triple r). For two relations R, S, we define the relation $\Theta_{R,S}$ as the relation that contains exactly those variables in mon($\Theta_{R,S}$), ctrl($\Theta_{R,S}$), and des($\Theta_{R,S}$) that appear in at least one of R or S in the respective vectors, with $\Theta_{R,S}$ being the largest relation doing so. This allows us to define the composition of relations as the "intersection" $R \hat{\cap} S \stackrel{\text{def}}{=} \{r \mid r \in \Theta_{R,S} \wedge r{\downarrow}_R \in R \wedge r{\downarrow}_S \in S\}$.

Basic Structure of the Design

For the moment, we assume that we design a single feature only, with no other features already in the environment. Below, we remove this restriction and discuss the general case of many features.

Figure 8.1(a) shows the components of the requirements document. We group the variables (both monitored and controlled) into three vector triples, as shown. The first, the vector triple of *semantic variables*, describes the semantic signals by the users. Furthermore, we split the description of the relevant environment into two relations. The first relation *USR* describes what the users might do on the semantic variables (USR is strongly non-deterministic since many aspects of user behaviour are not relevant for the system). The second relation *IOHARD* describes some pre-existing input/output hardware (and maybe software), by relating a vector triple of *physical variables* to a vector triple of *software variables*. The requirements of the feature are described by the relation REQ. IOHARD and the low-level physical

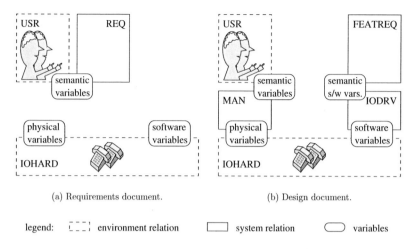

(a) Requirements document.   (b) Design document.

legend: ⌐ ⌐ ⌐ environment relation   ▭ system relation   ⬭ variables

Figure 8.1: Structure of the documents.

and software variables have not yet any connection to REQ. We deviate from the standard approach insofar as we define REQ only over the semantic variables, not over all variables mentioned. Nevertheless, (USR∩̂IOHARD)∩̂REQ still describes the allowed behaviour of the system, using the definition of composition by intersection from the previous section. The entire environment NAT can be derived from the composition of USR and IOHARD:

$$\text{NAT} \; \overset{\text{def}}{=} \; \text{USR}\hat{\cap}\text{IOHARD}$$

In Figure 8.1(b), we propose a *design structure* for these requirements that encapsulates the user interface. There are two important aspects in this design. First, we introduce a software reflection of the semantic variables (which cannot be observed directly by any machine). These design variables, the *semantic software variables*, separate the software into an input/output driver part *IODRV* and another version of the feature's requirements *FEATREQ*. FEATREQ is usually very similar to or identical to REQ, modulo variable renaming; the difference is that the semantic software variables can be observed by the software, while the semantic variables in the users' minds cannot.

The second important aspect is how the semantic variables in the users' minds are related to the physical variables in the design. We propose to describe this relation by an explicit relation *MAN*. It documents explicitly how the users translate their decisions on the semantic level into physical actions, and how physical actions translate to users' perceptions. These translations do not exist before the system is designed, therefore MAN is part of the design. The system designer conceives these translation rules, and usually he documents them in a user manual (hence the name MAN).

For the verification and validation purposes in Section 8.4, we need to write down this relation explicitly and formally. It should be noted that the formal document supports verification and validation, but we should also provide an informal version that is structured differently, which the users can understand easily.

The user interface relation, for short *UIF*, is composed of the relations MAN, IOHARD, and IODRV:

$$\text{UIF} \stackrel{\text{def}}{=} \text{MAN} \hat{\cap} \text{IOHARD} \hat{\cap} \text{IODRV}$$

The user interface relation is a part of the design, since some of its components do not exist before the system is constructed. The user interface UIF is a *module in the information-hiding sense*, as discussed in Section 8.2.1. Its *secret* is how the high-level semantic variables are mapped to the low-level syntactic physical and software variables. This encapsulation becomes possible by introducing an explicit user manual relation MAN.

Overall, all the relations in Figure 8.1(b) with solid lines together form the design *DSGN* and must implement the relation REQ in Figure 8.1(a), in the given environment. Formally, we write this as:

$$(\text{DSGN} \hat{\cap} \text{NAT}) \; \hat{\subseteq} \; (\text{REQ} \hat{\cap} \text{NAT})$$

with $\text{NAT} \stackrel{\text{def}}{=} \text{USR} \hat{\cap} \text{IOHARD}$
and $\text{DSGN} \stackrel{\text{def}}{=} \text{MAN} \hat{\cap} \text{IODRV} \hat{\cap} \text{FEATREQ}$

Analogously to the composition $\hat{\cap}$, we define the variable-extended implication predicate $R \hat{\subseteq} S$ (for relations S that have no design variables)

$$R \hat{\subseteq} S \stackrel{\text{def}}{=} (\forall r \in R : r|_S \in S) \wedge$$
$$(\Theta_{R,S} = \Theta_{R,R}) \wedge (\{\underline{m}^t|_S \mid \underline{m}^t \in \text{mon}(R)\} = \text{mon}(S))$$

The Extensible User Interface in the Design

We have seen how the user interface aspects of *one* feature can be encapsulated in the design. But how can we coordinate this for many features, and with the base system? The answer is, of course, that there must be one single user interface module in the environment of all these features, and the concerns of the user interface must not be part of the design of the functionality of the features at all. That means that we have to provide once and for all an information-hiding module that provides a one-to-one relation between the semantic signals in the mind of the users and a representation of them as semantic software signals, as shown in Figure 8.2.

The user interface module must be *extensible*; the module must allow pairs of semantic mental variables and semantic software variables to be added to its interface. Now, we have split the job of implementing the requirements of a new feature into two parts: implementing the behaviour of the feature, and extending the user interface module, if necessary.

We have to stress that, as already mentioned in Section 8.2.1, a module in the information-hiding sense does not need to be implemented in one centralized spot.

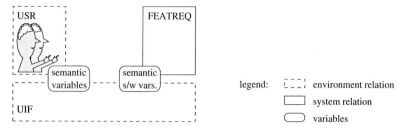

Figure 8.2: Design with a user interface that maps semantic variables one-to-one onto semantic software variables.

Adding new semantic variables to the user interface module may be done either offline during the feature design process, or it may be done dynamically by an online variable registration facility in the user interface. When a designer extends the user interface module offline, he can consider "good" human-computer interface design, and he can perform extensive verification and validation of his result, as discussed in Section 8.4 below. The drawback of offline extension is that all features that will access the user interface must be known beforehand. In a dynamic and heterogeneous network, this might prove difficult.

Alternatively, we can design a set of generic semantic variables beforehand, for which we design a workable mapping to the syntactic variables, and then let an automated agent within the user interface module assign these generic variables to arbitrary features on request. This assignment process must include a suitable online instruction of the affected users, for example announcements. If we decide for an automated registration agent, the user interface module must comprise some special variables that features can use to issue registration requests.

There has already been some work in the above direction. Zibman et. al. [ZWO+96] take a more general view and propose an architecture out of agents that separates concerns, in conjunction with a processing model. The architecture includes a terminal agent, which, amongst others, manages the dynamic assignment of signals to a new service. Since the authors focus more on general aspects, this is not detailed further; also, they present no formal model of their agent architecture. Keck [Kec98] proposes a service admission control scheme for the IN that keeps track of the resources relevant to a session and that notifies services in case of possible interactions. Also related is the work on Open Distributed Processing (ODP) [FLdM95], which attempts to identify several useful abstractions and to separate several communication-related concerns. Van der Linden [vdL94], for example, proposes to use an ODP architecture to beat feature interactions, and the TINA initiative [Ab+97] customizes the ODP ideas for telecommunication networks.

Our discussion on extending the user interface module did not comprise the question of how the functionality of the telecommunication system should be extended, i.e., how the relation FEATREQ in Figure 8.2 relates to and modifies the base system and other features. This is outside the scope of this chapter, it is basically the question of how to tackle feature interactions not related to the user interface.

8.3   Applications

We now show how our general approach can be applied concretely to a legacy telephone switching architecture and in a new communication system. We first show how
the approach can be applied to the widely used Intelligent Network telephone switching architecture. We then discuss how we applied our approach to the newly designed
requirements structure of our LAN messages service example from Section 6.5, and
how we applied it to our specification of the telephone switching system discussed in
Section 7.8.

8.3.1   Application to the Existing IN Architecture

We now show how our general approach can be applied concretely to the widely used
Intelligent Network [DuVi92, ITU01] telephone switching architecture. This architecture provides the concept of "Service Independent Building Blocks" (SIBs). We
propose a design architecture where a suitable SIB is used as part of an information-
hiding module that encapsulates the user interface.

Service Independent Building Blocks in the Intelligent Network Architec-
ture

The IN standard allows to build new services on top of the basic call processing
by using Service Independent Building Blocks (SIBs), and by connecting these with
so-called Service Logic [ITU01]. One of the SIBs defined in the IN CS-1 standard
is a "user interaction" SIB. The standard states that this SIB provides a call party
with information (e.g. announcements) and/or collects information from a call party.
The announcements can be, for example: DTMF tones, a customized or generic
audio message, or network progression tones (e.g. dial tone, busy tone, etc.). The
collected information can be, for example: DTMF tones, audio, or IA5 String text
[ITU93b]. The parameters of this SIB include, among others, the announcement ID,
the number of repetitions, and the number of the expected digits. Thus, the user
interaction SIB clearly provides a user interface at the syntactic level, according to the
model of Foley and Wallace.

Furthermore, there are other SIBs that share user interface related concerns, for
example "queue" (plays announcements), "verify" (performs a syntactic check of user
input), and "translate" (relies, e.g., on the structure of directory numbers).

Proposed Design Architecture

The IN SIBs are intended to be reusable software components. A suitable SIB can
be used as part of an information-hiding module that encapsulates the user interface
and that provides variables at the semantic level. Such a SIB can be used as part of
the environment of a new service to conceive.

For this, we need a redesigned set of SIBs where only the "user interface" (UIF)
SIB is concerned with the details of the user interface. In order that other concerns
can be encapsulated, too, SIBs should be designed to be built hierarchically one

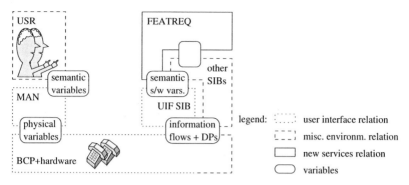

Figure 8.3: Encapsulated user interface in the IN architecture.

on another. Fortunately, the concept of hierarchical SIBs is introduced in IN CS-2 [ITU97c].

Furthermore, a UIF SIB will be so complex that its design should be broken down further into sub-SIBs. For example, there should be a registration agent, as discussed in the previous section.

Our overall design architecture looks like Figure 8.3, with the "software variables" now being the Informations Flows of the Distributed Functional Plane, plus the Detection Points, which together underly the definition of the SIBs. The "IODRV" module is now the rewritten UIF SIB. The user interface module is completed by the relevant aspects of the underlying Basic Call Process (BCP), and, of course, by the user manual relation MAN.

A certain difficulty with the concept of the Intelligent Network arises from its separation of the Basic Call Process and of IN service processing. The Basic Call Process performs user interaction, too, which can be controlled by the IN services only partially. Only when this user interaction leads to triggering a detection point, for example when a dialled number during call setup is completed, the IN service processing can notice and influence this user interaction. Furthermore, the behaviour of the Basic Call Process between the detection points cannot be changed by the IN service processing, which makes changes to the syntax of the user interface hard. For example, when a user goes on-hook, this can induce some irreversible state changes before the next detection point is triggered, thus we cannot reassign an arbitrary meaning to this syntactic signal. Therefore, the translation between syntactic and semantic signals has less degrees of freedom, leaving even less freely usable syntactic signals for new services.

Nevertheless, we can design a set of generic semantic variables for the user interface module with a workable mapping to the syntactic variables, as proposed above. But any service requesting dynamically for the assignment of such a generic variable must be prepared that no more variables are available, and the service must react by a graceful degradation. Alternatively, we might provide an arbitrary number of generic semantic variables, but with increasingly reduced quality of usage comfort, such that a service has to decide whether to accept an assignment offered by the registration agent, or to degrade gracefully, again.

The semantic variables of the user interface are each associated to only one user, since they reflect mental processes. Therefore, the corresponding syntactic physical variables of one user are associated to one physical Service Control Point (SCP) only. As long as a user always employs the same line, all user interface processing related to him can be performed at the same location. As soon as a user is allowed to roam and to use his IN services on different lines, the UIF SIB becomes distributed. Now, the implementation of the UIF SIB incurs substantial additional organizatorial and technical complexity. Nevertheless, the UIF SIB still should be regarded as a single module, and its problems should be separated from other concerns of IN service functionality. In this case, the UIF SIB certainly has a sub-structure. For example, the variable registration agent can be a sub-module of its own, encapsulating the assignment strategy for the generic semantic variables.

8.3.2   Application in Our LAN Message Services Example

We now discuss how we applied our approach to the newly designed requirements structure of our LAN messages service example from Section 6.5. The actual specification is in Appendix A; Figure 6.7 on page 113 shows its module structure.

The requirements module structure follows our template structure from Sect. 5.3.1. At the top level, the specification is divided into the requirements on the behaviour of the software system to build and into the requirements on its environment. The environment comprises the communicating entities, the messages they want to exchange, and the existing hardware and software that that can be made use of. The specification of the behaviour of the software system describes what the system does to the communicating entities and the messages, without referring to any details of the existing hardware or software.

All aspects concerning the users (and other kinds of communicating entities, such as automated agents) are encapsulated in the chapter communicating_entities. This module hides the differences between the interfaces that allow the software to interact with the communicating entities. In particular, the module hides the differences between the various types of messages, and it hides the difference between the interfaces to human users and to automated agents. The module provides abstractions for communicating entities and communication events, for the messages which are communicated, and for the devices that allow the software to interact with the communicating entities.

The module provides an abstract interface with stable semantic signals. Its interface section comm_base provides the notions of communicating entities and of communication events. A communication event can be a submission event or a delivery event. The other interface section comm_params_base states that the submission and delivery events each have three basic parameters associated: both have a message, both have a point in time where they are submitted/delivered, a submission also has exactly one sender, and a delivery has a non-empty set of receivers instead.

The syntactic details of the user interface are encapsulated in the chapter user_interface, which is a sub-chapter of the chapter communicating_entities. This user interface module hides the differences between the possible kinds of interfaces to human users. In particular, there may be a graphical user interface, and there may be a textual user interface. The sub-chapter's interface section user_base introduces a set of human users which are part of the communicating entities. The private section graphical_user_interface hides the differences between the possible kinds of graphical user interfaces; it provides abstractions of the graphical devices that allow the software to interact with the human users. The private section textual_user_interface does the same for textual user interfaces.

We did not work out the details of the syntactic signals in this specification anymore, however. This specification of requirements modules is not intended to be complete. It contains the important abstractions, and it contains also some details in sub-modules. This shows how we can describe such details. But we did not elaborate all details, since we do not actually want to build such systems. A complete specification would need space beyond what fits into an appendix.

8.3.3 Application in Our Telephone Switching System Example

We also applied our approach to our specification of the telephone switching system discussed in Section 7.8 [Bre01, Bre00a, Bre99]. We sketch this application only briefly here because it still misses the distinction between features and requirements modules (Sect. 7.2) and because it still misses multi-level requirements modules (Sect. 5.3).

In this specification, we have a Basic Connection module/feature. It provides the basic notion of a connection, and describes how a connection can be set up and torn down. No details are yet provided on the users' interface for this. Neither do we yet say what kind of connection is provided; there might be, e.g., voice channel or video channel modules/features that build on this module/feature.

The module provides stable semantic signals. For connection setup, it provides the fundamental events *connectReq*, *connectInd*, *connectRsp*, and *connectCnf*. The events denote a request for a connection, the indication of an offered connection request to the callee, the response to such a request by the callee, and the confirmation to the original caller. We expect these signals to be usable for all kinds of telephony-like connections, because of their generality. The syntactic details of the user interface are not part of this module. (Suitable other modules with these details are not worked out anymore in this specification, as above.)

8.4 Verification and Validation of the User Interface

Modelling a feature's behaviour at the semantic level, and separating the concerns of the user interface, additionally allows for a formal verification and validation specifically of the user interface. The design specification for the feature's user interface states a set of one-to-one correspondences between semantic signals in the mind of the users and a representation of them as software signals (compare Figures 8.1(b), 8.2, and 8.3). A successful design of the extended user interface must provide a pair of mutually inverse mapping relations to syntactic signals. This task may be difficult when there are few syntactic signals. But the design can be verified formally, and iterated until it is proven correct.

There are two kinds of properties that we can check. First, we can verify whether the design indeed implements the *functional requirements* we have stated formally, that is, whether there is indeed a one-to-one mapping of mental to software semantic signals. Possible errors include (a) a *translation to an incorrect*, i.e., another, semantic *signal*, when the two mapping functions MAN and IODRV do not fit properly, and, in particular, (b) a *non-deterministic interpretation* of syntactic signals, which constitutes one of the dreaded signalling ambiguities.

Even without having an explicit relation MAN, we can do a check for a non-deterministic interpretation, by generating and checking all permutations of syntactic signals. This is a common approach [DBL97, ChOh95, BoVe94], but a disadvantage is that it may lead to false warnings, since there are (possibly many) state/signal combinations that are reachable only when the system is not used according to its usage rules, and the users then should not expect the system's features to work as intended anyway.

The second kind of properties of the user interface design that we can check are on *usability*. In the area of human-computer interface research, there have been identified numerous properties which are desirable or undesirable (cf., e.g., [Shn97]), and several of them can be checked even formally [Jac83]. For example, (a) *almost-alike states* of the user interface [Par69] tend to confuse users, (b) *interactive deadlock* [DDH83] prevents users from leaving a state due to (in particular) insufficient help available, and (c) the amount of *character level ambiguity* [Thi82] should be minimized, which is a measure derived from the number of different modes in which each keystroke has different meanings. The latter optimization is of particular interest in our context, where there are many more semantic signals than syntactic signals. Verifying the absence of interactive deadlock and reducing undesired ambiguities is part of a validation of the usability of the user interface.

In this book, we are only concerned about how to gather the information necessary for a verification or validation step, as one of its preconditions. We do not discuss how to actually perform such a step.

8.5   Outlook

The user interface is only one of the resources of a telecommunication system. Therefore, a telecommunication system architecture that avoids (at least many) feature interaction problems should encapsulate the details of other resources, too. More work on this is necessary. The advent of a host of new features of telecommunications systems, which we expect to work concurrently and independently, is with some respects comparable to the concurrency and its problems when multi-user time-sharing processing was introduced for computer operating systems. The basic ideas of encapsulation developed at that time are not new anymore, but important tasks are now (a) to apply this knowledge to the specific structure of telecommunication systems, while they change and become more and more complex; and (b) to combine this with formal methods and the tool support these methods provide.

Chapter 9

User Interface Behaviour Requirements and Mode Confusion Problems

A technical system, even if showing its specified behaviour, is useful and safe only when its user can operate it. This becomes difficult or impossible when the user gets confused about the mode the system is currently in. An article titled "How in the world did we ever get into that mode?" [SaWo95] pointedly sums up the users' despair.

Many safety-critical systems today are shared-control systems. These are interdependently controlled by an automation component and a user. Examples are modern aircraft and automobiles. Shared-control systems can cause automation surprises, and, in particular, mode confusions.

The American Federal Aviation Administration (FAA) considers *mode confusion* to be a significant safety concern in modern aircraft. For instance, consider the crash of an Airbus A320 near Strasbourg, France, in 1992 [Bil97]. Probably due to heavy workload because of a last-minute path correction demanded by the air traffic controller, the pilots confused the "vertical speed" and the "flight path angle" modes of descent. The display read "3.3", meaning 3,300 feet per minute. But the crew intended to descend at 3.3 degrees, which translates into about 1,000 feet per minute. There was no ground view due to night and poor weather. As a result, the Air Inter machine descended far too steeply, crashed, and 87 people were killed. Another example is the often cited kill-the-capture bust [Pal95]: an MD-88 jet plane was supposed to climb to 5,000 feet. The captain set the capture mode of the autopilot for this. But the aircraft climbed dangerously higher than 5,000 feet. The captain had adjusted the vertical speed before. This had disarmed the capture mode without the pilot's knowledge. The literature contains considerable research work on mode confusions. Nevertheless, it remains surprisingly unclear what a mode confusion actually is.

This chapter is structured as follows. We introduce to the research work on mode confusions in safety-critical systems. We then present a rigorous definition of mode confusion. This allows us to classify mode confusions, and we use this classification to derive recommendations for avoiding some of the problems. We validate our definitions against the informal notions in the literature. Our approach supports the automated detection of remaining mode confusion problems; we therefore apply this practically to a wheelchair robot.

9.1 Mode Confusions in Safety-Critical Systems

A mode confusion occurs when the observed behaviour of a technical system is out of sync with the user's mental model of its behaviour. We now introduce to mental models of behaviour, we give an informal intuition of the meaning of mode confusion, and we briefly recapitulate the pertinent research results on mode confusions.

9.1.1 Mental Models of Behaviour

People form internal, *mental models* of themselves and of the things with which they are interacting [Nor83]. (The term "mental model" has also another, different meaning in the pertinent literature. We refer to the above one, introduced by Norman [Nor83].) There is ongoing research on the nature of such mental models, and on how people use them when interacting with their environment.

Here, we restrict our interest to mental models of the behaviour of a technical system, in particular of an automated system. We exclude the aspects unrelated to behaviour. For example, we are not interested in how people mentally represent spatial relations. We concentrate on shared-control, automated, technical systems, because many safety-critical systems are shared-control systems. We concentrate on their behaviour, because the notion of safety is usually defined with respect to the behaviour, for these systems. An advantage of this restriction is that we have powerful mathematical tools for analyzing models of behaviour.

Mental models of the behaviour of technical systems appear to be based on state transition rules. This motivated many experiments to derive an explicit description of a mental model, in form of a *state machine* with modes and mode transitions. Mental models have been extracted from training material, from user interviews, and by user observation. For example, Cañas *et al.* [CnAQ01] survey work on this. They also performed three experiments with 115 participants. They exposed these users to different knowledge elicitation tasks and made conclusions about their mental models.

Extracting a mental model from an individual user is notoriously difficult and expensive. In particular, mental models are unstable [Nor83]. The user constantly learns and therefore adapts his/her mental model. The user also forgets. Furthermore, the model which is the user's long-term knowledge, the *conceptual model*, is different from the user's current working abstraction. When performing a task, the user concentrates on the part of his/her knowledge which he/she assumes to be relevant [CnAQ01].

Nevertheless, even imperfect descriptions of mental models have value. If they are extracted from individuals by interview or by observation, they will have some randomness. If they are extracted from training material, they are generic only.

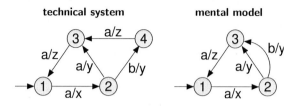

(a) The automata.

input sequence	output sequence		mode confusion observed?
	technical system	mental model	
a a a a	x y z x	x y z x	no
a b a a	x y z <u>z</u>	x y z <u>x</u>	yes

(b) Reactions of the automata to different input sequences.

Figure 9.1: Example with potential for mode confusion.

The value is that any mode confusion problem showing up here has some chance to repeat itself with other individuals. We should therefore try to find its causes and tackle them. This is in line with Rushby's argument on this issue [Rus01b]: "most automation surprises reported in the literature are not the result of an errant operator holding a specific and inaccurate mental model but are instead due to the design of the automation being so poor that *no* plausible mental model can represent it accurately." A basic assumption of our work is that one can produce descriptions of mental models at all that have at least some resemblance to the actual mental models of individuals.

9.1.2   An Informal Intuition of Mode Confusion

Intuitively, a mode confusion occurs when the observed behaviour of a technical system is out of sync with the user's mental model of its behaviour. Figure 9.1 shows the modes and mode transitions of some technical system and of some mental model of its behaviour. These automata are "similar": for the sequence of inputs given first, the outputs are the same. But the mental model misses one mode. For the second input sequence, the observed behaviour is different from the expected behaviour. The user will be surprised, probably unpleasantly. Even more, the surprise happens only later (after the fourth input), not when the modes actually get out of sync (after the second input). In Figure 9.1(a), circles denote modes, and arrows denote mode transitions, labelled with the corresponding inputs and outputs.

9.1.3   Survey of Work on Mode Confusions

We briefly recapitulate the pertinent state of the art here. Since the early 1990s, a number of research groups from the human factors community, in particular the aviation psychology community, work on mode confusions in shared-control systems. Recently, people from the computer science community, especially the formal methods community, also became interested. There are some promising results with respect to tool supported detection of mode confusion problems (see below). But it remains surprisingly unclear what a mode confusion actually is.

Definitions of Mode and Mode Confusion.   While some relevant publications give no [CJR00, BMPC98, CaHa01] or only an implicit definition [Rus01a, HoJo01a] of the notions "mode" and "mode confusion", there are others that present an explicit informal definition [SaWo95, DSK99, But01, LPS+97].

Doherty [Doh98] presents a formal framework for interactive systems and also gives an informal definition of "mode error".

Thimbleby [Thi90] develops his "mode" definition over some stages from a generic and informal one ("a mode is a variable information in the computer system affecting the meaning of what the user sees and does", [Thi90, p. 228]) to a formal one. Doing so, he focuses his scope to the pure two-agent interaction between the human and the machine. He does not consider the physical environment. The latter is a third agent relevant in shared-control systems. As a result, he defines a mode to be a "mathematical function mapping commands to their meanings within the system" [Thi90, p. 255]. Thimbleby does not deal with the mode confusion problem. He therefore does not provide a rigorous definition of the notion "mode confusion".

Wright and colleagues give explicit but example driven definitions of the notions "error of omission" and "error of commission" by using the language CSP to specify user tasks [WFH94].

Modelling and Tool Support.   Interestingly, the way of modelling often seems to be influenced significantly by the tool that is meant to perform the final analysis.

Degani and Heymann use the language StateCharts to model separately the technical system and the user's mental model of its behaviour [HeDe02a]. Then they compose both models and search for certain composite states (so-called "blocking", "error", and "augmenting" states) which indicate mode confusions.

Butler *et al.* use the theorem prover PVS to examine the flight guidance system of a civil aircraft for mode confusion situations [BMPC98]. They do not consider the mental model of the pilot as an independent entity in their analysis.

Campos and Harrison [CaHa01] use the model checker SMV. They specify the system as a state transition system. They specify selected properties of the mental model as assertions in temporal logic.

Leveson and her group specify the black-box behaviour of the system in the language SpecTRM-RL that is intended to be both well readable by humans and processable by computers [LPS+97, RZK+00, ZRI+00]. In [LPS+97], they give a categorisation of different kinds of modes and a classification of mode confusion situations.

Joshi, Miller, and Heimdahl [JMH03] build on this work. They use the cousin language RSML^{-e} for modelling the system. They use the model checker NuSMV and the theorem prover PVS to explore the state space for "off-normal" use cases, which might confuse a pilot.

Thimbleby (see above) uses the so-called PIE modelling approach [Thi90] that describes human-machine interaction by specifying a sequence of user commands, the **Program**. Such a program is interpreted by the technical system by an **Inter**pretation function and causes some **Effect**. PIE models are also readable by humans and processable by computers.

Sage and Johnson [SaJo02] describe a rapid prototyping approach for an air traffic control system. They are able to verify safety properties based on a system specification in the language LOTOS. They claim that their method can support the operator directed design process proposed in [VaHa02] (see below). Nonetheless, they do not specify the mental model of the user.

Rushby and his colleagues employ the model-checking tool Murϕ [RCP99, Rus01a, CJR00]. Technical system and mental model are coded together as a single set of so-called Murϕ rules. In each step, all rules are "fired" of which the condition is true; i. e. some manipulation of global state variables is performed. Furthermore, a set of invariants is checked. The mode confusion situations are detected with these invariants.

Lüttgen and Carreño examine the three state-exploration tools Murϕ, SMV, and Spin with respect to their suitability in the search for mode confusion potential [LüCa99]. They find that each tool has its advantages but also its drawbacks: Spin supports the designer to find the sources of mode confusion situations by the animation of diagnostic information. SMV bears the advantages that it integrates temporal logics. And Murϕ provides the best specification language.

Buth [But01] and Lankenau [Lan01] clearly separate the technical system and the user's mental model in their CSP specification of the well-known MD-88-"kill-the-capture" scenario and in a service-robotics example, respectively. The support of this clear separation is one reason why Buth's comparison between the tool Murϕ and the CSP tool FDR favours the latter [But01, pages 209-211].

Meanwhile, also Rushby [Rus02] acknowledges this need to separate both entities. For mode confusion detection, he affirms the advantages of model-checking tools for process algebras such as FDR over tools such as Murϕ. A conformance relation between two descriptions has to be checked. The concepts of refinement and abstraction are required for this. They are provided directly by FDR.

Case Studies.   Almost all publications refer to the aviation domain when examining a case study: an MD-88 [Pal95, SaWo95, LPS$^+$97, RCP99, But01], an Airbus A320 [CJR00, HoJo01a], or a Boeing 737 [Rus01a]. For a non-aviation case study, refer to Thimbleby's running (pedagogical) example, a calculator [Thi90].

Recommendations.   The literature has several recommendations for avoiding mode confusions.

Reason [Rea90] is concerned with human error in general. He recommends to minimize the affordances for error. He takes up the design principles of Norman's "Psychology of Everyday Things" [Nor88]: use both knowledge in the world and in the head in order to promote a good conceptual model. Simplify the structure of tasks. Make both the execution and the evaluation sides of an action visible. Exploit natural mappings. Exploit the power of constraints, both natural and artificial. Design for error; make it easy to reverse operations and hard to carry out non-reversible ones; exploit forcing functions. When all else fails, standardize.

Sarter and Woods [SaWo95] propose several measures against mode confusions: reduce the number and complexity of modes (if possible). Focus training on knowledge activation in context. Train skill at controlling attention. Provide better indications of what mode the system is in and how future conditions may produce changes. Maybe provide displays for the history of interaction. Also use nonvisual, e. g., aural or kinesthetic, channels to reduce load on the visual channel. Use forcing functions to guide the user, if the system has enough overall context to do it sensibly.

Butler *et al.* [BMPC98] propose to create a clear, executable formal model of the automation and use it to drive a (flight-deck) mockup for (pilot) training. It can be augmented with an additional display, for training only, that directly exposes the internal structure of the automation and its internal changes.

Leveson *et al.* [LPS+97, BaLe01] have identified six categories of system design features that can contribute to mode confusion errors (and thus should be avoided): ambiguous interfaces, inconsistent system behaviour, indirect mode transitions, lack of appropriate feedback, operator authority limits, and unintended side effects.

Degani and Heymann [DeHe02] propose to check formally whether all necessary information is presented to the user in order to avoid mode confusion. This requires a formal model of both the machine and of user's mental model. They also propose an algorithm to generate automatically the interface to the machine and the corresponding user manual information [HeDe02a, HeDe02b].

Rushby proposes a procedure to develop automated systems which pays attention to the mode confusion problem [Rus01b]. The main part of his method is the integration and iteration of a model-checking based consistency check and the mental model reduction process introduced by [Jav98, CJR00].

Vakil and Hansman, Jr. [VaHa02] recommend three approaches to reduce mode confusion potential in modern aircraft: pilot training, enhanced feedback via an improved interface, and, most substantial, a new design process (ODP, for operator directed design process) for future aircraft developments. ODP aims at reducing the complexity of the pilot's task, which may involve a reduction of functionality.

Critique. Hourizi and Johnson [HoJo01a, HoJo01b] criticize that automation surprises are not only due to mode error, but also due to a "task knowledge gap". It is more than a perceptual slip. The underlying problems are a (mode) confirmation bias and selective (mode-confirming) perception of the human user.

9.2 A Rigorous Definition of Mode Confusion in Safety-Critical Systems

Interestingly, none of the work surveyed above defines the notions of "mode" and "mode confusion" rigorously. We therefore propose such definitions. They will help to tackle mode confusion problems.

We will present our definitions in several steps. We start with a brief introduction to a suitable notion of formal refinement. It will be the base of our definition. We then introduce the notions that are part of our definition: the behaviour of the technical system, the mental model of the behaviour of the technical system, the user's senses, and the safety-relevant abstractions of all of these. The actual rigorous definitions conclude this section.

9.2.1 Brief Introduction to Refinement

We use a kind of specification/implementation relation in the following. Such relations can be modelled rigorously by the concept of *refinement*. There exist a number of formalisms to express refinement relations. We use CSP [Hoa85] as specification language and the refinement semantics proposed by Roscoe [Ros97]. Additionally we use the extension to Timed CSP by Schneider [Sch00, Sch95]. One reason for using CSP is that there is good tool support for performing automated refinement checks with the tool FDR [Ros97]. This section shall clarify the terminology for readers who are not familiar with the concepts.

In CSP, one describes the externally visible behaviour of a system by a so-called process. Processes are defined over events. CSP offers a set of operators. One can use them to specify processes.

In CSP, the meaning of a process P can be described by the set $traces(P)$ of the event sequences it can perform. Since we must pay attention to what can be done as well as to what can be *not* done, the traces model is not sufficient in our domain. CSP offers the enhanced *failures model* for this case.

Definition 1 (Failure) *A* failure *of a process P is a pair (s, X) of a trace s ($s \in traces(P)$) and a so-called* refusal *set X of events that may be blocked by P after the execution of s.*

If an output event o is in the refusal set X of P, and if there also exists a continuation trace s' which performs o, then process P may decide internally and non-deterministically whether o will be performed or not.

Definition 2 (Failures Refinement) *P refines S in the failures model, written $S \sqsubseteq_F P$, iff $traces(P) \subseteq traces(S)$ and also $failures(P) \subseteq failures(S)$.*

This means that P can neither accept an event nor refuse one unless S does; S can do at least every trace which P can do, and additionally P will refuse not more than S does. Failures refinement allows to distinguish between external and internal choice in processes, i.e. whether there is non-determinism. As this aspect is relevant for our application area, we use failures refinement as the appropriate kind of refinement relation.

Timing problems contribute to mode confusions, at least in some domains. An example is the telephony domain, discussed in the next chapter. Our formalism therefore should be able to express timing. The extension to Timed CSP by Schneider [Sch00, Sch95] adds operators to express a delay of a specified amount of time. Accordingly, each event in a timed trace is associated with a real number meaning the point in time at which the event occurs. A set of timed refusals associates time intervals to every event that may be blocked. The rest is exactly analogous to the untimed case. A timed failure is a pair of a timed trace and a timed refusal set. The definition of timed failures refinement is:

Definition 3 (Timed Failures Refinement) *P refines S in the timed failures model, written* $S \sqsubseteq_{TF} P$, *iff* $traces_T(P) \subseteq traces_T(S)$ *and also* $failures_T(P) \subseteq failures_T(S)$.

We can abstract away the concrete timing from a specification in Timed CSP. Meyer [Mey01] has proven that we can decompose a specification in Timed CSP into a finite set of simple timer processes running in parallel with an untimed specification.

9.2.2 The Behaviour of the Technical System

We must use a *black-box view* of a running technical system for the definition. This is because the user of such a system has a strict black-box view of it and because we want to solve the user's problems. As a consequence, we can observe (only) the environment of the technical system, not its internal workings. When something relevant happens in the environment, we call this an *event*. The user can cause such events, too.

There must be a general consensus on what the events are. This is a basic assumption of our approach about the domain where we apply it. In the safety-critical systems domain, this assumption is true. For example, there is no argument between pilots and cockpit designers about whether the lighting of a sign or the pressing of a button is relevant for flying a plane.

The technical system has been constructed according to some *requirements* document REQ. We can describe REQ entirely in terms of observable events, by referring to the *history* of events until the current point of time. For this description, no reference to an internal state is necessary. Usually, several histories of events are equivalent with respect to what should happen in the future. Such equivalences can greatly simplify the description of the behaviour required, since we might need to state only a few things about the history in order to characterise the situation.

During any run of the technical system, it is in one specific state at any point of time. The (possibly infinite) state transition system specified by REQ defines the admissible system runs.

9.2.3 The Mental Model of the Behaviour of the Technical System

We call the user's mental model of the behaviour of the technical system REQ^M. Ideally, REQ^M should be "the same" as REQ. During any run of the technical system, REQ^M is also in one specific state at any point of time. You may think of the behaviour of REQ^M as a "parallel universe" in the user's mind. Ideally, it is tightly coupled to reality. Each time an event happens and the technical system changes into another state, the user keeps track of what has happened and adjusts his/her expectations about future events accordingly.

Our approach is based on the motto *"the user must not be surprised"*. This is an important design goal for shared-control systems. We must make sure that the reality does not exhibit any behaviour which cannot occur according to the mental model of its behaviour. Additionally, the user must not be surprised because something expected does *not* happen. When the mental model prescribes some behaviour as necessary, reality must not refuse to perform it. For example after dialling a number, a phone must either produce an alert tone or a busy tone, and it must never ring itself.

The rule of non-surprise means that the relationship between the reality's behaviour and the user's mental model of its behaviour must be a *relationship of implementation to specification*. The reality should do exactly what the mental model prescribes, no less and no more. In case that the user does not know what to expect, but knows that he/she does not know, then the reality is free to take any of the choices. A common example is that the user does not know the exact point of time at which the technical system will react to an event, within some limits.

We can describe such an implementation/specification relationship formally by a refinement relation. In CSP, *timed failures refinement* is precisely the relation described above.

9.2.4 The Senses

The user does not always notice when his/her mental model of the behaviour REQ^M is not the same as the behaviour of the reality REQ. This is because the user's mind does not take part in *any* event in the environment. The user perceives the reality through his/her senses only.

The user's senses SENSE translate from the set of events in the environment to a set of events in the user's mind. SENSE is not perfect. Therefore we must distinguish these two sets. For example, the user might not hear a signal tone in the phone due to loud surrounding noise. Or the user might not listen to all of a lengthy announcement text, or he/she might not understand the language of the announcement. At the very least, there is always a larger-than-zero delay between any environment event and the respective mental event. In all these cases, what happens in reality, as described by REQ, is different from what happens according to the user's perception of it, as described by SENSE(REQ).

The user is surprised only if the *perceived* reality does not behave the same as his/her expectations. This is why the user does not always notice a difference between the actual reality REQ and the "parallel universe" REQ^M in his/her mind.

We cannot compare the perceived reality SENSE(REQ) to the mental model of the reality REQ^M directly. They are defined over different sets of events (mental/environment). We need a translation.

The user has a mental model of his/her own senses $SENSE^M$. $SENSE^M$ translates the behaviour of the mental model of the technical system REQ^M into events in the user's mind. It does this in the same fashion as SENSE does it for REQ.

The user's knowledge about the restrictions and imprecisions of his/her own senses is also part of $SENSE^M$. Ideally, the user should know about them precisely, such that $SENSE^M$ matches SENSE exactly. The user is not surprised if the process SENSE(REQ) is a timed failures refinement of the process $SENSE^M(REQ^M)$.[1]

9.2.5 The Abstractions

We restrict our definition of mode confusion to safety-critical systems. This is because traditionally the safety-critical systems community has perceived mode confusions as a problem. As a consequence, we need to abstract to the *safety-relevant* aspects of the technical system.

When the user concentrates on safety, he/she performs an on-the-fly simplification of his/her mental model REQ^M towards the safety-relevant part REQ^M_{SAFE}. This helps him/her to analyse the current problem with the limited mental capacity. Psychological studies show that users always adapt their current mental model of the technical system according to the specific task they carry out [CnAQ01]. The "initialisation" of this adaptation process is the static part of their mental model, the *conceptual model*. This model represents the user's knowledge about the system and is stored in the long term memory.

Analogously to the abstraction performed by the user, we perform a simplification of the requirements document REQ to the safety-relevant part of it REQ_{SAFE}. REQ_{SAFE} can be either an explicit, separate chapter of REQ, or we can express it implicitly by specifying an abstraction function, i.e., by describing which aspects of REQ are safety-relevant. We abstract REQ out of three reasons: REQ^M_{SAFE} is defined over a set of abstracted events, and it can be compared to another description only if it is defined over the same abstracted set; we would like to establish the correctness of the safety-relevant part without having to investigate the correctness of the entire mental model REQ^M; and our model-checking tool support demands that the descriptions are restricted to certain complexity limits.

We express the abstraction functions mathematically in CSP by functions over processes. Mostly, such an abstraction function maps an entire set of events onto a single abstracted event. Other transformations are hiding (or concealment [Hoa85]) and renaming. But the formalism also allows for arbitrary transformations of behaviours; a simple example being a certain event sequence pattern mapped onto a new abstract event. We use the abstraction functions $\mathcal{A}_R$ for REQ and $\mathcal{A}_M$ for

---

[1]In [BrLa02], we used the name MMOD for $SENSE^M(REQ^M)$. We did not define $SENSE^M$ and REQ^M separately. We now make a distinction between these two different kinds of mental model for clarity.

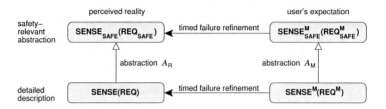

Figure 9.2: Relationships between the different refinement relations.

REQ^M, respectively.

The relation SENSE must be abstracted in an analogous way to $SENSE_{SAFE}$. They are relations from processes over environment events to processes over mental events. It should have become clear by now that $SENSE_{SAFE}$ needs to be rather true, i.e., a bijection which does no more than some renaming of events. If $SENSE_{SAFE}$ is "lossy", we are already bound to experience mode confusion problems. $SENSE^M_{SAFE}$ accordingly is the user's mental model of $SENSE_{SAFE}$.

Figure 9.2 shows the relationships among the different descriptions. In order not to surprise the user with respect to safety, there must be a timed failures refinement relation on the abstract level between $SENSE_{SAFE}(REQ_{SAFE})$ and $SENSE^M_{SAFE}(REQ^M_{SAFE})$.

9.2.6   The Definitions

In the following, let REQ_{SAFE} be a black-box requirements specification, abstracted to the safety-relevant aspects, let REQ^M_{SAFE} be a mental model of the behaviour of REQ_{SAFE}, and let $SENSE_{SAFE}$ and $SENSE^M_{SAFE}$ be relations from processes over environment events to processes over mental events representing the user's senses and the mental model of them, respectively.

The definition of mode needs a precise definition of a potential future behaviour. We take it directly from the timed failures model of CSP (compare Def. 1).

Definition 4 (Potential future behaviour) *A* potential future behaviour *is a set of timed failures.*

A state is a potential future behaviour. We can distinguish two states of a system only if the system may behave differently in the future. This is because of the black-box view.

Definition 5 (Automation surprise) An *automation surprise* between $SENSE(REQ)$ and $SENSE^M(REQ^M)$ occurs if and only if $SENSE(REQ)$ is not a timed failures refinement of $SENSE^M(REQ^M)$, i.e., iff $SENSE^M(REQ^M) \not\sqsubseteq_{TF} SENSE(REQ)$.

The user is surprised if any detail of the technical system contradicts to his/her expectations.

A mode is just a state. But we reserve the word for the "states" of abstracted descriptions, i.e., of $\mathrm{SENSE_{SAFE}(REQ_{SAFE})}$ and of $\mathrm{SENSE^M_{SAFE}(REQ^M_{SAFE})}$. We can distinguish two modes only if the system may behave differently in the future with respect to safety.

Definition 6 (Mode) *A* mode *of* $\mathrm{SENSE_{SAFE}(REQ_{SAFE})}$ *is a potential future behaviour. And, a* mode *of* $\mathrm{SENSE^M_{SAFE}(REQ^M_{SAFE})}$ *is a potential future behaviour.*

We now finally can present our central definition for mode confusion:

Definition 7 (Mode confusion) A *mode confusion* between $\mathrm{SENSE_{SAFE}(REQ_{SAFE})}$ and $\mathrm{SENSE^M_{SAFE}(REQ^M_{SAFE})}$ occurs if and only if $\mathrm{SENSE_{SAFE}(REQ_{SAFE})}$ is not a timed failures refinement of $\mathrm{SENSE^M_{SAFE}(REQ^M_{SAFE})}$, i.e., iff
$$\mathrm{SENSE^M_{SAFE}(REQ^M_{SAFE})} \not\sqsubseteq_{TF} \mathrm{SENSE_{SAFE}(REQ_{SAFE})} \ .$$

A (safety-critical) mode confusion is an automation surprise, but only if it is safety-relevant.

Every time a user's $\mathrm{REQ^M_{SAFE}}$ changes, one must decide anew whether a mode confusion occurs. Our definition of mode confusion is based on the (rather strong) assumption that $\mathrm{REQ^M_{SAFE}}$ is stable over time. The user generates $\mathrm{REQ^M_{SAFE}}$ on-the-fly from $\mathrm{REQ^M}$ and must re-generate it later when he/she needs it again. This re-generation might lead to a different result. In particular, the re-generation requires the user's recollection of the current mode. A user's lapse [Rea90] here can result in a mode confusion. This happens when the user selects a mode as initial mode which does not match the reality's current mode.

9.3   Classification of Mode Confusions

We classify mode confusions into four classes. The classification follows directly from the above definition of mode confusion. Each part where something can go wrong leads to a class.

1. Mode confusions which arise from *incorrect knowledge* of the human about the technical system and its environment.

   If $\mathrm{REQ^M}$ does not match REQ, then the timed failures refinement relation can break.

2. Mode confusions which arise from the *incorrect abstraction* of the user's knowledge to the safety-relevant aspects of it.

   If the mental abstraction function $\mathcal{A}_M$ does not match the abstraction function for the technical system $\mathcal{A}_R$, then the timed failures refinement relation can break (compare Figure 9.2 above).

3. Mode confusions which arise from an *incorrect observation* of the technical system or its environment. This may have *physical* or *psychological* reasons.

   The sense organs may be physically imperfect; for example, eyes which cannot see behind the back. Or an event is sensed physically, but is not recognised consciously; for example because the user is distracted, or because the user currently is flooded with too many events. ("Heard, but not listened to.") If SENSE does not match SENSE^M, the timed failures refinement relation can break. We could call this class also the mode confusions which arise from incorrect knowledge of the human about his or her own senses. The confusion disappears when the human knows about the senses' limitations.

4. Mode confusions which arise from an *incorrect processing* of the abstracted mental model by the user. There can be a memory lapse or a "rule-based" mistake [Rea90], i.e., a mode transition that is not part of the correctly interpreted model.

   An "execution failure" can spoil an otherwise perfect abstracted mental model. The model's semantics depends on the executing "machine".

In contrast to previous classifications of mode confusions, this classification is *by cause* and not phenomenological, as, e.g., the one by Leveson [LPS$^+$97].

9.4 Recommendations for Avoiding Mode Confusions

The above causes of mode confusions lead directly to recommendations for avoiding them. We now list and discuss these recommendations. We then also show how they are reflected by syntactic properties in our formal model.

9.4.1 The List of Recommendations

S1: Make the technical system deterministic. Non-determinism increases the user's effort for processing the mental model. The user must simultaneously track several alternative paths in the model. This can quickly exceed the user's mental processing capabilities and lead to incorrect processing. Therefore, the requirements of the technical system should allow as little non-deterministic internal choices as possible. To eliminate a non-deterministic internal choice, we must change the system requirements. We must add an environment event controlled by the machine and observed by the user which indicates the software's choice.

This recommendation generalises and justifies the recommendation by others to eliminate "hidden mode changes" [BaLe01, DSK99].

S2: Check that the user can physically observe all safety-relevant events. This avoids incomplete observation. To also avoid incorrect observation, we must check that the user's senses are sufficiently precise to ensure an accurate translation of these environment events to mental events. To prevent observation problems, we can apply the same measure as used against non-deterministic internal choices: we add an environment event controlled by the machine which indicates the corresponding software input event.

Improving the user's knowledge about his/her own senses has little potential for avoiding mode confusion problems. If the user knows that some things may happen, but he/she cannot perceive them, then they are non-deterministic choices to the user's mind. Again, the user will have difficulties with the complexity of tracking alternative outcomes.

Timeout events without immediate notification are inherently bad. Humans do have a sense for physically observing time. But it is rather inaccurate. Any silent timeout therefore leads to non-determinism.

S3: Check that the user can psychologically observe all safety-relevant events. This avoids an incorrect observation because of a psychological reason. We must check that observed safety-relevant environment events become conscious reliably. The knowledge-based approach of Hourizi and Johnson [HoJo01a, HoJo01b] can be a starting point here.

S4: Document the requirements explicitly and rigorously. This helps to establish a correct knowledge of the user about the technical system and its environment. It enables us to produce user training material, such as a manual, which is complete with respect to functionality.

S5: Document the safety-relevant part of the requirements separately, or mark it clearly. This helps to produce training material which aids the user to concentrate on safety-relevant aspects. Such training material, in turn, helps the user to abstract correctly to the safety-relevant parts. It makes explicit the safety-relevance abstraction function for the machine, $\mathcal{A}_R$.

We must also *minimize the affordances for human error* in general. We already cited the respective recommendations of Reason [Rea90] on page 197 above. Reason distinguishes three basic types of human error: skill-based slips and lapses, rule-based mistakes, and knowledge-based mistakes. Slips appear as incorrect observation for psychological reasons in our classification, and knowledge-based mistakes appear as incorrect knowledge. Lapses and rule-based mistakes cause incorrect processing.

9.4.2 The Recommendations as Syntactic Properties in the Formal Model

Our recommendations are reflected by syntactic properties in our formal model. If one follows our recommendations, some simple syntactic properties of the formal specifications should be satisfied. By checking whether these formal properties are satisfied, we can check whether the recommendations have been followed.

S1: Make the technical system deterministic. To be precise, the specification of the safety-relevant part of the technical system REQ_{SAFE} should be deterministic. A specification in Timed CSP is deterministic, if it contains only deterministic constant processes, operators that preserve determinism, other operators in cases that do not introduce non-determinism, and constructive recursions. The operators that preserve determinism are prefixing, 1–1 renaming, alphabetized parallel, sequential composition, timed prefixing, and delay. Roscoe [Ros97, pp. 219] also discusses all other operators of CSP and more details. A specification can become non-deterministic by using the internal choice operator and the hiding operator, in particular.

S2/3: Check that the user can physically/psychologically observe all safety-relevant events. This is satisfied if the abstracted behaviour translation function $SENSE_{SAFE}$ contains nothing but 1–1 renaming operators for events. In particular, this is most likely *not* satisfied if $SENSE_{SAFE}$ contains a hiding operator.

S4: Document the requirements explicitly and rigorously. This is satisfied if the requirements REQ have been specified in Timed CSP.

S5: Document the safety-relevant part of the requirements separately, or mark it clearly. This is satisfied if the safety-relevant part of the requirements REQ_{SAFE} have been specified in Timed CSP.

9.5   Checking Our Definition Against Other's Notions of Mode Confusion

We now check whether our definitions of mode and of mode confusion indeed cover the informal notions in the literature.

9.5.1   Comparison

Thimbleby [Thi90] defines a mode to be a "mathematical function mapping commands to their meanings within the system". This is consistent with a mode being a potential future behaviour. Thimbleby does not deal with the mode confusion problem.

Doherty [Doh98, pp. 118] finds that any treatment of mode must be based on a user-relevant abstraction, because there will be sequences of input actions which can distinguish between virtually all states. This avoids treating all states as separate modes. This argument supports our choice of a mandatory abstraction function. Doherty defines modes as partitions of the state-space. A mode formally relates a trace of input actions to an outcome. This again is consistent with a mode being a potential future behaviour. Doherty has no explicit notion of mode confusion.

Sarter & Woods [SaWo95] have no explicit definition of mode. Concerning mode confusion, they refer to Norman [Nor88] and state that "a human user can commit an erroneous action by executing an intention in a way that is appropriate to one mode when the device is actually in another mode." This definition leaves open what "erroneous" and "inappropriate" mean. If we interpret them as "has an undesired outcome", we get close to our definition. One can argue that Sarter & Woods don't include situations with an unexpected but not undesired outcome. For example, the user might just not care about the different behaviour. We cover this aspect insofar as we first abstract the system to its safety-relevant behaviour. After that, all differing behaviour is undesired by definition.

Leveson *et al.* [LPS+97] explicitly view the system as a black box, exactly as us. For them, "a mode defines a mutually exclusive set of system behaviours." The term "mutually exclusive" alludes to the partitioning of the state space, again. The term "set of system behaviours" is precisely equivalent to our definition.

Leveson *et al.* allow more than one human controller and more than one automated controller. Nevertheless, the idea is the same to have separate models that must be consistent. We focus on one of the human users only and put all other humans into the environment. Both views can be translated into each other.

These authors distinguish three kinds of modes: supervisory modes, component operating modes, and controlled-system operating modes. This distinction is a direct consequence of their different view on controllers. With our view, the three kinds collapse into two kinds: the modes of the technical system and the modes of the human's mental model of it.

Leveson *et al.* define that "mode confusion errors result from divergent controller models." This definition is stronger than ours. It requires equivalence between the models, that is, refinement in both directions. We require refinement in one direction only. The latter covers situations where the user does not know how the system will behave, but where the user knows that he/she does not know. Such a situation does not lead to an automation surprise. Leveson *et al.* are right that this is undesirable. But we prefer to distinguish insufficient knowledge of the user from actual confusion situations.

The definition of Leveson *et al.* is informal, it does not define precisely the term "divergent". Therefore, it is not clear whether the models must have the same set of traces only or also the same set of failures. Only the latter ensures that no model can refuse an event when the other cannot. We clearly opted for the second choice. Otherwise, a surprise can still happen.

Rushby [Rus01a, Rus02] has implicit definitions of mode and mode confusion only. Rushby writes [Rus02]: "Complex systems are often structured into 'modes' [. . .], and their behavior can change significantly across different modes. 'Mode confusion' arises when the system is in a different mode than assumed by its operator; this is a rich source of automation surprises, since the operator may interact with the system according to a mental model that is inappropriate for its actual mode." We do not see any contradiction to our rigorous definitions.

Rushby describes his model-checking approach [Rus02]: "If we accept that automation surprises may be due to a mismatch between the actual behavior of a system and the operator's mental model of that behaviour, then one way to look for potential surprises is to construct explicit descriptions of the actual system behavior, and of a postulated mental model, and to compare them." This does not say yet how the models are compared. Otherwise, it matches our approach. Rushby's actual comparison of models is determined strongly by the tool he uses, Murϕ. Murϕ can check one model against a set of properties, but not two models against each other. Therefore, Rushby must encode the comparison indirectly. Buth [But01] discusses this in detail. In the end, Rushby explicitly agrees that the two-model approach of FDR and CSP (as we use it) would have been better.

Degani & Heymann *et al.*: Degani *et al.* [DSK99] "define a mode as a machine configuration that corresponds to a unique behavior." The term "unique behavior" matches our notion. The term "machine configuration" already reveals that they do not use a black-box view on the technical system. Together with Leveson *et al.*, we think that a black-box view is necessary. Because of their white-box view, Heymann and Degani [HeDe02b] propose a formal abstraction algorithm. This algorithm generates a (minimal) black-box description from an internal machine description that includes non-observable events. This is helpful if one does not have a (black-box) requirements document in the beginning. Nevertheless, we prefer to start with an explicit requirements document.

Degani *et al.* [DSK99] distinguish clearly between physical and actually observed events. This matches the respective part of our definition. They point out that the user must be able to sense the input events that trigger a transition, and that "the user's job of integrating events, some of which are located in different displays, is not trivial". These recommendations are close to our recommendations to check that the user can both physically and psychologically observe all safety-relevant events.

Degani *et al.* [DSK99] state a prerequisite for mode confusion: the user's inability to anticipate the future behavior of the machine leads directly to confusion and error. As with Leveson *et al.*, this description includes non-surprise situations where the user knows that he/she does not now what will happen.

Degani and Heymann [HeDe02a] add a formal verification algorithm. The models must "march in synchronization". This means automata equivalence, as with Leveson *et al.* They construct a "composite model" in a fashion similar to Rushby, and they state three correctness criteria for the composite model.

The check for equivalence is motivated by Degani's and Heymann's desire to construct a *minimal* safe mental model. We agree that a minimal safe mental model should be in an equivalence relation with the machine. However, we define correctness separately from minimality.

A prerequisite for their entire approach is that the machine is deterministic. This eliminates the difference between our failures refinement and the simpler traces refinement. Our approach can handle non-deterministic models that nevertheless do not imply a mode confusion.

Buth [But01, pp. 183] writes: "Modes are identifiable and distinguishable states of a system which differ with regard to the effect of interactions." This is exactly the same as our notion. She continues: "Mode confusion scenarios or in general automation surprises describe situations where the operator's assumption about the system mode differs from the actual mode of the system and may lead to potentially critical actions of the operator." This also is exactly our intuition.

Later (pp. 199), Buth uses failures refinement in CSP. We adopted this idea from her. A major part of her work is the comparison of Rushby's one-automaton approach to the two-automaton failures refinement approach, for checking the two models against each other. She finds that the failures refinement approach is better.

A difference to our approach is that Buth requires mutual failures refinement, i. e., equivalence. This is due to the notion of mode confusion that Rushby uses and which Buth investigates.

Buth does not consider senses, and she does not consider the task of abstraction formally. However, in one case she hides an event manually that the user cannot perceive. And she discusses abstraction, but only in the light of model checking and state space explosions, not with respect to safety-relevance (pp. 208).

Hourizi & Johnson [HoJo01a, HoJo01b] criticize the mode confusion detection efforts in the literature. They stress that the underlying problems are a (mode) confirmation bias and selective (mode-confirming) perception of the human user. These are covered by our definition, too. They manifest themselves as a lossy relation SENSE$_{\text{SAFE}}$ whose lossiness depends on the current mode.

We already stated that *any* imperfect relation SENSE$_{\text{SAFE}}$ is bound to cause trouble. One should fix the perception first and then perform the formal verification of the rest. Therefore, it does not matter that it would indeed be rather difficult to obtain an explicit SENSE$_{\text{SAFE}}$ that is sufficiently precise in its mode-dependent lossiness.

9.5.2 Discussion

We conclude that all authors, including us, agree about what a mode is. Only Degani & Heymann *et al.* disagree in one sub-topic. They have a white-box view of the system instead of the usual black-box view.

The abstraction from states to modes is discussed by only a few authors. Most just implicitly assume that it has been done. Some use abstraction for a different purpose. They use it to reduce the size of the state space such that model checking becomes feasible. Doherty makes a case to have a user-relevant abstraction. We specialize this to a safety-relevant abstraction.

All authors who use a model-checking tool require that the two models must be in some equivalence relation to avoid mode confusion. Here, we disagree. We require a (timed failures) refinement relation in one direction only. Equivalence would mean refinement in both directions. Our position gets some support from Sarter & Woods: a problem arises only if the user does something wrong.

We claim that equivalence is stronger than necessary. If the mental model is in a specification/implementation relation, i. e., a refinement relation, with the technical system, then no automation surprise will arise. We agree that a non-deterministic mental model can cause a problem indirectly. Non-determinism can quickly exceed the user's mental capacity, leading to incorrect processing of the model. But this does not happen necessarily. Therefore we prefer to distinguish an outright wrong mental model from an execution failure on a correct model.

We suspect that the general insistence on an equivalence relation roots in the tools used. There are many model checking tools, but only one can check for failures refinement. This is FDR, the tool we use. Without FDR, one needs to check for a more than sufficient condition if one wants tool support at all.

It is generally accepted that two models must be compared. Nevertheless, all model checking tools except FDR require to encode the two models into a single composite automaton. Buth's idea to use FDR makes the comparison much more natural.

Only few authors consider "incorrect observation" explicitly. Degani & Heymann *et al.* do it, and Hourizi & Johnson, too. We can probably safely assume that all other authors would agree that this can happen, even if they did not include it in their particular approach. Buth, for example, hides a non-perceivable event manually. Our rigour made it obvious that one needs an explicit translation from environment events to mental events.

No author except us appears to consider timing. All their formalisms are un-timed. Time-dependent user interfaces are rare in the safety-critcal systems domain. They are generally considered as bad design. For example, a displayed value that disappears after a timeout is bound to cause problems for a heavily loaded operator. Nevertheless, we generalized our formalism from CSP to Timed CSP because we are interested in other domains, too. An example is the telephony domain. Timeouts are quite common there. We discuss it in the next chapter.

Our approach does not allow to have more than one human controller or more than one automated controller, as Leveson *et al.*'s approach does. But both views can be translated into each other.

Our approach is specific to safety-critical systems. Other, earlier literature discusses mode confusion in (moded) text editors. We can adapt our definition by abstracting to other than safety-relevant aspects. We do this in the next chapter, for the telephony domain.

All above tool-supported approaches use the term "mental model" in the restricted sense of "mental model *of the behaviour* of the technical system". They furthermore assume that an explicit, useful description of such a mental model can be extracted. We follow them in our attempt to clarify the definitions. This restriction loses the wider general meaning of mental model. But it also enables us to propose definitions for mode and mode confusion with mathematical rigour, and it enables us to exploit the analytical power of the tools.

All above tool-supported approaches check for *any* kind of automation surprise. This includes our approach. One might argue that automation surprises exist that are no mode confusions. We are convinced firmly that we need a black-box view of the technical system. But this implies that we can distinguish two modes *only* by their potential future behaviour. If two behaviours are different, that is, if there is a surprise, then there must be two different modes. Our solution therefore is to have a suitable abstraction from states to modes. An automation surprise is no mode confusion if it is abstracted away.

9.6 Application: Mode Confusion Analysis for an Automated Wheelchair

We demonstrate the usefulness of our definition and of our recommendations by an application in the service robotics domain. We analyze the cooperative obstacle avoidance behaviour of a wheelchair robot. We specify its behaviour formally and then we analyze it with an automated tool. This reveals several mode confusion problems. We then resolve these problems.

9.6.1 The Bremen Autonomous Wheelchair "Rolland"

The Bremen Autonomous Wheelchair "Rolland" is a shared-control service robot, that realizes intelligent and safe transport for handicapped and elderly people. The vehicle is a commercial off-the-shelf power wheelchair Meyra Genius 1.522. It has been equipped with a control PC, a ring of sonar proximity sensors, and a laser range finder (Fig. 9.3).

Rolland is jointly controlled by its user and by a software module, in contrast to other service robots. Depending on the active operation mode, either the user or the automation is in charge of driving the wheelchair. Conflict situations, often caused by mode confusions, arise if the commands issued by the two control instances contradict each other.

System Architecture

The user controls the commercial version (no control PC, no sensors) of the wheelchair with a joystick. The command set via the joystick determines the speed and the steering angle of the wheelchair.

The *safety module* [RöLa00] wiretaps the control line from the joystick to the motor. Only those commands that won't do any harm to the wheelchair and its user are passed unchanged. If there is an obstacle dangerously close to the wheelchair, the safety module performs an emergency brake by setting the target speed to zero. The notion "dangerously" refers to a situation in which there is an object in the

Figure 9.3: The autonomous wheelchair Rolland that was model-checked for mode confusion problems.   Photo: Rolf Müller

surroundings of the wheelchair that would be hit, if the vehicle was not decelerated to a standstill immediately. Thus, this fundamental module ensures safe travelling in that it guarantees that the wheelchair will never actively collide with an obstacle.

Higher-level skills provide additional functionality above the safety module. Obstacle avoidance (i. e., smoothly detouring around objects in the path of the wheelchair), assistance for passing the doorway, behaviour-based travelling (wall following, turning on the spot, etc.) and others. These modules have been combined to the *driving assistant* [LaRö01]. It provides the driver with various levels of support for speed control and for steering.

Obstacle Avoidance Skill

The obstacle avoidance skill must satisfy two requirements. Firstly, the automation must support the handicapped user when braking or detouring around objects. The goal is a smooth and comfortable driving behaviour. Secondly, the user must not be surprised. Whatever the automation decides to do, it has to be consistent with the user's expectation.

This intelligent shared-control behaviour is realized by projecting the anticipated path of the wheelchair into a local obstacle occupancy grid map. Figure 9.4 shows a situation in which the wheelchair is supposed to pass through a doorway. The right doorpost is a relevant obstacle since it is on the current path of the vehicle. The distance before collision is visualised for positions on this path by the grey-shaded area: the darker the sooner some part of the wheelchair will reach the corresponding position. The joystick command shown on the photo in the upper right corner of the figure indicates a narrow right curve. Since the corresponding projected path (upper

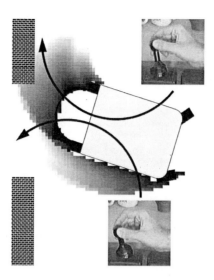

Figure 9.4: Deciding on which side the user wants the obstacle to be passed.

arrow) points to the right of the doorpost, this command is interpreted as "do not pass through the doorway". The lower photo shows a joystick command indicating a left curve. Since the corresponding projected path (lower arrow) points to the left of the doorpost (i. e. through the doorway), this command is interpreted as "pass through the doorway".

The algorithm chooses the speed and steering angle depending on the side on which the projected path, indicated with the joystick, passes the obstacle. If the driver directly steers toward an obstacle, the algorithm infers that he or she wants to approach the object. Then it does not alter the steering angle. As a result, obstacles are smoothly detoured if desired, but they can be directly approached if need be. If the automation realizes that the projected path of the vehicle happens to be free after an avoidance manoeuvre, it again accelerates up to the speed indicated by the user via the joystick.

The transition to the obstacle avoidance mode is an "indirect" one [LPS+97]. The mode is not invoked by the user on purpose. Thus, the driver probably does not adapt to the new situation after an obstacle has been detoured, because he or she did not notice that the operation mode changed from operator-control to obstacle avoidance. It is very likely that the user would not react immediately after the avoidance manoeuvre and steer back to the original path. Instead, he or she would probably not change the joystick command. The driver would be surprised that the wheelchair follows a wrong track after the obstacle.

An additional feature of the obstacle avoidance algorithm fixes this obvious mode confusion problem. It steers back to the heading of the original path after the obstacle has been passed. If the user does not adapt to the new situation, i. e., he or she does not change the joystick position after a detouring manoeuvre, the algorithm interprets the command in the frame of reference that was current when the manoeuvre began.

The algorithm therefore is able to navigate through a corridor full of people or static obstacles by simply pointing forward with the joystick. If there is an object that has to be detoured, the user keeps the joystick in an unchanged position and thereby enables the obstacle avoidance algorithm to steer back to the orientation of the original path.

Please note that we extend the narrow safety notion introduced here during our case study: Any behaviour of the wheelchair that contributes to its obstacle avoidance skill is considered to be safety-relevant.

9.6.2 Obtaining Specifications of the Behaviour

We obtained an explicit specification of the motion behaviour of the wheelchair robot, and we obtained an example of an explicit mental model of the wheelchair's motion behaviour, in order to demonstrate our mode confusion analysis approach.

Methodology

Our goal is to prove that our mode confusion analysis can be applied successfully to a problem of practical size. This requires that two explicit specifications are available for comparison. It is not our goal to explore suitable ways for the extraction of a mental model of behaviour. This is outside of our research focus and of our expertise.

A basic assumption of our work is that an explicit mental model of the safety-relevant aspects of the wheelchair's behaviour can be made available. Mental models have been extracted from training material, from user interviews, and by user observation (see Sect. 9.1.1). There is dispute about how reliable user observations are, in particular (see, e.g., [CnAQ01]). Even in a user interview, one has to take into account that the user may actually believe in one thing, but act in a different manner [Nor83]. Solutions to such difficulties are outside the focus of our work.

We selected a simple way of obtaining an example of a mental model of behaviour. It is sufficient to prove the feasibility of our approach under the above assumption. We performed a naive user interview. The resulting explicit description probably does not match exactly the actual model of the user. Furthermore, the user interviewed is an expert user. This prevents us from detecting mode confusion problems that are specific to novice users. Nevertheless, we believe that the resulting explicit model has sufficient resemblance to an actual mental model to prove the feasibility of our approach. In addition, we think that the insights from the example analysis are still of value to a designer of an automated wheelchair, despite some limitations.

The Events

The relevant events are obvious for the wheelchair. The basic assumption from Sect. 9.2.2 above therefore is satisfied that there is a general consensus about the events. There is a number of variables of the technical system visible to the user in a black-box view. These are the position of the joystick, the actual status of the wheelchair motors, the orientation of the wheelchair in the initial inertial system, the locations of obstacles, and the current command to the wheelchair motorics. We therefore specified events in CSP that denote a change in one of the variables.

The safety-relevant abstractions of the events required a little more work, but it was straightforward. First, we documented explicitly for the detailed data types that describe measured values and motor commands, which properties are safety-relevant. We then replaced the detailed data types by suitably abstracted ones. The latter only have two to three or sometimes four distinct values instead of some integer ranges. For example, we abstracted an integer-valued speed command range between -42 cm/s and 84 cm/s to the three values standStill, slowSpeed, and fastSpeed. They cover all distinct safety-relevant cases. We do not even distinguish between forward and backward driving, since the setting turned out to be symmetrical with this respect.

The most difficult abstraction was that of the virtual map of the obstacle situation. We kept only the closest obstacle on the current path of the wheelchair. An object in the surrounding is a relevant obstacle if driving further on the current path would cause some part of the wheelchair to collide with the object. We describe the position of the obstacle relative to the wheelchair by a potential wheelchair path and a distance. The path is defined by the steering angle that would be necessary for a collision of the centre of the wheelchair's front axle with the obstacle. The distance is the travel distance before impact. Since we are not interested in the distance as such, we abstract it to the corresponding criticality with respect to the current wheelchair speed: if the obstacle is far away, the required action is less demanding than it is if the obstacle is close.

Obtaining an Example Mental Model of the Behaviour

We "interviewed" a user who has built a mental model of the wheelchair robot through extensive use: our co-author [BrLa02] Axel Lankenau. Even though he has seen the source code of the software, he definitely does not use this knowledge while driving. Instead, he has built his own, intuitive, black-box mental model. This model is much easier to use for quick decisions. It also turned out that it is structured differently than the technical system. In addition, the user interviewed can express himself in CSP directly. This saved us from conducting a standard user interview for this research.

However, we conducted several interviews with different kinds of users for other purposes. We tried to optimize the different skills of the wheelchair such as obstacle avoidance, turning on the spot, etc. For this, we also experimented with wheelchair novices such as visitors and students.

Obtaining the Requirements Specification of the Behaviour

We extracted the CSP requirements specification of the behaviour of the wheelchair robot through "reverse engineering" from the source code. Unfortunately, no requirements document existed before this. (Of course, we did this only *after* we specified the mental model, in order not to spoil the latter by a fresh and close impression of the code.) The CSP specification is close to the source code. We restricted it to those parts related to motion. The rather complex sensor software is included at a high level of abstraction only.

The technical system is split into three parts: the input devices, the software, and the output devices. The requirements specification therefore follows the classical four-variable approach (Sect. 2.1). This separation is not present in the mental model. The mental model sees the entire technical system as a single black box.

The driver software of the sonar system provides "virtual sensors" [LaRö01]. They allow the other software to inspect a virtual map of the obstacle situation. This design structure of Rolland helped a lot for the specification of the requirements of the input devices. The mapping of physical obstacle locations to the software's input variables became a nearly trivial mapping because of this.

The wheelchair behaviour does not depend on specific timing values. Therefore, we used untimed CSP for the wheelchair requirements and for the mental model.

The safety-relevant abstraction of the behaviour is rather similar to the detailed specification. Mostly, the parameters of the detailed events were replaced by the simpler parameters of the abstracted events. All motion-related behaviour is potentially safety-relevant. Accordingly, the mental model of the safety-relevant part of the behaviour is rather similar to its detailed version, too. But with other applications, more simplifications might be possible and necessary.

Overview of CSP Specifications

There are the four specifications in CSP. We have versions for the technical system and for the mental model, both subdivided into a detailed version and an abstracted version. They partially share the definitions of events and types as appropriate. Ultimately, we combine them for a refinement check of the detailed descriptions on the one hand, and for an automated refinement check of the safety-relevant abstractions on the other hand. As expected, an automated refinement check at the detailed level is not possible since the state space is way too large.

The user's mental model of the behaviour of the wheelchair's obstacle avoidance module is specified by four major CSP processes: a "halt" process entered whenever the joystick is in neutral position, a "user controlled" process for user controlled driving, an "avoid" process for the obstacle avoidance skill of the wheelchair, and a "steer-back" process in which the wheelchair automatically returns to the original driving direction after an obstacle avoidance manoeuvre has been completed. Figure 9.5 shows the processes and the transitions among them.

The structure of the specification of the wheelchair behaviour requirements is different from that of the mental model. The specification of the wheelchair behaviour requirements REQ is the composition of the requirements on the technical system SYSREQ and of the requirements on its environment NATREQ. SYSREQ in turn is a composition of the input device requirements IN, the software requirements SOF, and the output device requirements OUT. SOF performs an infinite loop of reading sensors, choosing the appropriate software routine, processing the input, and setting

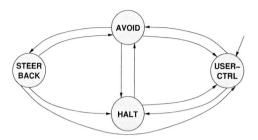

Figure 9.5: The user's mental model of the behaviour of the wheelchair represented by four CSP processes.

the actuators. In contrast, the specification of the mental model of the behaviour of the wheelchair REQ_M is the composition of the mental model of the behaviour of the technical system SYSREQ_M and of the mental model of the behaviour of its environment NATREQ_M. SYSREQ_M performs a loop of perception, calculation, and acting. There are no separate input/output relations, and the detailed structure of SYSREQ_M is also quite different from that of SOF. For each of the above, the structure of the detailed and of the abstracted specifications are identical.

The size of both safety-relevant abstractions together is about 1400 lines of commented CSP specification, or about 720 lines of pure CSP specification. The specification is available from us on request.

9.6.3 Mode Confusion Detected During Modelling

Our rigorous modelling process already revealed a first mode confusion problem:

Mode Confusion Due to Imperfect Vision

The user's vision is more restricted than one would think. We found out when we had to specify the user's senses SENSE explicitly. SENSE does a direct one-to-one mapping of monitored events to mental monitored events mostly (with some delay). But the explicit modelling made it obvious that there is one exception. The user cannot see obstacles behind his back. Of course, this is already a problem when driving backward. But they are likely to obstruct forward paths, too: when driving a curve, the back of the wheelchair swerves out to the side and may hit obstacles which are nearby alongside the wheelchair, but behind the user's head. The wheelchair robot will notice the danger, activate the obstacle avoidance skill, and change the motion into a safe one. The user will not notice the mode change, and he or she will be surprised. This is the reason why driving backward has the exactly same problems as driving forward. (It therefore can be ignored in our abstraction out of symmetry considerations.)

```
SENSE_M_SAFE(REQ_M_SAFE):
   performs:
      <mmJoystickCommand.100.straight>
   then accepts:
      {mcMotorsCommand.fastSpeed.straight}

SENSE_SAFE(REQ_SAFE):
   performs:
      <mmJoystickCommand.100.straight,
      mmJoystickCommand.100.right>
```

This proves that $\text{SENSE}^{\text{M}}_{\text{SAFE}}(\text{REQ}^{\text{M}}_{\text{SAFE}}) \not\sqsubseteq_F \text{SENSE}_{\text{SAFE}}(\text{REQ}_{\text{SAFE}})$, i.e., that the perceived reality is not an implementation of the mental model.

Figure 9.6: Counterexample by FDR proving the mode confusion due to fast and slow senses.

In our classification, the problem found is one arising from an incorrect observation of the environment by the user.

This mode confusion problem can be resolved by adding a feedback light to the user interface. It is on when the system is in the "avoid" or "steer-back" software routine.

9.6.4   Mode Confusions Detected by Model Checking

An automated analysis detected two mode confusion problems which were new to us. This happened despite the second author knows the wheelchair robot well, even its more obscure properties. Additionally, the automated analysis detected all expected mode confusion problems.

Mode Confusion Due to Fast and Slow Senses

The first new mode confusion problem occurs when the different senses of the user work at different speeds. The relation $\text{SENSE}_{\text{SAFE}}$ translates monitored events to mental monitored events. In a first version, we specified this translation independently for each of the user's senses (vision, tactile, motion-detection). This is realistic, since the organ of equilibrium can take some time before detecting a slow turning, and since the user might not see an obstacle in a complex surrounding immediately. These delays need not be correlated. And the joystick position is felt practically without delay by the user.

The automated model-checking tool FDR [Ros97] detected a violation of the refinement property resulting from this. Figure 9.6 shows one of the generated counter-examples. Initially, the wheelchair does not move. The user then fully tilts the joystick forward. Shortly after that, the user points the joystick to the right. The user expects to feel the acceleration (`mcMotorsCommand.fastSpeed.straight`) of the forward command after issuing it. Instead, the user has time to issue another command while he or she cannot feel any reaction of the wheelchair. This is a mode confusion. FDR allows to investigate the cause by inspecting the traces of the CSP sub-processes from which `SENSE_SAFE(REQ_SAFE)` is composed. The wheelchair indeed reacts as expected, but the user's senses delay the perception of the reaction. In practice, the situation is not really grave. Human senses are sufficiently fast to clear up any such confusions before driving at 6 km/h becomes difficult. Nevertheless, the tool correctly pointed out that in principle there is a problem.

In our classification, the problem found is one arising from an incorrect observation of the system by the user.

Really resolving this mode confusion is hard. In principle, we can educate the user about the timing problems. But the mental model will become much more non-deterministic. Strongly non-deterministic mental models are hard to handle for the user. They can easily go beyond his or her mental processing capabilities. This leads to mode confusion problems because of incorrect processing. The most viable solution is to keep the timing of the system so slow that we can make the explicit assumption that the user's senses will not delay events noticeably. This was what we did in our case.

The mode confusion problem found will occur in most shared-control systems. It occurs if the user uses different senses, and if these can have different delays for perception. With this respect, a complex visual scene can already count as being perceived by different senses, like the collection of aircraft cockpit panels.

Mode Confusion Due to Wrong Knowledge About the Halting Wheelchair

The second mode confusion problem revealed by the FDR tool is caused by an erroneous simplification of the acquired mental model by the user. Rushby denotes this process of irregularly generalising often used knowledge as *inferential simplification* [Rus01b]. The user simplified his model of the behaviour of the "halt" routine (see above) such that the wheelchair was assumed to re-set the steering angle to its initial "straight" position whenever the intended user speed was set to zero. As a consequence, according to this mental model the wheelchair could not change its steering to a value other than `straight` when standing still. But the technical system allows this.

The FDR tool reported the refinement violation shown in Fig. 9.7: the user intends to steer to the right while the wheelchair stands still. Both, the perceived reality as well as the mental model of the reality engage in the corresponding mental monitored event `mmJoystickCommand.0.right`. The technical system correctly maps this joystick command to the corresponding motor command `mcMotorsCommand.standStill.right`. Due to the inferential simplification mentioned above, the mental model refuses to engage in this event, it only accepts `mcMotorsCommand.standStill.straight` here.

Please note that this mode confusion is safety-relevant: if the user's mental model does not allow to change the steering angle during a standstill, the user might lose

```
SENSE_M_SAFE(REQ_M_SAFE):
   performs:
      <mmJoystickCommand.0.right>
   then accepts:
      {mcMotorsCommand.standStill.straight}

SENSE_SAFE(REQ_SAFE):
   performs:
      <mmJoystickCommand.0.right,
      mcMotorsCommand.standStill.right>
```

This proves that $\text{SENSE}^M_{\text{SAFE}}(\text{REQ}^M_{\text{SAFE}}) \not\sqsubseteq_F \text{SENSE}_{\text{SAFE}}(\text{REQ}_{\text{SAFE}})$, i.e., that the perceived reality is not an implementation of the mental model.

Figure 9.7: Counterexample by FDR proving the mode confusion in the "halt" routine.

track of the automation behaviour: consider a situation in which it is necessary to set the steering angle to its maximum value on either side to avoid a certain object in front of the wheelchair. If your mental model refuses to steer while standing still, you might not be able to set the steering angle soon enough while driving. This is because the curve radius increases when you steer while you are already driving (even at a very low speed level). Therefore, this mode confusion may decide about whether or not it is possible to pass an obstacle, and is thus safety-relevant.

In our classification, this mode confusion results from incorrect knowledge of the user about the system caused by an erroneous inferential simplification.

We resolved this mode confusion by refreshing the second author's knowledge about the "halt" routine: The corrected version of his mental model allows to change the steering angle while the wheelchair is in a standstill. This enhanced version of the mental model is used in the following.

Detecting the Known Mode Confusion

The automated analysis also detected the mode confusion problem which we already found during modelling. We specified the user's senses in non-matching versions for reality and for the mental model of it. The mental model $\text{SENSE}^M_{\text{SAFE, ideal}}$ maps all physical events to mental events perfectly. The reality $\text{SENSE}_{\text{SAFE}}$, however, may replace the visual perception of the closest obstacle by a less critical one.

The model-checking tool generated example traces for a mode confusion situation (Fig. 9.8 shows one of them). The wheelchair appears to change its motion behaviour without a cause. In the beginning, the user fully tilts the joystick to forward right. The wheelchair accordingly moves in a right curve at full speed. The user then sees an obstacle on the path. It is a bit to the left of the middle of the path, and still at a

```
SENSE_M_SAFE_IDEAL(REQ_M_SAFE):
    performs:
        <mmJoystickCommand.100.right,
        mcMotorsCommand.fastSpeed.right,
        mmObsLocChange.left.nonCriticalDist>
    then accepts:
        {mcMotorsCommand.fastSpeed.right}

SENSE_SAFE(REQ_SAFE):
    performs:
        <mmJoystickCommand.100.right,
        mcMotorsCommand.fastSpeed.right,
        mmObsLocChange.left.nonCriticalDist,
        mcMotorsCommand.standStill.right>
```

This proves that $\text{SENSE}^{\text{M}}_{\text{SAFE, ideal}}(\text{REQ}^{\text{M}}_{\text{SAFE}}) \not\sqsubseteq_F \text{SENSE}_{\text{SAFE}}(\text{REQ}_{\text{SAFE}})$, i. e., that the perceived reality is not an implementation of the mental model.

Figure 9.8: Counterexample by FDR proving the mode confusion due to imperfect vision.

non-critical distance. Suddenly, the wheelchair brakes to a stand-still. The cause for the braking action is a second, much closer obstacle on the path which is out of the user's vision. The user is confused. He thinks the wheelchair is in the user control mode, while in reality it is in the avoid mode. He cannot explain this behaviour as long as he assumes that his vision is perfect. Therefore the failures refinement check fails and produces this counter-example.

In our classification, such a mode confusion arises from an incorrect observation of the environment: the "wrong" obstacle is assumed to be the closest obstacle.

We resolved the mode confusion by updating the user's knowledge about his senses: we replaced $\text{SENSE}^{\text{M}}_{\text{SAFE, ideal}}$ by $\text{SENSE}^{\text{M}}_{\text{SAFE}}$. The latter mental model of the senses includes the restricted vision and is identical to the physical senses $\text{SENSE}_{\text{SAFE}}$.

The above mode confusion is very common in manned robotics: the human driver of the robot (here: the wheelchair) is not correctly aware of the obstacle situation in the surrounding of the robot. As a consequence, the user is surprised if the automation intervenes where there seems to be no reason for such an intervention. Or, vice versa, the user cannot track the automation's behaviour if it does *not* intervene while the user expects it should do so.

Proving the Absence of Further Mode Confusions

The automated analysis proved the absence of further mode confusions after we resolved the above problems as described. The model-checking tool investigated all traces of events theoretically possible and thereby conducted a mathematical proof by exhaustive enumeration. Of course, the proof holds only for the mental model of this specific user, and only as long as the actual mental model does not change. The expanded transition graphs to be explored during one of the refinement checks are in the order of 100,000 states and 300,000 transitions.

9.7 Summary

We present a rigorous way of modelling the user and the machine in a shared-control system. This enables us to propose precise definitions of "mode" and "mode confusion" for safety-critical systems. We then validate these definitions against the informal notions in the literature. Our definition is an improvement with two respects: First, it "sharpens" the relation between the two models involved. We demonstrate that a mathematically weaker relation is sufficient to avoid automation surprises. Instead of an equivalence relation, a specification/implementation relation is sufficient. Second, our definition adds precision to many details. For example, an abstraction step from states to modes is necessary, and one must consider a possibly incorrect observation of the environment by the user.

A new classification of mode confusions by cause is another result of our definitions. It leads to a number of design recommendations for shared-control systems which help to avoid mode confusion problems.

Our approach supports the automated detection of remaining mode confusion problems. A tool to model-check our specific specification/implementation relation exists. We demonstrated our approach practically by applying it to a wheelchair robot. Our rigorous modelling process already revealed a mode confusion problem. Our automated analysis detected two other mode confusion problems, which were new to us. We then could resolve these problems.

The automated detection is obviously restricted to a particular instance of a mental model of behaviour that has been extracted. The success of reducing mode confusion potential in this way therefore depends on the suitable selection of one or more typical users. It also requires that sufficiently accurate methods are available for extracting a mental model by a user interview or by user observation. As an exception, a mental model derived from training material will be relevant for most users of a safety-critical system without further effort.

If one had applied our recommendations already while building the automated wheelchair, it would have been easier to use. One should have kept an up-to-date requirements document, with a separate section on the safety-relevant behaviour. This could have prevented the above problem with the "halt" process. One also should have made the display show which part of the wheelchair is about to collide with an obstacle. This could have prevented confusion because of the user's insufficient lateral obstacle observation abilities.

Our work lends itself to extension into at least two directions. First, we can apply our recommendations while building a new system. Second, the notions of mode and mode confusion need not be restricted to safety-critical systems, e. g., aviation and robotics. The next chapter investigates the telephony domain.

Chapter 10

Mode Confusion Problems in Telephony

In telephony, call control is shared between users and many modern telephony features. Some examples are call screening, call forwarding, voice mail, and credit card calling. Multi-party features such as three-way calling let all users involved share call control to some extent. In contrast to many shared-control systems, telephones usually are not immediately safety-critical. Nonetheless, users expect a comparably high reliability which must not be impaired by undesired feature interactions.

We found that a considerable number of undesired telephony feature interactions in the feature interaction benchmark of Cameron *et al.* [CGL+94] are also shared-control mode confusions. The benchmark was written by practitioners from the telecom industry. It provides representative examples of a broad range of undesired feature interactions.

Table 10.1 summarizes the mode confusions we found in the feature interaction benchmark. There are 12 mode confusion problems in 8 of the 22 examples of the feature interaction benchmark. This shows that mode confusions are definitely a relevant cause for feature interaction problems. (Obviously, there are other causes, too. We discuss them briefly in the end of Section 10.2.)

The aim of this chapter is to present the new way in which one can view and tackle feature interactions. First, we adapt the definition of mode confusion to telephony. We then report from our investigation of the feature interaction benchmark in detail. The wealth of mode confusion examples demonstrates that our effort is worthwhile. Afterwards, we apply our classification of mode confusion causes to the examples. The distribution of causes turns out to be still reasonable. This further supports our new view on feature interactions. The benefit of our view is that we can apply the measures from the shared-control area for preventing mode confusions in telephony, too. Additionally, we recommend some specific measures for telephony. Attention to mode confusions helps to design features and sets of features with less undesired surprises.

Table 10.1: A summary of the mode confusions found in the feature interaction benchmark of Cameron *et al.* [CGL+94].

benchmark example no.	benchmark example ID	number of mode confusions	benchmark example no.	benchmark example ID	number of mode confusions
1	CW&AC	–	12	OCS&CF/2	–
2	CW&TWC	2	13	CW&ACB	–
3	911&TWC	1	14	CW&CW	2
4	TCS&ARC	–	15	CW&TWC/2	1
5	OCS&ANC	–	16	CND&UN	–
6	Operator&OCS	–	17	CF&CF	–
7	CCC&VM	2	18	ACB&ARC	–
8	MBS-ED&CENTREX	–	19	LDC&MRC	1
9	CF&OCS	–	20	Hotel	2
10	CW&PCS	1	21	Billing	–
11	OCS&MDNL-DR	–	22	AIN&POTS	–

10.1 Adapting the Definition of Mode Confusion to Telephony

We must use a different kind of abstraction relation in telephony. Clearly, the abstraction to safety-relevant aspects from Chapter 9 is not suitable here. The telephone user does not abstract to the safety-relevant behaviour REQ_{SAFE}^M. Instead, the user abstracts his/her knowledge about the behaviour of the telephone switching system REQ^M to the behaviour REQ_R^M of those features which are "relevant".

The relevant features are those that are currently active or can become active. They must be active for the user considered and in the scope of time considered. A feature is active if it can contribute to the visible behaviour of the system. A feature can be activated either by the user considered or by another user in the telephone network. The relevant scope of time ends when all features involved become inactive. Often this is the end of the current call. Sometimes, the scope of time is not limited at all, if the effects of a feature's behaviour are permanent. An example is the billing of calls from hotel rooms. The money spent will never return.

We can abstract the actual behaviour of the entire telephone switching system REQ to the behaviour of the relevant features REQ_R in the same way as the user abstracts REQ^M to REQ_R^M. The same holds for $SENSE/SENSE_R$ and $SENSE^M/SENSE_R^M$. We need all these for the adapted definition of mode confusion.

The same criterion for the relevance of a feature applies. The adapted definition is:

Definition 8 (Mode confusion in telephony) A *mode confusion in telephony* between $\mathrm{SENSE_R(REQ_R)}$ and $\mathrm{SENSE_R^M(REQ_R^M)}$ occurs if and only if $\mathrm{SENSE_R(REQ_R)}$ is not a timed failures refinement of $\mathrm{SENSE_R^M(REQ_R^M)}$, i.e., iff $\mathrm{SENSE_R^M(REQ_R^M)} \not\sqsubseteq_{TF} \mathrm{SENSE_R(REQ_R)}$.

The difference of mode confusion in telephony to mode confusion in safety-critical systems is in the abstraction function. In safety-critical systems, the abstracted mental model of the behaviour is stable, at least more or less. In telephony, the abstracted mental model of the behaviour depends on the set of features that are relevant currently. If this set changes, the abstracted mental model of the behaviour must change. This is an additional challenge for the user. However, this difference is not that big in the end. A user of a safety-critical system will occupy himself/herself also with other, non-safety-critical issues. After some time, this user will have to re-generate the abstracted mental model of the behaviour, too.

10.2 Mode Confusion Problems in the Feature Interaction Benchmark

This section contains a description and a discussion of those feature interaction examples that are also mode confusion problems. All descriptions of feature interactions are quoted from Cameron *et al.* [CGL+94] (except one variant in Section 10.2.3 and one extra example of ours in Section 10.2.11). For completeness, we also briefly sketch the wide range of causes from the other feature interaction examples.

10.2.1 Example 2 – Call Waiting and Three-Way Calling (CW & TWC)

Description [CGL+94]. "The signalling capability of customer premises equipment (CPE) is limited. As a result, the same signal can mean different things depending on which feature is anticipated. For example, a flash-hook signal (generated by hanging up briefly or depressing a 'tap' button) issued by a busy party could mean to start adding a third party to an established call (Three-Way Calling) or to accept a connection attempt from a new caller while putting the current conversation on hold (Call Waiting). Suppose that during a phone conversation between **A** and **B**, an incoming call from **C** has arrived at the switching element for **A**'s line and triggered the Call Waiting feature that **A** subscribes to. However, before being alerted by the call-waiting tone, **A** has flashed the hook, intending to initiate a three-way call. Should the flash-hook be considered the response for Call-Waiting, or an initiation signal for Three-Way Calling?"

Discussion. This feature interaction can be resolved by a precedence rule. An activated Call-Waiting feature should have a higher precedence than the Three-Way

Calling feature, with respect to the interpretation of the flash-hook. This allows both features to work most of the time without introducing a new user signal.

The mode confusion problem in the above particular situation remains, though. The mode of the switching element has changed, but the user issuing the flash-hook signal has not yet noticed it. He/she therefore will be surprised by an unexpected reaction of the system.

The cause of the mode confusion is a race condition between the notification tone for the mode change and the user signal. (A mode change not apparent to the user is called a *hidden mode change* in the literature on human-computer interaction [BaLe01, DSK99].) When **A** plans how to perform the three-way call, **A** will use his/her knowledge about the behaviour of the system, but he/she will concentrate on the "relevant" part for efficiency. This will probably make **A** exclude the Call Waiting feature, even when **A** usually is aware of it. The result is the mode confusion in which **A** expects a dial tone but is connected to the new party instead.

A careful user **A** can avoid the mode confusion, but still remains in an uncomfortable situation. **A** must expect a non-deterministic reaction of the system to the flash-hook signal. **A** can find out the actual current mode only by waiting a short amount of time whether a dial tone becomes audible. Only after this re-synchronization, **A** can either proceed with his/her plan, or adjust it to the new situation of an incoming call.

10.2.2 Example 2b – Plain Old Telephone Service and Plain Old Telephone Service (POTS & POTS)

There is another mode confusion problem in the same example of the benchmark. Cameron *et. al.* do not consider it as a feature interaction for the technical reason that no *incremental* features to the Plain Old Telephone Service (POTS) are involved.

Description, continued [CGL+94]. "A similar situation occurs when lifting a handset is interpreted as accepting the incoming call, even though the user's intention is to initiate a call – remember the cases when one picks up the phone in the absence of ringing and somebody is already at the other end of the line. The call processing is behaving just as it was designed to, but some users may be momentarily puzzled."

Discussion. This mode confusion is very similar to the previous one. The cause for the mode confusion is the same.

10.2.3 Example 3 – 911 and Three-Way Calling (911 & TWC)

The following example has been presented by several other authors in a more dangerous and also more concise variant. We also include this variant, using our own words.

Description [CGL⁺94]. "A Three-Way Calling subscriber must put the second party on hold before bringing a third party into the conversation. However, the 911 feature[1] prevents anyone from putting a 911 operator on hold. Suppose that **A** wishes to aid a distressed friend **B** by connecting **B** to a 911 operator using the Three-Way Calling service. If **A** calls **B** first and then calls 911, **A** can establish the three-way call, since **A** still has control of putting **B** on hold before calling 911. However, if **A** calls 911 first, then **A** cannot put the 911 operator on hold to call **B**; therefore **A** cannot make the three-way call. [...]"

Description of a more dangerous variant (911 and Consultation Call). "**A** calls **B**; **B** suddenly gets distressed, and **A** does a successful Consultation Call to the 911 operator. Then **A** wants to switch back to **B** for further information, but **A** can't do this because **A** first must put the 911 operator on hold, which is prevented by the 911 feature."

Discussion. The second scenario in the upper description where **A** cannot make the desired Three-Way Call is a mode confusion. **A** would succeed in a normal call, but does not in a 911 call. It is likely that **A** is not aware of the mode change concerning call control in an emergency situation. Again, when **A** plans the three-way call, **A** will concentrate on the "relevant" part of the behaviour of the features for efficiency. **A** does not intend to play tricks on the 911 operator and therefore excludes call control aspects from his abstracted mental model of the behaviour of the system.

Discussion of the variant. The system and **A**'s abstracted mental model of its behaviour are clearly in different modes here. The cause is the same as for the mode confusion above. A correct plan for **A** would have been to initiate a Three-Way Calling call instead of a Consultation Call.

10.2.4   Example 7 – Credit-Card Calling and Voice-Mail service (CCC & VM)

Description [CGL⁺94]. "Instead of hanging up and then dialling the long distance access code again, many credit-card calling services instruct callers to press [#] for placing another credit-card call. On the other hand, to access voice mail messages from phones other than his/her own, a subscriber of some Voice-Mail service such as *Aspen* can (1) dial the Aspen service number, (2) listen to the introductory prompt (instruction), (3) press [#] followed by the mailbox number and passcode to indicate that the caller is the subscriber, and then (4) proceed to check messages. However, when a customer places a credit-card call to Aspen, the customer does not know exactly when the Credit-Card Calling feature starts passing signals to Aspen instead of interpreting them itself. Suppose that **A** has frequently called Aspen and knows how to interact with Aspen. When **A** places a credit-card call to Aspen, **A** may hit

---

[1]In North America, dialling 911 connects to an emergency service.

[#] immediately without waiting for the Aspen's introductory prompt. However, the [#] signal could be intercepted by the credit-card call feature; hence it is interpreted as an attempt to make a second call."

Discussion. The abstracted mental model of the system's behaviour already has switched to the voice mail mode, while the system still is in credit-card mode. The user wanted to plan a shortcut in the voice mail service. In order to do this, he/she constructed an abstraction of the relevant parts of the telephone system. But in the abstraction step he/she made the mistake of dropping the entire Credit-Card Calling feature, even though it was still latently active.

Even with a correct abstraction, a potential for mode confusion remains. The user cannot observe when the system switches from credit-card mode to voice-mail mode. This happens somewhere between dialling the last digit of the Aspen access number and the end of Aspen's introductory prompt. We have a hidden mode change, again. The user can re-synchronize only by waiting, as above.

10.2.5 Example 10 – Call Waiting and Personal Communication Services (CW & PCS)

Description [CGL+94]. "Call Waiting is a feature assigned to a *directory number*. However, Call Waiting uses the status of the *line* with which the number is associated to determine whether the feature should be activated: at present in a public switched telephone network, if a non-ISDN line is in use, then it is busy; a second call to the same line will trigger the switching element to send out a call-waiting tone. PCS[2] customers may not all be subscribers of Call Waiting. Suppose that **X** and **Y** are both PCS customers currently registered with the same CPE[3]; **X** has Call Waiting but **Y** does not. We further assume that **Y** is on the phone when somebody calls **X**. Since **X** has Call Waiting and the line is busy, the new call triggers the Call Waiting feature of **X**. But is it legitimate to send the call-waiting alert through the line to interrupt **Y**'s call? If not, then **X**'s Call Waiting feature is ignored."

Discussion. If **Y** is alerted, this will cause a mode confusion for **Y** due to incorrect knowledge about the system. **Y** has no Call Waiting and does not know about the additional alerting mode the system can get into. When **Y** is alerted, **Y** probably does not know how to leave the mode that causes this annoying signal.

Personal Communication Services (PCS) will show mode confusions when combined with several other features, too. When a user shares a line with other users through PCS, his/her mental model of the system's behaviour must also comprise a significant part of the features of the other users. Since this often will not be the case, the system can easily get into modes he/she does not know of, similar as in the above example.

---

[2]personal communication services
[3]customer premises equipment

10.2.6   Example 14 – Call Waiting and Call Waiting (CW & CW)

We have two mode confusion problems here.

Description, first part [CGL⁺94]. "Call Waiting allows a subscriber to put the other party on hold. However, it does not protect the subscriber from being put on hold. Confusion can arise when two parties exercise this type of control concurrently. Suppose that both **A** and **B** have Call Waiting, and **A** has put **B** on hold to talk to **C**. While on hold, **B** decides to flash the hook to answer an incoming call from **D**, which puts **A** on hold as well. If **A** then flashes the hook expecting to get back to the conversation with **B**, **A** will be on hold instead, unless either **B** also flashes the hook to return to a conversation with **A** or **D** hangs up automatically returning **B** to a conversation with **A**."

Discussion.   **A**'s mental model of the system's behaviour does not include the possibility of being put on hold while exercising the Call Waiting feature. This incorrect knowledge about the system causes the mode confusion.

Description, second part [CGL⁺94]. "An ambiguous situation arises, when **B** hangs up on the conversation with **D** while **A** is still talking to **C**; there are two separate contexts in which to interpret **B**'s action. Assume that CW1 refers to the Call Waiting call among **C-A-B** and CW2 refers to the one among **A-B-D**. According to the specification of Call Waiting, in the context of CW2 **B** will be rung back (because **A** is still on hold) and, upon answering, become the held party in the CW1 context and hear nothing. But in the context of CW1 the termination **B** will be interpreted as simply a disconnection, thus **A** and **C** are placed in a normal two-way conversation, and **B** is idled. The question is: Should **B** be rung back or should **B** be idled?"

Discussion.   **B**'s incorrect knowledge about the implemented system can cause a mode confusion. The incomplete requirements specification for this combinations of features must be disambiguated by the implementers, in one way or the other. The choice is not obvious. User **B** must also disambiguate the situation, but may well take the opposite choice, even without noticing that there are others. In case that **B** expects to be idled after hanging up, but actually is rung back, this results in a mode confusion for **B**. **B** interprets the ringing as a new incoming call but then hears nothing when answering. In case that **B** is idled but expects to be rung back, this results in a period of mode confusion while **B** waits to be called back in vain.

10.2.7   Example 15 – Call Waiting and Three-Way Calling (revisited) (CW & TWC / 2)

Description [CGL⁺94]. "Consider how Call Waiting and Three-Way Calling might interact in the situations where a user can exercise both features simultaneously on the same line. The call control relationship can now become quite complicated. Suppose that **A** has both Call Waiting and Three-Way Calling, and **A** is talking to **B**. Now **C** calls **A**, so **A** uses Call Waiting to put **B** on hold and talks to **C**. **A** may decide to have **B** join his conversation with **C**, so he puts **C** on hold, makes a second call to **B**, and after **B** answers the call with Call Waiting, **A** brings **C** back into the conversation to establish a three-way call. There are three contexts in this establishment: a Call Waiting call and a Three-Way Calling call, both established by **A** among **B-A-C**, and a Call Waiting call established by **B** as **A-B-A**. Now, if **B** hangs up, then according to the contexts established by **A**, the session becomes a two-way call between **A** and **C**; according to the contexts established by **B** though, **B** should get a ring-back because **B** still has **A** on hold."

Discussion. **B**'s incorrect knowledge about the implemented system can cause a mode confusion exactly as in the previous example.

10.2.8   Example 19 – Long distance calls and Message Rate Charge services (LDC & MRC)

Description [CGL+94]. "Each long distance call consists of at least three segments – two local accesses at each end and one provided by an interexchange carrier in between. Should a customer be charged for the segments that have been successfully completed even if the call did not reach its final destination? Would it be counted as one unit toward the total local units allowed per month for a Message Rate Charge service?"

Discussion. First of all, this is a problem of ambiguous requirements, but there can also be a mode confusion because of incorrect knowledge about the behaviour of the system. Because of the difficult billing questions, the user can easily have false expectations on the behaviour. A call segment may be in a charged connection mode earlier than expected. The user will notice this confusion only much later, when he receives the bill. For example, he might be charged for long distance call attempts that he knows were never completed. An overrun of the allowed Message Rate Charge units could in principle also be a surprise, but it is much less likely that the user really counts all his local calls.

10.2.9   Example 20 – Calling from hotel rooms (Hotel)

Description [CGL+94]. "Many hotels contract with independent vendors to collect access charges for calls originated from phones in their premises. Without being able to access to the status of call connections, some billing applications developed by these vendors use a fixed amount of time to determine if a call is complete or not – thus one can be billed for incomplete calls that rang a long time, or not billed for very short duration calls (even long distance)."

Discussion. This is another mode confusion with a particularly long delay. The user will detect it several days later when paying the hotel bill. The cause is incorrect knowledge about the behaviour of the system. The user is usually not informed about the unusual way to determine the start of billing by a timer and incorrectly assumes that completing a connection starts billing. In case that the user knows the behaviour of the system correctly, a mode confusion due to the hidden mode change can still occur, that is, due to incorrect observation. This happens when the system and the user perceive a call duration just below / just above the threshold due to imprecise time measurement.

10.2.10 Benchmark Feature Interactions Which are No Mode Confusions

The remaining examples present undesired feature interactions with a wide range of causes. Often, there are ambiguous, incomplete, or conflicting requirements. In some examples, the restrictions of the current implementation cause a problem, or the implementation is just deficient. In all of these examples, there are either no surprising modes, or the user is not actively involved.

10.2.11 A Non-Benchmark Example – Key Lock and Volume Adjust (Lock & Vol)

This example is not from the benchmark, but its causes are particularly interesting with respect to our classification. Our colleague Axel Lankenau experienced this problem, we report it here.

Description (by ourselves). "Our colleague's mobile phone has the feature to lock its keys. This prevents unintended commands while carrying it in the pocket. The lock mode is indicated permanently by a small key symbol on the display. The lock can be released only by pressing the pound key for a long time. If any key is pressed, the lock mode is shown clearly on the display ("press '#' to unlock"), such that the user knows that he must unlock the phone before any further usage. There is one exception to the lock: when the phone rings, the user can press the hook button to accept the call. The phone remains locked otherwise. The phone also has two buttons at the side of its case which allow to adjust the volume of the speaker. It happened that our colleague carried his phone in the pocket in locked mode, and the phone rang. He took out the phone, pressed the hook button to accept the call, and held the phone to his ear. He then noticed that the volume level was not right and tried to adjust it. This did not work, and it surprised and annoyed him."

Discussion. This problem has three causes: incorrect processing by the user, incorrect observation for psychological reasons, and incorrect observation for physical reasons. First, there was a slip of memory when our colleague did not remember that his phone was in locked mode after some time of non-use. This was incorrect processing. Second, he committed a lapse as he did not look at the display while

Table 10.2: The causes of the mode confusions in the benchmark and of our one extra example.

cause \ no. ID	CW&TWC 2	POTS&POTS 2b	911&TWC 3	CCC&VM 7	CW&PCS 10	CW&CW 14	CW&TWC/2 15	LDC&MRC 19	Hotel 20	Lock&Vol —
incorrect knowledge				•	•	••	•	•	•	
incorrect abstraction	•	•	•	•						
incorrect observation									•	••
incorrect processing										•

accepting the call. He can do it without looking and therefore missed to check the mode. This was an incorrect observation for psychological reasons. Afterwards, he could not see the display of the phone while it was close to his ear. This was an incorrect observation for physical reasons.

A solution to the problem could be: when the user presses any key in the locked mid-call mode, the phone not only shows a textual warning message, but also generates an unambiguous warning beep tone. Another solution could be to redesign (and weaken) the lock feature such that it releases the lock entirely when the user accepts a call.

10.3 Applying the Classification of Causes to Telephony

Our classification of causes for mode confusions in safety-critical systems shows a distribution of causes in telephony which is still reasonable. Table 10.2 classifies all mode confusions in the feature interaction benchmark of Cameron *et.al.* [CGL$^+$94] and also our one extra example according to their causes. The dominant cause is incorrect knowledge of the user about the system (7 cases). Also important is an incorrect abstraction of the user's knowledge to the relevant parts of it (4 cases). Rare is an incorrect observation by the user (1 case). One cause does not appear in the benchmark, but in our extra example: incorrect processing by the user (1 case). This extra example also shows more incorrect observations by the user (2 cases).

Two of the four classes appear to be less important for telephony: incorrect observation by the user and incorrect processing by the user. One can suspect that this is only because the authors of the benchmark concentrated on "technical" problems and were not interested in human factors problems here. But we would need more empirical data to support this.

If incorrect processing by the user should occur only rarely, this is even an advantage for our approach. The user then sticks more closely to the mental model on which our mode confusion analysis is based.

10.4   Recommendations for Avoiding Mode Confusions in Telephony

Attention to mode confusions helps to design features and sets of features with less undesired surprises. We can adapt many of the recommendations for safety-critical systems from the literature and from Sect. 9.4 to telephony. And we have some specific recommendations for avoiding mode confusions in telephony ourselves.

10.4.1   Adapted Recommendations from Safety-Critical Systems

We can adapt many of the recommendations for safety-critical systems from the literature to telephony. We already surveyed them briefly in Section 9.1.3 above.

L1: Reduce the number and complexity of modes, if possible [SaWo95].

We put this recommendation first to underline that having different modes for the user is fundamentally bad. Unfortunately, the restricted hardware in telephony does not allow us to add sufficiently many controls and displays to get rid of modes.

L2: Annunciate the current mode. This avoids ambiguous interfaces where the interpretation of input or output events is not clear [LPS$^+$97, SaWo95].

Unfortunately, the restricted hardware in telephony does not even allow us to display constantly the complete current mode. The best solution available therefore is to annunciate all mode changes, and to repeat important parts of the current mode from time to time. This can be done by audible tones or by voice announcements.

In the benchmark example 7 (Credit Card Calling & Voice Mail), the switch from credit-card input mode to voice mail input mode should be annunciated. In the benchmark example 20 (Calling from hotel rooms), the start of billing should be annunciated.

L3: The interpretation of mode annunciations should not depend on the current mode, if possible [LPS$^+$97].

In telephony this means that the same tone should mean the same mode that is changed to, independent of the current mode. If the number of distinguishable tones is too small, voice announcements are a relief.

L4: Associate a similar task or goal with similar or identical actions. This avoids inconsistent system behaviour. Consistent behaviour makes it easier for the operator to learn how a system works, to build an appropriate mental model of the automation, and to anticipate system behaviour [LPS+97, CaOl88].

We can apply this to telephony if we encode an action as several button presses. These encoded actions, at least, should be consistent across the entire user interface. This requires a coordination and encapsulation of features, as discussed in Chapter 8.

In the benchmark example 7 (Credit Card Calling & Voice Mail), the inconsistent interpretation of the [#] button is obvious.

L5: Make the technical system deterministic. This avoids inconsistent system behaviour [LPS+97, HeLe96].

This is a fundamental recommendation. We already discussed it in Section 9.4. In telephony, non-determinism usually results from events that the user cannot observe. We therefore must annunciate all events that are relevant to the user.

Annunciating the exact timing of mode changes would have helped in the benchmark examples 7 (Credit Card Calling & Voice Mail) and 20 (Calling from hotel rooms).

L6: Extract a mental model from the user training material and check formally whether a mode confusion is possible. If it is, the training material and/or the technical system must be changed, and then the process is iterated [Rus01b, DeHe02].

Our rigorous definition of mode confusion is a suitable foundation for such a tool supported development process. A potential obstacle for this model-checking approach is the complexity of a complete telephone switching system. The analysis might be infeasible because of the state space explosion problem. A potential solution is to analyse small sets of features at a time. We need statistical information for this about which features are used together most often. These combinations are most likely to annoy customers if they are prone to mode confusions.

L7: Produce the user training material directly after the system requirements specification, even before the software requirements specification. This is part of the operator directed design process (ODP) that Vakil and Hansman, Jr. propose for future aircraft developments. It aims at reducing the complexity of the pilot's task through the early articulation of a model for the operator. The reduction of complexity may involve a reduction of functionality [VaHa02].

The same process can be applied to telephone switching. Note that the commonly done specification of use cases is something very different than the production of user training material. The point is to find out early, not whether the goal of the feature can be achieved at all, but whether the feature is usable conveniently.

L8: Minimize the affordances for human error. All the general recommendations of Reason [Rea90] and Norman [Nor88] apply, see Sect. 9.1.3, "recommendations". These are crucial basic recommendations. We do not rehearse them here since they are not specific to mode confusion problems. Nevertheless, you should read and practice these recommendations before you try to apply the more specific ones here.

Some recommendations from the safety-critical systems literature cannot be applied to telephony. One notable difference is user training. Telephony providers have orders of magnitude less opportunity to train the users. We therefore cannot adapt most recommendations related to training. Another major difference is that a telephone feature designer usually has no choice of hardware. He/she is not allowed to improve the physical interface. The customer usually is not prepared to pay up for a new, improved customer premises equipment.

10.4.2   Adapting the Recommendations Resulting From Our Classification of Mode Confusions

We can also apply most of our recommendations for safety-critical systems from Sect. 9.4 above that result from our new classification of mode confusions by cause. The same arguments for these recommendations apply.

S1: Make the technical system deterministic.

See recommendation L5 above.

S3: Check that the user can psychologically observe all [safety-]relevant events.

Our feature interaction between Key Lock and Volume Adjust above might have been avoided if the designers would have investigated how a frequent user scans the visual display. Frequent users do not always check it before commissioning an action. Therefore, an additional audible beep tone could be an adequate feedback to invalid input attempts in Key Lock mode.

S4: Document the requirements explicitly and rigorously.

In the benchmark example 20 (Calling from hotel rooms), the usual instruction leaflet in the hotel room should state the precise conditions for billing.

Two of our recommendations are less relevant in telephony. Recommendation S2 on physical observability is not important with standard telephone hardware; only the inaccurately observed timout events are important, see recommendation T7 below. Recommendation S5 on separating the documentation of the abstracted-to part has little relevance in telephony. It means that we need to separate the documentation of features from each other that are activated separately. In telephony, this is usually the case anyway.

10.4.3 Specific Recommendations for Telephony

We have some specific recommendations for avoiding mode confusions in telephony ourselves. The largest share of recommendations results from the specific kind of abstraction relation used in telephony:

T1: Provide feedback on active and inactive features. The correct abstraction to the relevant features is difficult for a user. Table 10.2 shows this. In particular, it is difficult to determine which features are active currently. Enhanced feedback helps the user to abstract to his/her mental model. We must check if it is obvious to the user whether a feature becomes or is active or not. If not, a status notification might be appropriate. This recommendation is also an instantiation of recommendation L2 above on annunciating the current mode.

Accordingly, the benchmark example 7 (Credit Card Calling & Voice Mail) can serve as an illustration again. The announcement of the voice mail service must make clear the point of time from which on voice mail commands may be entered. The credit card feature must announce from which point of time on its command processing is suspended.

T2: Check whether the user perceives a feature as a single entity. If a feature is perceived as more than one entity, then the user's idea of the set of currently active features can become inconsistent. If necessary, the design must be changed. Correct abstraction is easier if the active features are simple.

In the benchmark example 3 (911 & Three-Way Calling), party **A** perceives the aid provided by the 911 operator as separate from the complete passing of call control to the 911 operator. Even if **A** knows about the latter, he/she abstracts it away as irrelevant when planning the three-way call. A solution could be to decouple these two sub-features partially: the 911 operator should not only be able to terminate the call, but also to pass back call control to the caller if necessary.

T3: Keep the number of active features small. This helps the user to abstract his/her mental model. Reducing the number of active features while keeping the features simple can mean to reduce the functionality of the system. If the system's functionality exceeds the user's ability to build a correct mental model, it becomes a burden instead of a wealth.

T4: Keep the duration of a feature's activation short. This reduces the complexity of the abstracted mental model. The longer a feature is active, the higher is the chance that its period of activity overlaps the period of activity of other features. This increases the number of features that the user must include into his/her abstracted mental model.

A feature should terminate its activity after the end of a call, if possible. The purpose of some features does not allow this. In this case the user should get appropriate feedback on the set of active features, at least.

Examples of features with long durations of activity are Credit Card Calling (because of the re-authorization shortcut), Key Lock, and of course all billing features.

Some more recommendations are instantiations of our recommendations for safety-critical systems in the particular settings of telephony features:

T5: Allow remote activation of a feature only after feedback and proper delay. This is an instantiation of our recommendation S3 to check that the user can psychologically observe all relevant events. It avoids race conditions between the execution of user actions and the mental perception process of the user.

In the benchmark example 2 (Call Waiting & Three-Way Calling), the interaction persists even after a precedence rule has been added. The call waiting feature has modified the meaning of flash-hook, but the user has not yet noticed that call waiting has become active. The problem is that the user must perform the abstraction step again to get a new, extended mental model before he/she can process further events. This re-generation needs a little time.

We can avoid such problematic race conditions if a remotely activated feature like the call waiting feature proceeds in two steps: first, it informs the user about its activation. Second, only after it has completed this, it changes the system's behaviour, for example by accepting hook flashes. For this, the feature could either use two signals with, e. g., a delay of one second, or it could just make the system ignore hook flashes for one second, starting with the signal tone, until the user must have noticed the mode change.

T6: Provide the user with complete information about the system's behaviour. Preferably, a features's behaviour should be intuitive to understand. "Knowledge in the world" [Nor88], for example through suitably formed controls and other cues, is a preferred means to achieve this. Unfortunately, this is often impossible due to the restricted hardware interface.

Alternatively, the user should be trained suitably. This can be done by training material or by on-the-fly training, for example through voice announcements. Our telephone provider offers us a few use-cases only as the description of a newly provisioned feature. These leave many questions about the behaviour open. Research on better teaching material is required here.

This recommendation is an instantiation of the general recommendation S4 to document the requirements explicitly and rigorously, in order to produce suitable training material. The instruction leaflet in the hotel room that we discuss with S4 is a concrete place for good training material.

T7: Check that every timeout event is annunciated immediately. This avoids the non-determinism due to the inaccurate observation of time by humans. It is a specialization of our recommendation S2 to check that the user can physically observe all relevant events, and also of recommendation L2 to annunciate the current mode.

In the benchmark example 20 (Calling from hotel rooms), the expiration of the start-of-billing timer should be annunciated. An audible tone or a short voice announcement can serve this purpose.

Our final recommendations result from our experience with investigating the feature interaction benchmark:

T8: Take advantage of a richer hardware interface for feedback, if the user owns one. Examples are a text display or many indicator lights. Unfortunately, we cannot generally improve the feedback by a richer hardware interface. The hardware costs prevent us from installing better customer premises equipment everywhere at the same time. If a specific customer premises equipment is restricted, improved switch-side feedback is possible, nevertheless. In particular, voice announcements can help.

Of course, the access to such flexible and variable feedback means must be coordinated between different features. Chapter 8 discusses this issue.

In our feature interaction between Key Lock and Volume Adjust above, an additional audible tone would have been an improvement over only using the visual display. The hardware even would have been available completely in this case.

T9: Redesign a feature if the user has no chance to learn its behaviour. An example is the activation of Call Waiting (CW) and Personal Communication Services (PCS) on the line of another PCS user not subscribed to CW (example 10 in the benchmark). CW-PCS must not "hi-jack" the line without telling its current user what is going on. A model-checking approach (see recommendation L6) might be used to detect such situations.

10.5   Summary and Outlook

Summary

We present a new way in which one can view and tackle feature interactions. Many undesired telephony feature interactions are also shared-control mode confusions. For this view, we can take our existing definition of mode confusion for safety-critical systems, and we only need to insert a different abstraction relation from states to modes. Instead of to the safety-relevant aspects, it must abstract to the currently relevant features. The wealth of mode confusion examples that we found demonstrates that our approach is worthwhile. We show how one can apply many of the measures from the shared-control area for preventing mode confusions in telephony, too. Additionally, we recommend some specific measures for telephony. Attention to mode confusions helps to design features and sets of features with less undesired surprises.

Outlook

We could have a still more general notion of abstraction in the definition of mode confusion. This would broaden its applicability to even more domains. This is an interesting area for future research.

The above recommendations to avoid feature interactions need to be applied and tried out practically. This should be done by people who actually develop new telephony features.

The relation between ease of abstraction and the structure of the features deserves more research. Many feature interaction problems are abstractability failures. Are there any additional feature design rules that help the user to abstract to the currently active set of feature behaviour correctly? Research in shared-control systems is interested in the minimal safe mental model [Jav98, Jav02]. We have shown that this model is the "smallest" abstraction that is failures equivalent to the safety-relevant part of the behaviour of the technical system [Lan02]. We should find out how the user can have smaller abstracted mental models of the telephone switching system's behaviour without experiencing mode confusions.

The automotive domain starts to experience substantial problems with mode confusions and with feature interactions. The application of our results to the automotive domain therefore is promising. Car drivers increasingly get support from automated electronic assistants, and more and more car components contain an embedded computer.

Automated assitants for car drivers increase the complexity of the behaviour of a car. Mode confusions are bound to happen. The parallels with aircraft cockpits become stronger. Both kinds of systems are safety-critical. In the automotive domain, we even have to deal with humans which are less well trained, and which are less capable to handle complex situations than in the avionics domain.

Computerized car components increase the complexity of a car in general. High-end cars today already contain dozens of embedded computers. This leads to more and more feature interaction problems, as discussed in the outlook in Section 7.10.6.

Appendices

Appendix A

Software Requirements Module Base for a Family of LAN Message Services

At an example, we demonstrate our approach for requirements modules and for families and features from Chapters 5 to 7. This appendix contains the requirements module base, Appendix B contains the configuration rule base for it, and Appendix C presents specifications of some family members, as discussed in Sect. 7.4.2.

The example is about a family of LAN message services. The basic idea is that computer users on a local area network (LAN) can send each other short messages that are displayed immediately. These systems can have less or more functionality. A very simple version just unconditionally opens a graphical window at the receiving side and displays one line of text. This can be convenient to alert one's colleagues on the same floor that one will cut a birthday cake in five minutes. Other family members can support individual addressing, message blocking, message re-routing, output on a text console, delayed messages, and so on. This specification is a software requirements specification. The boundary between the system and its pre-existing environment is roughly between the software and the hardware.

This specification of requirements modules is not intended to be complete. It contains the important abstractions, and it contains also some details in sub-modules. This shows how we can describe such details. But we do not elaborate all details, since we do not actually want to build such systems. A complete specification would not contribute much further to our demonstration of its structure. But it would need space beyond what fits into an appendix.

The specification in the appendix is written in a part of the language Z_F, see Sect. 7.4.2 and 6.3.4. The chapter headings and the section headings in this appendix are part of the formal description. They are typeset in a suitable font and with a suitable numbering by the LaTeX style file which we developed, see Chap. 7.7. We type-checked the Z part of the specification sucessfully with the tool CADiZ [To⁺02], see Chap. 7.7.

The document structure shall help the reader to locate the information quickly which he or she is looking for. A tree structure of the document shall enable an efficient search. Each node starts with an overview that shall allow to decide which is the relevant sub-node.

Each formal paragraph is preceded by an informal explanation, for two reasons. First, the explanation shall help the reader to quickly get the idea of what the formulae are about. But the informal explanation sometimes does not discuss all tiny aspects. Therefore, the formal paragraph is always the authoritative version. Second, the informal text also links the formal constructs to real-world entities.

The module structure of the specification is shown in Table A.1. Section 5.3.1 discusses the general structure. And Section 6.5 discusses the structure of this particular specification. Figure 6.7 on page 113 shows both its module structure and its dependency relation.

At the top level, the specification is divided into the requirements on the behaviour of the software system to build and into the requirements on its environment. The environment comprises the communicating entities, the messages they want to exchange, and the existing hardware and software that that can be made use of. The specification of the behaviour of the software system describes what the system does to the communicating entities and the messages, without referring to any details of the existing hardware or software. We expect that changes in the hardware devices will happen independently from changes to the high-level behaviour of the system. For example, a change from a textual user interface to a graphical user interface will be independent of whether there is a message broadcast scheme or an individual message addressing scheme.

The specification follows the inverted four-variable model in order to link the mathematical theory to the real world, as discussed in Section 7.5.1. There are input transitions, monitored transitions, controlled transitions, output transitions, and operations. A naming convention identifies them (*"in_"*, *"mon_"*, *"ctrl_"*, *"out_"*, and *"op_"*). Furthermore, there are input variables (*"vin_"*) and estimated monitored variables (*"vmon_"*).

The transition systems specified here are completed by descriptions of their initial state (*"init_"*), of state invariants (*"inv_"*), and of auxiliary definitions. There may be several Z schemas for each of these. Our convention composes them implicitly by logical conjunction for each family member, see Section 7.5.3. Accordingly, the meaning of the specification of each family member is given through one transition system built from the above parts.

We interpret transitions such that the system evolves by events that happen, as discussed in Section 2.2.2. An event is specified by a transition, then. The event has a name and is distinguishable from other events. The effect of the event is specified by the post-states of the transition. The event may happen only if the current state is in the set of pre-states. Additionally, an event belonging to the environment may happen only if the environment agrees, and the system must not refuse it. We call this an input event. This interpretation allows for systems without any externally visible state space. In this case, any definition of a state variable is just an auxiliary definition.

Table A.1: The module structure of the family of LAN message services.

A.1. chapter environment

The environment module specifies the relevant parts of the world that are assumed to exist by the system. If the pre-existing hardware or the pre-existing software changes, this module must be changed. The module hides the details of the world that vary for different family members. In particular, the module hides the varying details of the underlying computing platform and of the concrete devices that allow the software to achieve its goal in the physical world. The module provides common abstractions for the communicating entities, for messages, and for time. The module's secret is how the concrete details of the world relate to these abstractions. These details are part of the requirements because the system cannot be implemented without using them. But the essential behaviour of the system is expressed without referring to them.

A.1.1 chapter computing_platform

The computing platform module hides those characteristics of the underlying computing platform that vary from one family member to another. In particular, it hides the details of the platform's native data types, and of the platform's facilities for communication among the different, distributed locations of itself.

We omit further sub-chapters on other characteristics of the computing platform here for brevity.

This module does not specify that part of the hardware which allows the software to achieve its goal in the physical world. This part can be found in the device interface module.

A.1.1.1 chapter data_types

The data type module hides the varying details of the platform's native data types. For example, the module hides those characteristics of characters, of text strings, and of graphical images that vary from one family member to another. Instead, the module provides abstractions that are common to all family members.

We omit further sub-chapters on more data types here for brevity.

A.1.1.1.1 chapter characters

The character module hides those characteristics of characters that vary from one family member to another. For example, there may be different encodings, and there may be different memory sizes.

A.1.1.1.1.1 section character_base

parents standard_toolkit

There is a set of characters. Each individual character is modelled as the number of its UCS encoding. This follows the way of the CADiZ toolset [To⁺02]. It allows us to use the extension for text string literals from this toolset, if necessary.

$$\mid \quad CHAR : \mathbb{F}_1 \, \mathbb{A}$$

We omit the specification of concrete character encodings for brevity. There should be at least one private section that defines a mapping from characters to natural numbers.

endchapter characters

A.1.1.1.2 chapter text_strings

The text string module hides those characteristics of text strings that vary from one family member to another. For example, there may be zero-terminated C-style sequences of bytes, and/or Pascal-style sequences of bytes with a length field in front. The module provides the notion of a text string, the signatures of the standard operations on text strings, and a specification of the common behaviour of text strings.

We omit further sections on other kinds of text strings than the C-style ones or the Pascal-style ones here for brevity.

A.1.1.1.2.1 section text_string_base

parents character_base

There are the notion of a text string, the signatures of the standard operations on text strings, and a specification of the common behaviour of text strings.

There is a set of text strings.

$$[TEXT\_STRING]$$

A text string behaves like a sequence of characters. We model this by a mapping function.

$$\mid \quad str2seq : TEXT\_STRING \rightarrowtail \text{seq } CHAR$$

The environment provides the basic standard operations on text strings.

The operation *op_strI* provides access to the character "*c!*" which is at position "*i?*" of string "*s?*". The operation can be performed only if "*i?*" is not greater than the length of "*s?*".

_op_strI _____
$s? : TEXT\_STRING$
$i? : \mathbb{N}_1$
$c! : CHAR$
_____
$c! = (str2seq(s?))(i?)$
_____

The operation *op_strlen* returns the length "*len!*" of string "*s?*".

---
op_strlen

$s?: TEXT\_STRING$
$len!: \mathbb{N}$

$len! = \#str2seq(s?)$

The operation *op_strcat* returns the concatenation "*res!*" of the two strings "*s?*" and "*t?*". The operation can be performed only if the concatenation is in the set of text strings. For example, it must not be too long.

---
op_strcat

$s?: TEXT\_STRING$
$t?: TEXT\_STRING$
$res!: TEXT\_STRING$

$res! = (str2seq^{\sim})(str2seq(s?) \frown str2seq(t?))$

We omit further details for brevity here, for example further operations.

A.1.1.1.2.2 private default section c_text_string

parents text_string_base

Text strings must be implementable as zero-terminated C-style sequences of bytes. The sequences are numbered starting with zero. These text strings must not contain a null character or a character with a UCS encoding above 255. This restricts the set of possible text strings.

$str2cstr: TEXT\_STRING \rightarrow (\mathbb{Z} \nrightarrow (0..255))$

$\forall s: TEXT\_STRING; \; byte\_seq: seq(1..255); \; len: \mathbb{N} \mid$
$\quad byte\_seq = str2seq(s) \land len = \#byte\_seq \bullet$
$\quad (\forall i: 1..len \bullet str2cstr(s)(i-1) = byte\_seq(i)) \land$
$\quad str2cstr(s)(len) = 0$

A.1.1.1.2.3 private section pascal_text_string

parents text_string_base

Text strings must be implementable as Pascal-style sequences of bytes with a length field in front. These text strings must not contain a character with a UCS encoding above 255. They may not be longer than 255 characters. This restricts the set of possible text strings.

$str2pstr: TEXT\_STRING \rightarrow (\mathbb{N} \nrightarrow (0..255))$

$\forall s: TEXT\_STRING; \; byte\_seq: seq(0..255); \; len: \mathbb{N} \mid$
$\quad byte\_seq = str2seq(s) \land len = \#byte\_seq \bullet$
$\quad (\forall i: 1..len \bullet str2pstr(s)(i) = byte\_seq(i)) \land$
$\quad str2pstr(s)(0) = len \land$
$\quad \mathrm{dom}(str2pstr(s)) = 0..len$

endchapter text_strings

A.1.1.1.3 chapter graph_images

The graphical image module hides those characteristics of graphical images that vary from one family member to another. We only introduce the notion of a graphical image here and leave out the rest for brevity.

A.1.1.1.3.1 section graph_image_base

parents standard_toolkit

There is a set of graphical images.

[GRAPH_IMAGE]

endchapter graph_images

endchapter data_types

A.1.1.2 private default chapter distributed_processing

The distributed processing module hides the varying characteristics of the platform's facilities for communication among the different, distributed locations of itself. There may be different kinds of LAN interfaces that the software may use to achieve its goals. There also may be systems without any distribution at all; therefore, this module is "private", since it may be missing.

We omit the further description here; the specification would comprise a description of the distribution and it would provide sending and receiving events that allow to bridge this distribution. The formal specification of the events would be similar to the submission and delivery events below.

endchapter distributed_processing

endchapter computing_platform

A.1.2 chapter device_interfaces

The device interface module hides the varying details of the concrete devices that allow the software to achieve its goal in the physical world. In particular, the module hides the differences between the interfaces that allow the software to interact with the communicating entities, and the module hides the differences between the ways to access the time.

This module does not specify that part of the hardware that is internal to the computing platform and that makes no contact with the physical world. This part can be found in the computing platform module.

A.1.2.1 chapter time

The time module hides the differences of the ways in which the access to time can be specified. We always assume a global time, which is sufficient for our purposes. The module's secret is the concrete kind of time scale used, and the concrete way in which the software can obtain information about the current time. The module provides the notion of time and of time differences, and it provides an abstract global clock.

We specify an example of a concrete time scale, but otherwise we omit the descriptions of most of the varying parts, again.

A.1.2.1.1 section time_base

parents standard_toolkit

There is a set of points in time and a set of time differences (i.e., relative time), with base operations on them. The numeric value of points in time and of time differences is all that interests about them.

$$time : \mathbb{P} \, \mathbb{A}$$

$$rtime == \{x, y : time \bullet x - y\}$$

Note that we do not yet specify what kind of numbers to use. But the natural numbers are part of the "arithmos": $\mathbb{N} \subset \mathbb{A}$

The standard toolkit provides us with the base operations for natural numbers and for integers: comparison, difference, and addition. Using other kinds of values for points in time requires to define these operators suitably for such values.

The point in time is reflected by an input variable.

┌─ *soft_clock* ─────────────────────────────
│ $vin\_curr\_time : time$
└──────────────────────────────────────

The software's estimate of the point in time is an estimated monitored variable.

┌─ *clock* ──────────────────────────────────
│ $vmon\_curr\_time : time$
└──────────────────────────────────────

The system starts at some specific point in time, which is determined by the environment.

$$vin\_start\_time : time$$

```
┌─ init_clock ──────────────────────────────────────────────────────┐
│ soft_clock                                                          │
│ clock                                                               │
├───────────────────────                                             │
│ vin_curr_time = vin_start_time                                      │
│ vmon_curr_time = vin_start_time                                     │
└────────────────────────────────────────────────────────────────────┘
```

The environment can make time pass without further inputs. This input event increments the points in time, as perceivable to the software.

```
┌─ in_tick ─────────────────────────────────────────────────────────┐
│ Δsoft_clock                                                         │
│ time_step? : rtime                                                  │
├───────────────────────                                             │
│ vin_curr_time′ = vin_curr_time + time_step?                        │
│ vin_curr_time′ > vin_curr_time                                     │
└────────────────────────────────────────────────────────────────────┘
```

There is a precision with which the software perceives time.

$prec\_time : rtime$

The software can perceive that time has passed after the corresponding input event. It will do it at least with the above precision.

```
┌─ mon_tick ────────────────────────────────────────────────────────┐
│ Ξsoft_clock                                                         │
│ Δclock                                                              │
├───────────────────────                                             │
│ vmon_curr_time′ = vin_curr_time                                    │
│ vmon_curr_time′ − vmon_curr_time ≤ prec_time                       │
└────────────────────────────────────────────────────────────────────┘
```

A.1.2.1.2 *private default section time_milliseconds*

parents time_base

The time values are in milliseconds (with no fraction). The system starts at 0 ms.

$$time = \mathbb{N}$$
$$vin\_start\_time = 0$$

This implies a discrete time scale.

endchapter time

A.1.2.2 chapter communicating_entities

The communicating entity module hides the differences between the interfaces that allow the software to interact with the communicating entities. In particular, the module hides the differences between the various types of messages, and it hides the difference between the interfaces to human users and to automated agents. The module provides abstractions for communicating entities and communication events, for the messages which are communicated, and for the devices that allow the software to interact with the communicating entities.

A.1.2.2.1 chapter messages

The message module hides the differences between the various types of messages. In particular, there may be text messages and graphical messages. The message module provides the notion of an abstract message.

We omit further message types and combinations of message types for brevity, again.

A.1.2.2.1.1 section message_base

parents standard_toolkit

There is a set of messages.

$[MESSAGE]$

A.1.2.2.1.2 private default section text_message_base

parents message_base

There is a set of text messages which are part of the set of messages. Each text message has a number of lines. There is an upper limit on the number of lines.

$$TEXT\_MESSAGE : \mathbb{F}_1\ MESSAGE$$
$$max\_lines : \mathbb{N}_1$$

$$msg2line\_no : TEXT\_MESSAGE \rightarrow 0\mathbin{..} max\_lines$$

A.1.2.2.1.3 private default section text_message_only

parents text_message_base

Nothing but a text message can be a message.

$$TEXT\_MESSAGE = MESSAGE$$

A.1.2.2.1.4 private default section one_line_message

parents text_message_base

A message has at most one line.

$$max\_lines = 1$$

A.1.2.2.1.5 private section multi_line_message
parents text_message_base

A message can have multiple lines. This means at least 100 lines.

$$max\_lines \geq 100$$

A.1.2.2.1.6 private section max_lines2_message
parents text_message_base

A message has at most two lines.

$$max\_lines = 2$$

A.1.2.2.1.7 private section graphical_message_base
parents message_base

There is a set of graphical messages which are part of the set of messages.

$$GRAPH\_MESSAGE : \mathbb{F}_1 \, MESSAGE$$

endchapter messages

A.1.2.2.2 section comm_base
parents standard_toolkit

There are communicating entities and communication events. A communication event can be a submission event or a delivery event.

$$[COMM\_ENTITY, EV\_SUBMIT, EV\_DELIVER]$$

We assume that both kinds of events can be ordered totally over time. Therefore, we model their histories as injective sequences.

```
┌─ hist_comm ──────────────────────────────────────────────
│  hist_submit : iseq EV_SUBMIT
│  hist_deliver : iseq EV_DELIVER
└──────────────────────────────────────────────────────────
```

A.1.2.2.3 section comm_params_base
parents comm_base, message_base, time_base

The submission and delivery events each have three basic parameters associated: both have a message, both have a point in time where they are submitted/delivered, a submission also has exactly one sender, and a delivery has a non-empty set of receivers instead.

$ev\_sub2msg : EV\_SUBMIT \rightarrow MESSAGE$
$ev\_deliv2msg : EV\_DELIVER \rightarrow MESSAGE$
$ev\_sub2time : EV\_SUBMIT \rightarrow time$
$ev\_deliv2time : EV\_DELIVER \rightarrow time$
$ev\_sub2sender : EV\_SUBMIT \rightarrow COMM\_ENTITY$
$ev\_deliv2receivers : EV\_DELIVER \rightarrow \mathbb{F}_1 \, COMM\_ENTITY$

A.1.2.2.4 private default section comm_behaviour

parents comm_params_base

The behaviour of communicating entities consists of message submission and message delivery events, it is not restricted in any way, as far as they are concerned.

$$
\begin{array}{|l}
\underline{init\_hist\_comm} \\
hist\_comm \\
\hline
hist\_submit = \varnothing \\
hist\_deliver = \varnothing \\
\end{array}
$$

$$
\begin{array}{|l}
\underline{mon\_submit} \\
m? : MESSAGE \\
s? : COMM\_ENTITY \\
\Delta hist\_comm \\
\hline
\exists\, e : EV\_SUBMIT \mid ev\_sub2msg(e) = m? \land ev\_sub2sender(e) = s? \bullet \\
\quad hist\_submit' = hist\_submit \frown \langle e \rangle \\
hist\_deliver' = hist\_deliver \\
\end{array}
$$

$$
\begin{array}{|l}
\underline{ctrl\_deliver} \\
m! : MESSAGE \\
r! : \mathbb{F}_1 \, COMM\_ENTITY \\
\Delta hist\_comm \\
\hline
\exists\, e : EV\_DELIVER \mid ev\_deliv2msg(e) = m! \land ev\_deliv2receivers(e) = r! \bullet \\
\quad hist\_deliver' = hist\_deliver \frown \langle e \rangle \\
hist\_submit' = hist\_submit \\
\end{array}
$$

A.1.2.2.5 private default section comm_io_base

parents standard_toolkit

There are input and output events by which the software interacts with the communicating entities through the devices.

$[EV\_INPUT, EV\_OUTPUT]$

We assume that these events can be ordered totally over time. Therefore, we model the history of these events as an injective sequence.

```
┌─ hist_io ──────────────────────────────────────────────┐
│ hist_input : iseq EV_INPUT                              │
│ hist_output : iseq EV_OUTPUT                            │
└────────────────────────────────────────────────────────┘
```

A.1.2.2.6 private default section comm_io_params_base

parents comm_io_base, comm_base, message_base, time_base

The input and output events each have three basic parameters associated: both have a message, both have a point in time where they occur, an input event also has exactly one sender, and an output event has a non-empty set of receivers instead.

$ev\_input2msg : EV\_INPUT \rightarrow MESSAGE$
$ev\_output2msg : EV\_OUTPUT \rightarrow MESSAGE$
$ev\_input2time : EV\_INPUT \rightarrow time$
$ev\_output2time : EV\_OUTPUT \rightarrow time$
$ev\_input2sender : EV\_INPUT \rightarrow COMM\_ENTITY$
$ev\_output2receivers : EV\_OUTPUT \rightarrow \mathbb{F}_1 \, COMM\_ENTITY$

There is no addressing yet, different schemes can be added.

A.1.2.2.7 private default section comm_io_behaviour

parents comm_io_params_base, comm_params_base

When a submission event is input, then a corresponding estimated monitored event will be computed; and when a delivery event is output, then a corresponding estimated controlled event has been computed before.

There are an input event at the software and an output event by the software:

```
┌─ in_submit ────────────────────────────────────────────┐
│ m? : MESSAGE                                            │
│ s? : COMM_ENTITY                                        │
│ Δhist_io                                                │
│ Ξclock                                                  │
├────────────────────────────────────────────────────────┤
│ ∃ e : EV_INPUT |                                        │
│     ev_input2msg(e) = m? ∧ ev_input2sender(e) = s? ∧    │
│     ev_input2time(e) = vmon_curr_time •                 │
│     hist_input' = hist_input ⌢ ⟨e⟩                      │
│ hist_output' = hist_output                              │
└────────────────────────────────────────────────────────┘
```

```
┌─ out_deliver ─────────────────────────────────────────────────┐
│ m! : MESSAGE                                                    │
│ r! : 𝔽₁ COMM_ENTITY                                            │
│ Δhist_io                                                        │
│ Ξclock                                                          │
├────────────────────────────────────────────────────────────── │
│ ∃ e : EV_OUTPUT |                                               │
│     ev_output2msg(e) = m! ∧ ev_output2receivers(e) = r! ∧       │
│     ev_output2time(e) = vmon_curr_time •                        │
│     hist_output' = hist_output ⌢ ⟨e⟩                            │
│ hist_input' = hist_input                                        │
└────────────────────────────────────────────────────────────────┘
```

In the beginning, the input and output histories are empty:

```
┌─ init_hist_io ────────────────────────────────────────────────┐
│ hist_io                                                         │
├────────────────────────────────────────────────────────────── │
│ hist_input = ∅                                                  │
│ hist_output = ∅                                                 │
└────────────────────────────────────────────────────────────────┘
```

There is a fixed upper time bound for the input delay, and another one for the output delay:

```
│ max_input_delay : rtime
│ max_output_delay : rtime
```

There is a fixed upper time bound until the estimated monitored submission event will be computed after the corresponding input event; and there is a fixed upper time bound between the computation of an estimated controlled delivery event and the corresponding output event.

```
│ max_mon_delay : rtime
│ max_ctrl_delay : rtime
```

For each submission event that has been input, there has been exactly one corresponding estimated monitored event, except maybe for those input events which are too new; also, no other estimated monitored submission events are computed. That means that there is a suitable mapping between the history of estimated monitored events and a suitable prefix of the input history.

$$\begin{array}{|l}
\_\_ \textit{inv\_hist\_input} _____ \\
\textit{hist\_comm} \\
\textit{hist\_io} \\
\textit{clock} \\
\hline
\exists\, h\_i, h\_j : \text{iseq}\ EV\_INPUT \mid h\_i \frown h\_j = hist\_input\ \wedge \\
\quad (\forall\, e : \text{ran}\ h\_j \bullet ev\_input2time(e) + max\_mon\_delay > vmon\_curr\_time) \bullet \\
\quad hist\_submit \, {}_9^\circ\, ev\_sub2msg = h\_i \, {}_9^\circ\, ev\_input2msg\ \wedge \\
\quad hist\_submit \, {}_9^\circ\, ev\_sub2sender = h\_i \, {}_9^\circ\, ev\_input2sender\ \wedge \\
\quad \exists\, tshift : time \rightarrow time \mid (\forall\, t : time \bullet tshift(t) = t - max\_input\_delay) \bullet \\
\quad\quad hist\_submit \, {}_9^\circ\, ev\_sub2time = h\_i \, {}_9^\circ\, ev\_input2time \, {}_9^\circ\, tshift
\end{array}$$

For each estimated controlled delivery event that has been computed, there has been exactly one corresponding output event, except maybe for those estimated controlled events which are too new; also, no other delivery output events occur. That means that there is a suitable mapping between the history of output events and a suitable prefix of the estimated controlled event history.

$$\begin{array}{|l}
\_\_ \textit{inv\_hist\_output} _____ \\
\textit{hist\_comm} \\
\textit{hist\_io} \\
\textit{clock} \\
\hline
\exists\, tshift : time \rightarrow time \mid (\forall\, t : time \bullet tshift(t) = t + max\_output\_delay) \bullet \\
\quad \exists\, h\_d, h\_e : \text{iseq}\ EV\_DELIVER \mid h\_d \frown h\_e = hist\_deliver\ \wedge \\
\quad\quad (\forall\, e : \text{ran}\ h\_e \bullet \\
\quad\quad\quad ev\_deliv2time(e) + max\_ctrl\_delay > tshift(vmon\_curr\_time)) \bullet \\
\quad hist\_output \, {}_9^\circ\, ev\_output2msg = h\_d \, {}_9^\circ\, ev\_deliv2msg\ \wedge \\
\quad hist\_output \, {}_9^\circ\, ev\_output2receivers = h\_d \, {}_9^\circ\, ev\_deliv2receivers\ \wedge \\
\quad hist\_output \, {}_9^\circ\, ev\_output2time \, {}_9^\circ\, tshift = h\_d \, {}_9^\circ\, ev\_deliv2time
\end{array}$$

A.1.2.2.8 private default chapter user_interface

The user interface module hides the differences between the possible kinds of interfaces to human users. In particular, there may be a graphical user interface, and there may be a textual user interface.

A.1.2.2.8.1 section user_base

parents comm_base

There is a set of human users which are part of the communicating entities.

$$user : \mathbb{F}_1\ COMM\_ENTITY$$

A.1.2.2.8.2 private default chapter graphical_user_interface

The graphical user interface module hides the differences between the possible kinds of graphical user interfaces. The module provides abstractions of the graphical devices that allow the software to interact with the human users.

We specify the common abstractions only here and omit the varying details for brevity.

A.1.2.2.8.2.1 section gui_comm_base

parents comm_base

Some of the events that denote a submission by a communicating entity are submissions through the GUI. The same holds for deliveries. A submission through the GUI means that a user enters a message via a graphical input box. A delivery through the GUI means that the GUI software displays an alert box with a message to one or more users.

$ev\_gui\_submit : \mathbb{P}_1 \ EV\_SUBMIT$
$ev\_gui\_deliver : \mathbb{P}_1 \ EV\_DELIVER$

A.1.2.2.8.2.2 private default section gui_io_base

parents gui_comm_base, comm_io_base

Some of the software input events that are related to a submission by a communicating entity are input events of the GUI. The same holds for output events and deliveries.

$ev\_gui\_input : \mathbb{P}_1 \ EV\_INPUT$
$ev\_gui\_output : \mathbb{P}_1 \ EV\_OUTPUT$

The GUI submission events are always associated with the GUI input events, and the GUI output events are associated with the GUI delivery events.

---
inv_gui_io

hist_comm
hist_io

$hist\_input(\!| \ \mathrm{dom}(hist\_submit \rhd ev\_gui\_submit) \ |\!) \subseteq ev\_gui\_input$
$hist\_deliver(\!| \ \mathrm{dom}(hist\_output \rhd ev\_gui\_output) \ |\!) \subseteq ev\_gui\_deliver$

---

endchapter graphical_user_interface

A.1.2.2.8.3 private chapter textual_user_interface

The textual user interface module hides the differences between the possible kinds of textual user interfaces. The module provides abstractions of the textual devices that allow the software to interact with the human users.

We specify the common abstractions only here and omit the varying details for brevity.

A.1.2.2.8.3.1 section tui_comm_base

>   parents comm_base

Some of the software input events that are related to a submission by a communicating entity are input events of the textual user interface. The same holds for output events and deliveries.

> $ev\_tui\_submit : \mathbb{P}_1\ EV\_SUBMIT$
> $ev\_tui\_deliver : \mathbb{P}_1\ EV\_DELIVER$

We omit the further specification here for brevity.

endchapter textual_user_interface

endchapter user_interface

A.1.2.2.9 private chapter automated_agent_interface

The automated agent interface module hides the differences between the possible kinds of interfaces to automated agents.

A.1.2.2.9.1 section agent_base

>   parents comm_base

There is a set of automated agents which are part of the communicating entities.

> $agent : \mathbb{F}_1\ COMM\_ENTITY$

Some of the events that denote a submission by a communicating entity are submissions from agents. The same holds for deliveries.

> $ev\_agi\_submit : \mathbb{P}_1\ EV\_SUBMIT$
> $ev\_agi\_deliver : \mathbb{P}_1\ EV\_DELIVER$

We omit the further specification here for brevity. For example, automated agents could be passive receivers of messages only, while there would be no such restriction on the behaviour of human users.

endchapter automated_agent_interface

endchapter communicating_entities

endchapter device_interfaces

endchapter environment

A.2. chapter system_behaviour

The system behaviour module specifies what the system to build effects in its environment. The module hides this behaviour as its secret. The behaviour is specified in terms of the abstractions provided by the environment module. The module is composed of a function driver module and a shared services module that supports the function driver module.

A.2.1 chapter function_drivers

The function driver module consists of a set of individual modules called function drivers; each function driver is the sole controller of a set of closely related outputs. Outputs are closely related if it is easier to describe their values together than individually. Note that the behaviour is specified in terms of the abstractions provided by the environment module, not in terms of concrete devices.

At the moment, there is only one function driver, which is concerned with message delivery. If other kinds of output are added, there might be more function drivers.

A.2.1.1 chapter message_delivery

The message delivery module hides the relationship from message submission to message delivery. The behaviour is composed from a selection of properties. The selection of properties includes a timely message delivery, a correct message delivery, and a broadcast message delivery.

A.2.1.1.1 private default section message_delivery_reord
> parents standard_toolkit

The submission events may be reordered in transit before they are delivered (however, below are some restrictions on the reordering). We model this by a bijective reordering function that maps the numbering of the submission event history to the numbering of the delivery event history:

$$\mid \quad reord\_delivery : \mathbb{N}_1 \rightarrowtail\!\!\!\rightarrow \mathbb{N}_1$$

A.2.1.1.2 private default section timely_message_delivery
> parents comm_params_base, message_delivery_reord

After a fixed time bound, any submitted message will have been delivered.
There is a fixed upper time bound for the message delivery delay:

$$\mid \quad max\_msg\_delivery\_delay : rtime$$

After the maximum message delivery delay, any submitted message will have been delivered. For this, we consider only those submission events which are at least sufficiently old. We then consider that part of the reordering function that reorders only these events and discards all later events. In this setting, the corresponding reordered numbers in the delivery event history all must actually be there, and also the associated messages must be unaltered:

---
inv_timely_msg_delivery

hist_comm
clock

$\forall\, h\_s : \text{iseq}\, EV\_SUBMIT \mid h\_s \text{ prefix } hist\_submit \land h\_s \neq \langle\rangle \land$
$\quad ev\_sub2time(last(h\_s)) + max\_msg\_delivery\_delay < vmon\_curr\_time \bullet$
$\quad \exists\, reord : \mathbb{N}_1 \nrightarrow \mathbb{N}_1 \mid reord = (\text{dom}\, h\_s) \lhd reord\_delivery \bullet$
$\quad\quad \text{ran}(reord) \subseteq \text{dom}\, hist\_deliver \land$
$\quad\quad h\_s \,\mathring{,}\, ev\_sub2msg = reord \,\mathring{,}\, hist\_deliver \,\mathring{,}\, ev\_deliv2msg$

A.2.1.1.3 private default section correct_message_delivery

parents comm_params_base, message_delivery_reord

The system won't deliver a message unless the message has been submitted before. For this, we consider the backward direction of the reordering function, and only that part of it that has the numbers of the delivery events that already occurred. The rest is similar as before. The corresponding numbers in the submission event history all must actually be there, and also the associated messages must be unaltered:

---
inv_hist_correct_msg

hist_comm

$\exists\, ireord : \mathbb{N}_1 \nrightarrow \mathbb{N}_1 \mid ireord = (\text{dom}\, hist\_deliver) \lhd (reord\_delivery^{\sim}) \bullet$
$\quad \text{ran}\, ireord \subseteq \text{dom}\, hist\_submit \land$
$\quad hist\_deliver \,\mathring{,}\, ev\_deliv2msg = ireord \,\mathring{,}\, hist\_submit \,\mathring{,}\, ev\_sub2msg$

A.2.1.1.4 private default section broadcast_message_delivery

parents comm_params_base

Any delivery of a message will be to all communicating entities that exist ("broadcast").

---
inv_hist_broadcast_msg

hist_comm

$\forall\, e\_d : \text{ran}\, hist\_deliver \bullet ev\_deliv2receivers(e\_d) = COMM\_ENTITY$

---

endchapter message_delivery

endchapter function_drivers

A.2.2 chapter shared_services

The shared services module specifies those aspects that are common to several function drivers. The module is empty for now. This might change when more function drivers are specified.

endchapter shared_services

endchapter system_behaviour

Appendix B

Configuration Rule Base for the Family of LAN Message Services

We continue to demonstrate our approach with the configuration rule base for the requirements module base in the preceding appendix. The configuration rule base contains the definitions of features for the family. The definitions are written in the language Z_F, see Sect. 7.4.2. A feature is a list of sections added and a list of sections removed. The list of added sections is differentiated into essential and into changeable sections. The add list and the remove list can also refer to entire chapters instead of individual sections. Adding a chapter is equivalent to adding all its default sections. The formal definitions are typeset in a suitable font by the LaTeX style file which we developed, see Chap. 7.7.

The following specifications of features are not complete. In the requirements module base, we only specified enough modules and properties to demonstrate our structuring approach. Accordingly, we here reference only those properties that we specified.

feature note_to_all:
The users can write a note to everybody. A note is a text message. A note by default is short. That means only one line.

+ broadcast_message_delivery
+ text_message_base
(+) one_line_message

feature multi_line_text_message:
Text messages can have multiple lines.

+ multi_line_message
− one_line_message

feature scroll_text_message:
Text messages can be scrolled vertically to allow for longer messages. This requires a graphical user interface and excludes a textual user interface.

+ multi_line_message

- one_line_message
+ graphical_user_interface
- textual_user_interface

Note that we mention the graphical user interface in the list, despite that it is a default, to make it essential for this feature.

feature birthday_cake_picture:

One can send everybody a picture of the birthday cake that one is about to cut. This requires a graphical user interface for displaying.

+ broadcast_message_delivery
+ graphical_message_base
- text_message_only
+ graphical_user_interface

feature lunch_alarm:

An (external) automated alarm clock informs everybody when it is time for the lunch break. By default, the alarm is a short text message.

+ automated_agent_interface
+ broadcast_message_delivery
(+) text_message_base

feature deskPhoneXY_hardware:

The system uses the hardware of the office desk phones of brand XY instead of computer terminals. These phones only have a small text display with two lines. The associcated software platform is restricted to the language Pascal.

- graphical_user_interface
+ textual_user_interface
+ max_lines2_message
+ pascal_text_string
- c_text_string

feature standardPC_hardware:

The system uses the hardware of standard PCs. These machines have a graphical user interface, and they can display windows with text messages, too. But the associated software platform does not offer the language Pascal anymore. Instead, we can use the language C.

(+) textual_user_interface
- pascal_text_string

Note that a graphical user interface and C-style text strings are the default in our family of requirements anyway; we do not need to mention them to allow their use.

Appendix C

Some Family Members of the Family of LAN Message Services

We complete the demonstration of our approach with the specifcations of some family members of the family in the preceding two appendices. A family member is specified by a list of selected features. The features are defined in the configuration rule base in the preceding appendix. The specifications are written in the language Z_F, see Sect. 7.4.2. Each of the sections of this appendix specifies one complete family member.

The "Lunch Phone" System

The Lunch Phone system informs everybody that it is time for the lunch break, using only the hardware of the office desk phones (of brand XY) instead of computer terminals. The system's features are:

> lunch_alarm
> deskPhoneXY_hardware

The "Classic PC" Edition

The Classic PC edition is a "plain" version without any particular specialties; it would be sold for a comparably low price. The users can write a note of several lines to everybody, and the system uses the hardware of standard PCs. The system's features are:

> note_to_all
> multi_line_text_message
> standardPC_hardware

The "Deluxe PC" Edition

The Deluxe PC edition is a "premium" version to be sold at a higher price than the Classic PC edition. This version has many more, attractive-sounding features than the Classic PC edition: lunch alarm, birthday cake picture, and scroll text message. The system's features are:

lunch_alarm
birthday_cake_picture
note_to_all
multi_line_text_message
scroll_text_message
standardPC_hardware

List of Figures

List of Tables

Bibliography

[3GP]   *3rd Generation Partnership Project.* www.3gpp.org.

[Ab⁺97]   Abarca, C. et al.. *Service architecture.* Deliverable, TINA-Consortium, www.tinac.com (16 June 1997). Version 5.0.

[ABB⁺99]   Atlee, J., Bartussek, W., Bredereke, J., Glinz, M., Khedri, R., Prechelt, L., and Weiss, D. *Requirements.* In Denert, E., Hoffman, D., Ludewig, J., and Parnas, D., editors, "Software Engineering Research and Education: Seeking a new Agenda", no. 230 in Dagstuhl-Seminar-Report, ISSN 0940-1121, pp. 9–16 (Feb. 1999). www.dagstuhl.de.

[AFHB⁺92]   Alspaugh, T. A., Faulk, S. R., Heninger Britton, K., Parker, R. A., Parnas, D. L., and Shore, J. E. *Software requirements for the A-7E aircraft.* Report NRL/FR/5530–92-9194, Naval Research Lab., Washington DC 20375·5000, USA (31 Aug. 1992). Revision of NRL Memorandum Report 3876.

[AHMS02]   Autexier, S., Hutter, D., Mossakowski, T., and Schairer, A. *The development graph manager MAYA.* In Kirchner, H. and Ringeissen, C., editors, "Proc. 9th Int'l. Conf. on Algebraic Methodology And Software Technology (AMAST 2002)", vol. 2422 of "LNCS", pp. 495–501. Springer (2002).

[AKGM00]   Amer, M., Karmouch, A., Gray, T., and Mankovskii, S. *Feature-interaction resolution using fuzzy policies.* In Calder and Magill [CaMa00], pp. 94–112.

[Ame02]   Amey, P. *Correctness by construction: Better can also be cheaper.* Crosstalk – The Journal of Defense Software Engineering pp. 24–28 (Mar. 2002).

[AmLo03]   Amyot, D. and Logrippo, L., editors. *Feature Interactions in Telecommunications and Software Systems VII.* IOS Press, Amsterdam (June 2003).

[And01]   Andexer, J. *Design guidelines and documentation paradigms for object oriented programs.* Masters thesis, McMaster Univ., Hamilton, Canada (Sept. 2001). SERG Report 397.

[Art95]   Arthan, R. D. *Modularity for Z*. ZSRC Document 182 (5 Sept. 1995).
            www.lemma-one.com/zstan_docs/wrk059.ps.

[AuAt97]   Au, P. K. and Atlee, J. M. *Evaluation of a state-based model of feature
            interactions*. In Dini et al. [DBL97], pp. 153–167.

[BaLe01]   Bachelder, E. and Leveson, N. *Describing and probing complex sys-
            tem behavior: A graphical approach*. In "Proceedings of the Aviation
            Safety Conference", Seattle, USA (Sept. 2001). Society of Automotive
            Engineers, Inc. Paper number 01D-22.

[BBK95]   Blom, J., Bol, R., and Kempe, L. *Automatic detection of feature in-
            teractions in temporal logic*. In Cheng and Ohta [ChOh95], pp. 1–19.

[BCP+04]   Bond, G. W., Cheung, E., Purdy, K. H., Zave, P., and Ramming, J. C.
            An open architecture for next-generation telecommunication services.
            ACM Transactions on Internet Technology **4**(1), 83–123 (Feb. 2004).

[Bil97]   Billings, C. E. *Aviation automation: the search for a human-centered
            approach*. Human factors in transportation. Lawrence Erlbaum Asso-
            ciates Publishers, Mahwah, N.J. (1997).

[BJBJ04]   Broch Johnsen, E. and Lüth, C. *Theorem reuse by proof term trans-
            formation*. In Slind, K., Bunker, A., and Gopalakrishnan, G., editors,
            "Int'l. Conf. on Theorem Proving in Higher-Order Logics TPHOLs
            2004", vol. 3223 of "LNCS", pp. 152–167. Springer (Sept. 2004).

[BMPC98]   Butler, R. W., Miller, S. P., Potts, J. N., and Carreño, V. A. *A
            formal methods approach to the analysis of mode confusion*. In "Proc.
            of the 17th Digital Avionics Systems Conf.", Bellevue, Washington,
            USA (1998).

[BoVe94]   Bouma, L. G. and Velthuijsen, H., editors. *Feature Interactions in
            Telecommunications Systems*. IOS Press, Amsterdam (1994).

[Bow05]   Bowen, J. *Z Home Page* (2005). http://vl.zuser.org.

[Bre98]   Bredereke, J. *Requirements specification and design of a simplified
            telephone network by Functional Documentation*. CRL Report 367,
            McMaster University, Hamilton, Ontario, Canada (Dec. 1998). ISSN
            0381-9337.

[Bre99]   Bredereke, J. *Modular, changeable requirements for telephone switch-
            ing in CSP-OZ*. Tech. Rep. IBS-99-1, University of Oldenburg, Old-
            enburg, Germany (Oct. 1999).

[Bre00a]   Bredereke, J. *Families of formal requirements in telephone switching*.
            In Calder and Magill [CaMa00], pp. 257–273.

[Bre00b]   Bredereke, J. *genFamMem 2.0 Home Page*. University of Bremen
            (2000). www.tzi.de/~brederek/genFamMem.

[Bre00c]   Bredereke, J. *genFamMem 2.0 Manual – a Specification Generator
            and Type Checker for Families of Formal Requirements*. University of
            Bremen (Oct. 2000). www.tzi.de/~brederek/genFamMem.

[Bre01]   Bredereke, J. *A tool for generating specifications from a family of
            formal requirements*. In Kim, M., Chin, B., Kang, S., and Lee, D.,
            editors, "Formal Techniques for Networked and Distributed Systems",
            pp. 319–334. Kluwer Academic Publishers (Aug. 2001).

[Bre05a]   Bredereke, J. *Homepage for Typesetting Z Specifications with Fam-
            ily Constructs*. University of Bremen (2005). www.tzi.de/~brederek/
            latex-z-fam.

[Bre05b]   Bredereke, J. *Homepage for Vim Editor Syntax Highlighting for CSP
            and for Z*. University of Bremen (2005). www.tzi.de/~brederek/vim.

[BrLa02]   Bredereke, J. and Lankenau, A. *A rigorous view of mode confusion*. In
            Anderson, S., Bologna, S., and Felici, M., editors, "Computer Safety,
            Reliability and Security – 21st Int'l Conf., SafeComp 2002, Proc.", vol.
            2434 of "LNCS", pp. 19–31, Catania, Italy (Sept. 2002). Springer.

[BrLa05]   Bredereke, J. and Lankenau, A. *Safety-relevant mode confusions –
            modelling and reducing them*. Reliability Engineering & System Safety
            88(3), 229–245 (June 2005).

[BrSc01]   Bredereke, J. and Schlingloff, B.-H. *Specification based testing of the
            UMTS protocol stack*. In "Proc. of the 14th Int'l. Software & Internet
            Quality Week – QW2001", San Francisco, USA (29 May – 1 June
            2001). On CD ROM.

[BrSc02]   Bredereke, J. and Schlingloff, B.-H. *An automated, flexible testing
            environment for UMTS*. In Schieferdecker, I., König, H., and Wolisz,
            A., editors, "Testing of Communicating Systems XIV – Application
            to Internet Technologies and Services", pp. 79–94. Kluwer Academic
            Publishers (Mar. 2002).

[Bry86]   Bryant, R. E. *Graph-based algorithms for boolean function manipula-
            tion*. IEEE Trans. Comput. **35**(8), 677–691 (1986).

[But01]   Buth, B. *Formal and Semi-Formal Methods for the Analysis of In-
            dustrial Control Systems*. Habilitation thesis, University of Bremen,
            Germany (2001).

[CaHa01]   Campos, J. C. and Harrison, M. D. *Model checking interactor specifi-
            cations*. Automated Software Engineering **8**, 275–310 (2001).

[CaMa00]   Calder, M. and Magill, E., editors. *Feature Interactions in Telecommunications and Software Systems VI*. IOS Press, Amsterdam (May 2000).

[CaOl88]   Carroll, J. M. and Olson, J. R. *Mental models in human-computer interaction*. In Helander, M., editor, "Handbook of Human-Computer Interaction", pp. 45–65. Elsevier (1988).

[CGL+94]   Cameron, E. J., Griffeth, N. D., Lin, Y.-J., et al.. *A feature interaction benchmark in IN and beyond*. In Bouma and Velthuijsen [BoVe94], pp. 1–23.

[CGS91]   Cunis, R., Günter, A., and Strecker, H., editors. *Das PLAKON-Buch – Ein Expertensystemkern für Planungs- und Konfigurierungsaufgaben in technischen Domänen*. Springer (1991).

[CHJB95]   Cattrall, D., Howard, G., Jordan, D., and Buf, S. *An interaction-avoiding call processing model*. In Cheng and Ohta [ChOh95], pp. 85–96.

[ChOh95]   Cheng, K. E. and Ohta, T., editors. *Feature Interactions in Telecommunications III*. IOS Press, Amsterdam (1995).

[CJR00]   Crow, J., Javaux, D., and Rushby, J. *Models and mechanized methods that integrate human factors into automation design*. In Abbott, K., Speyer, J.-J., and Boy, G., editors, "Proc. of the Int'l Conf. on Human-Computer Interaction in Aeronautics: HCI-Aero 2000", Toulouse, France (Sept. 2000).

[CKMRM02] Calder, M., Kolberg, M., Magill, E. H., and Reiff-Marganiec, S. *Feature interaction: a critical review and considered forecast*. Comp. Networks **41**, 115–141 (2002).

[CnAQ01]   Cañas, J. J., Antolí, A., and Quesada, J. F. *The role of working memory on measuring mental models of physical systems*. Psicológica **22**, 25–42 (2001).

[CoWe98]   Conradi, R. and Westfechtel, B. *Version models for software configuration management*. ACM Comput. Surv. **30**(2), 232–282 (June 1998).

[CrSu96]   Croxford, M. and Sutton, J. *Breaking through the V and V bottleneck*. In "Ada in Europe 1995", vol. 1031 of "LNCS". Springer (1996).

[CzEi00]   Czarnecki, K. and Eisenecker, U. W. *Generative Programming*. Addison-Wesley (2000).

[DBL97]   Dini, P., Boutaba, R., and Logrippo, L., editors. *Feature Interactions in Telecommunication Networks IV*. IOS Press, Amsterdam (June 1997).

[DDH83]   Darlington, J., Dzida, W., and Herda, S. *The role of exursions in interactive systems.* Int'l. Jour. of Man-Machine Studies **18**(2), 101–112 (Feb. 1983).

[DeHe02]   Degani, A. and Heymann, M. *Formal verification of human-automation interaction.* Human Factors **44**(1), 28–43 (2002).

[DeM79]   DeMarco, T. *Structured Analysis and System Specification.* Computing Series. Yourdon Press, Englewood Cliff, NJ (1979).

[DGL86]   Dittrich, K., Gotthard, W., and Lockemann, P. *DAMOKLES, a database system for software engineering environments.* In Conradi, R., Didriksen, T. M., and Wanvik, D. H., editors, "Proc. of the Int'l Workshop on Advanced Programming Environments", vol. 244 of "LNCS", pp. 353–371, Trondheim, Norway (June 1986). Springer.

[dKTG00]   de Keijzer, J., Tait, D., and Goedman, R. *JAIN: A new approach to services in communication networks.* IEEE Commun. Mag. **38**(1), 94–99 (Jan. 2000).

[Doh98]   Doherty, G. *A Pragmatic Approach to the Formal Specification of Interactive Systems.* PhD thesis, University of of York, Dept. of Computer Science (Oct. 1998).

[DSK99]   Degani, A., Shafto, M., and Kirlik, A. *Modes in human-machine systems: Constructs, representation and classification.* Int'l Journal of Aviation Psychology **9**(2), 125–138 (1999).

[DuVi92]   Duran, J. M. and Visser, J. *International standards for Intelligent Networks.* IEEE Commun. Mag. **30**(2), 34–42 (Feb. 1992).

[EFH+89]   Ehrig, H., Frey, W., Hansen, H., Lowe, M., and Jacobs, D. *Algebraic software development concepts for module and configuration families.* In Madhavan, V., editor, "Proc. of the 9th Conf. on Foundation of Software Technology and Theoretical Computer Science", vol. 405 of "LNCS", pp. 181–192, Bangalore (Dec. 1989). Springer.

[EHS97]   Ellsberger, J., Hogrefe, D., and Sarma, A. *SDL – Formal Object-oriented Language for Communicating Systems.* Prentice-Hall (1997).

[Est85]   Estublier, J. *A configuration manager: The Adele data base of programs.* In "Proc. of the Workshop on Software Engineering Environments for Programming-in-the-Large", pp. 140–147, Harwichport, MA, USA (June 1985).

[Fau01]   Faulk, S. R. *Product-line requirements specification (PRS): An approach and case study.* In IEEE [IEE01], pp. 48–55.

[FBWK92]   Faulk, S., Brackett, J., Ward, P., and Kirby, Jr., J. *The Core method for real-time requirements.* IEEE Software **9**(6), 22–33 (Sept. 1992).

[Fis97]   Fischer, C. *CSP-OZ: a combination of Object-Z and CSP*. In Bowman, H. and Derrick, J., editors, "Formal Methods for Open Object-Based Distributed Systems (FMOODS'97)", vol. 2, pp. 423–438. Chapman & Hall (July 1997).

[Fis00]   Fischer, C. *Combination and implementation of processes and data: from CSP-OZ to Java*. PhD thesis, report of the Comp. Sce. dept. 2/2000, University of Oldenburg, Oldenburg, Germany (Apr. 2000).

[FJKFM93]   Faulk, S. R., James Kirby, J., Finneran, L., and Moini, A. *Consortium requirements engineering guidebook*. Tech. Rep. SPC-92060-CMC, version 01.00.09, Software Productivity Consortium Services Corp., Herndon, Virginia, USA (Dec. 1993).

[FLdM95]   Farooqui, K., Logrippo, L., and de Meer, J. *The ISO reference model for Open Distributed Processing: an introduction*. Comp. Networks and ISDN Syst. **27**(8), 1215–1229 (July 1995).

[FoWa74]   Foley, J. D. and Wallace, V. L. *The art of natural graphic man-machine conversation*. Proc. of the IEEE **62**(4), 462–471 (Apr. 1974).

[FvDFH90]   Foley, J. D., van Dam, A., Feiner, S. K., and Hughes, J. F. *Computer Graphics: Principles and Practice*. Addison-Wesley, 2nd ed. (1990).

[GBGO98]   Griffeth, N., Blumenthal, R., Gregoire, J.-C., and Ohta, T. *Feature interaction detection contest*. In Kimbler and Bouma [KiBo98], pp. 327–359. www.tts.lth.se/FIW98/contest.html.

[GFd98]   Griss, M., Favaro, J., and d'Allesandro, M. *Integrating Feature Modeling with RSEB*. Hewlett-Packard Comp. (1998).

[GHH+02]   Günter, A., Herzog, O., Hollmann, O., Ranze, C., Schlieder, C., Scholz, T., and Wagner, T. *A structure based configuration tool: Drive Solution Designer – DSD*. In "AAAI'02 / IAAI'02", pp. 845–852. AAAI (2002).

[GHJV95]   Gamma, E., Helm, R., Johnson, R., and Vlissides, J. *Design Patterns – Elements of Reusable Object-Oriented Software*. Addison-Wesley (1995).

[Gib97]   Gibson, J. P. *Feature requirements models: Understanding interactions*. In Dini et al. [DBL97], pp. 46–60.

[GiRy00]   Gilmore, S. and Ryan, M., editors. *Proc. of Workshop on Language Constructs for Describing Features*, Glasgow, Scotland (15–16 May 2000). ESPRIT Working Group 23531 – Feature Integration in Requirements Engineering.

[GiRy01]   Gilmore, S. and Ryan, M. D., editors. *Language Constructs for Describing Features*. Springer (2001).

[GRKK93]   Garrahan, J. J., Russo, P. A., Kitami, K., and Kung, R. *Intelligent Network overview*. IEEE Commun. Mag. **31**(3), 30–36 (Mar. 1993).

[GrVe94]   Griffeth, N. D. and Velthuijsen, H. *The negotiating agents approach to runtime feature interaction resolution*. In Bouma and Velthuijsen [BoVe94], pp. 217–235.

[Gün95]   Günter, A., editor. *Wissensbasiertes Konfigurieren – Ergebnisse aus dem Projekt PROKON*. Infix, Sankt Augustin, Germany (1995).

[HABJ05]   Heitmeyer, C., Archer, M., Bharadwaj, R., and Jeffords, R. *Tools for constructing requirements specifications: The SCR toolset at the age of ten*. Int'l. Jour. of Comp. Systems Sce. & Engineering **5**(1), 95–114 (Jan. 2005).

[Hal98]   Hall, R. J. *Feature combination and interaction detection via foreground/background models*. In Kimbler and Bouma [KiBo98], pp. 232–246.

[Hal00]   Hall, R. J. *Feature combination and interaction detection via foreground/background models*. Comp. Networks **32**(4), 449–469 (Apr. 2000).

[HaPe02]   Haxthausen, A. E. and Peleska, J. *A domain specific language for railway control systems*. In IDPT'02 [IDP02].

[HaPe03a] Haxthausen, A. E. and Peleska, J. *Automatic verification, validation and test for railway control systems based on domain-specific descriptions*. In Tsugawa, S. and Aoki, M., editors, "Proc. of 10th IFAC Symp. on Control in Transportation Systems", Tokyo, Japan (Aug. 2003). Elsevier.

[HaPe03b] Haxthausen, A. E. and Peleska, J. *Generation of executable railway control components from domain-specific descriptions*. In Tarnai, G. and Schnieder, E., editors, "Proc. of Formal Methods for Railway Operation and Control Systems – FORMS'2003", pp. 83–90, Budapest, Hungary (May 2003).

[HBGL95]   Heitmeyer, C., Bull, A., Gasarch, C., and Labaw, B. *SCR*: A toolset for specifying and analyzing requirements*. In "Proc. Ninth Annual Conf. on Computer Assurance – COMPASS'95", pp. 109–122, Gaithersburg, MD, USA (June 1995).

[HBPP81]   Heninger Britton, K., Parker, R. A., and Parnas, D. L. *A procedure for designing abstract interfaces for device interface modules*. In "Proc. of the 5th Int'l. Conf. on Software Engineering – ICSE 5", pp. 195–204 (Mar. 1981). Reprinted in [HoWe01].

[HeBh00]   Heitmeyer, C. and Bharadwaj, R. *Applying the SCR requirements method to the light control case study.* Jour. of Universal Comp. Sce. **6**(7), 650–678 (2000).

[HeDe02a]   Heymann, M. and Degani, A. *Constructing human-automation interfaces: A formal approach.* In "Proc. of the Int'l Conf. on Human-Computer Interaction in Aeronautics: HCI-Aero 2002", pp. 119–125, Cambridge, MA, USA (Oct. 2002).

[HeDe02b]   Heymann, M. and Degani, A. *On the construction of human-automation interfaces by formal abstraction.* In Koenig, S. and Holte, R., editors, "SARA 2002", no. 2371 in LNAI, pp. 99–115. Springer (2002).

[HeLe96]   Heimdahl, M. P. E. and Leveson, N. *Completeness and consistency analysis of state-based requirements.* ACM Trans. Softw. Eng. (June 1996).

[HKPS78]   Heninger, K. L., Kallander, J. W., Parnas, D. L., and Shore, J. E. *Software requirements for the A-7E aircraft.* NRL Report 3876, Naval Research Lab., Washington DC, USA (Nov. 1978).

[HKW04]   Hotz, L., Krebs, T., and Wolter, K. *Knowledge-based product derivation – research topics of the ConIPF project.* Künstliche Intelligenz **04**(4), 58–61 (Nov. 4004).

[Hoa85]   Hoare, C. A. R. *Communicating Sequential Processes.* Prentice-Hall (1985).

[HoJo01a]   Hourizi, R. and Johnson, P. *Beyond mode error: Supporting strategic knowledge structures to enhance cockpit safety.* In "HCI 2001, People and Computers XIV", Lille, France (10–14 Sept. 2001). Springer.

[HoJo01b]   Hourizi, R. and Johnson, P. *Unmasking mode error: A new application of task knowledge principles to the knowledge gaps in cockpit design.* In "Interact'01, The 18th IFIP Conf. on Human Computer Interaction", Tokyo, Japan (9–14 July 2001). Springer.

[HoKr03]   Hotz, L. and Krebs, T. *Configuration – state of the art and new challenges.* In Hotz, L. and Krebs, T., editors, "Proc. Workshop Planen und Konfigurieren (PuK-2003)", pp. 145–157, Hamburg, Germany (15–18 Sept. 2003). German Conference on Artificial Intelligence (KI-2003). www.is.informatik.uni-oldenburg.de/~sauer/puk2003/paper/Proceedings.pdf.

[Hol97]   Holzmann, G. J. *The model checker Spin.* IEEE Trans. Softw. Eng. **23**(5), 279–295 (May 1997).

[HoWe01]   Hoffman, D. M. and Weiss, D. M., editors. *Software Fundamentals –
             Collected Papers by David L. Parnas*. Addison-Wesley (Mar. 2001).

[HsGu92]   Hsia, P. and Gupta, A. *Incremental delivery using abstract data types
             and requirements clustering*. In "Proc. of the 2nd Int'l Conf. on Sys-
             tems Integration", pp. 137–150. IEEE Computer Society (June 1992).

[IDP02]   *Proc. of the 6th Biennial World Conf. on Integrated Design and Process
             Technology – IDPT 2002*, Pasadena, Calif., USA (23–28 June 2002).

[IEE00]   IEEE. *Proc. of the 19th Digital Avionics Systems Conf.*, Philadelphia,
             PA, USA (7–13 Oct. 2000).

[IEE01]   *5th IEEE Int'l Symposium on Requirements Engineering (RE'01)*,
             Toronto, Canada (27–31 Aug. 2001). IEEE Computer Society Press.

[ISO93]   *ISO/IEC 10646-1:1993 Information Technology – Universal Multiple-
             Octet Coded Character Set (UCS) – Part 1: Architecture and Basic
             Multilingual Plane* (1993).

[ITU92]   ITU-T, Recommendation Q.1203. *Intelligent Network – Global Func-
             tional Plane Architecture* (Oct. 1992).

[ITU93a]   ITU-T, Recommendation Q.931. *Digital Subscriber Signalling System
             No. 1 (DSS 1) — ISDN User-Network Interface Layer 3 Specification
             for Basic Call Control* (Mar. 1993).

[ITU93b]   ITU-T, Recommendation Q.1213. *Global Functional Plane for Intelli-
             gent Network CS-1* (Mar. 1993).

[ITU97a]   ITU-T, Recommendation Q.1224. *Distributed Functional Plane for
             Intelligent Network Capability Set 2: Parts 1 to 4* (Sept. 1997).

[ITU97b]   ITU-T, Recommendation Q.1223. *Global Functional Plane for Intelli-
             gent Network Capability Set 2* (Sept. 1997).

[ITU97c]   ITU-T. *Q.122x-Series Intelligent Network Recommendations for Ca-
             pability Set 2* (1997).

[ITU99]   ITU-T, Recommendation Z.100 (11/99). *CCITT Specification and De-
             scription Language (SDL)* (Nov. 1999).

[ITU01]   ITU-T. *Q.12xx-Series Intelligent Network Recommendations* (2001).

[Jac83]   Jacob, R. J. K. *Executable specifications for a human-computer in-
             terface*. In Janda, A., editor, "Proc. ACM CHI'83 Human Factors in
             Computing Systems Conf.", pp. 28–34, Evanston, USA (12–15 Dec.
             1983). ACM, North-Holland.

[JAMS00]   Jain, R., Anjum, F. M., Missier, P., and Shastry, S. *Java call control, coordination, and transactions.* IEEE Commun. Mag. **38**(1), 108–114 (Jan. 2000).

[Jav98]   Javaux, D. *Explaining Sarter & Woods' classical results. The cognitive complexity of pilot-autopilot interaction on the Boeing 737-EFIS.* In "Proc. of HESSD '98", pp. 62–77 (1998).

[Jav02]   Javaux, D. *A method for predicting errors when interacting with finite state systems. How implicit learning shapes the user's knowledge of a system.* Reliability Engineering & System Safety **75**(2), 147–165 (Feb. 2002).

[JaZa98]   Jackson, M. and Zave, P. *Distributed feature composition: A virtual architecture for telecommunications services.* IEEE Trans. Softw. Eng. **24**(10), 831–847 (Oct. 1998).

[JMH03]   Joshi, A., Miller, S., and Heimdahl, M. *Mode confusion analysis of a flight guidance system using formal methods.* In "22nd IEEE Digital Avionics Systems Conf. (DASC'2003)", Indianapolis, USA (Oct. 2003).

[Joh96]   Johnston, W. *A type checker for Object-Z.* Tech. Rep. 96-24, Univ. of Queensland, Dept. of Comp. Sce., Software Verification Research Centre, Australia (Sept. 1996).

[KaHa83]   Kaiser, G. E. and Habermann, A. N. *An environment for system version control.* In "Digest of Papers of Spring CompCon '83", pp. 415–420, Los Alamitos, CA, USA (1983). IEEE Computer Society Press.

[Kat93]   Katz, S. *A superimposition control construct for distributed systems.* ACM Trans. Prog. Lang. Syst. **15**(2), 337–356 (Apr. 1993).

[KCH⁺90]   Kang, K., Cohen, S., Hess, J., Novak, W., and Peterson, A. *Feature-oriented domain analysis (FODA) feasibility study.* Tech. Report CMU/SEI-90-TR-021, Software Engineering Institute, Carnegie-Mellon University, Pittsburgh, USA (1990).

[Kec98]   Keck, D. O. *Requirements and a proposal for the prevention of a class of service interactions in Intelligent Networks.* In Margaria et al. [MSRP98], pp. 90–105.

[KeRi78]   Kernighan, B. W. and Ritchie, D. M. *The C Programming Language.* Prentice-Hall (1978).

[KiBo98]   Kimbler, K. and Bouma, L. G., editors. *Feature Interactions in Telecommunications and Software Systems V.* IOS Press, Amsterdam (Sept. 1998).

[Kin90]   King, P. *Printing Z and Object-Z LaTeX documents.* Univ. of Queensland, Dept. of Comp. Sce., Australia (29 May 1990).

[KLD02]   Kang, K. C., Lee, J., and Donohoe, P. *Feature-oriented product line engineering*. IEEE Software pp. 58–65 (July/Aug. 2002).

[KMMR00]   Kolberg, M., Magill, E. H., Marples, D., and Reiff, S. *Second feature interaction contest*. In Calder and Magill [CaMa00], pp. 293–310.

[KoMa98]   Kolberg, M. and Magill, E. H. *Service and feature interactions in TINA*. In Kimbler and Bouma [KiBo98], pp. 78–84.

[KSZ+04]   Kemnade, A., Stahlbock, A., Zhou, D., et al.. *TRACS Semesterbericht SS2004*. Interim report of the students' project (in German), University of Bremen, Germany (Oct. 2004). www.informatik.uni-bremen.de/tracs/.

[Lam86]   Lamport, L. *LaTeX– A Document Preparation System*. Addison-Wesley (1986).

[Lan01]   Lankenau, A. *Avoiding mode confusion in service-robots*. In Mokhtari, M., editor, "Integration of Assistive Technology in the Information Age, Proc. of the 7th Int'l Conf. on Rehabilitation Robotics", pp. 162–167, Evry, France (Apr. 2001). IOS Press.

[Lan02]   Lankenau, A. *The Bremen Autonomous Wheelchair 'Rolland': Self-Localization and Shared Control*. PhD thesis, University of Bremen, Germany (Aug. 2002).

[LaRö01]   Lankenau, A. and Röfer, T. *The Bremen Autonomous Wheelchair – a versatile and safe mobility assistant*. IEEE Robotics and Automation Magazine, "Reinventing the Wheelchair" **7**(1), 29–37 (Mar. 2001).

[Lis88]   Liskov, B. *Data abstraction and hierarchy*. SIGPLAN Notices **23**(5) (May 1988).

[LMB92]   Levine, Mason, and Brown. *Lex & Yacc*. O'Reilly & Associates Inc (1992).

[LPS+97]   Leveson, N. G., Pinnel, L. D., Sandys, S. D., Koga, S., and Reese, J. D. *Analyzing software specifications for mode confusion potential*. In "Workshop on Human Error and System Development", Glasgow, UK (1997).

[LüCa99]   Lüttgen, G. and Carreño, V. *Analyzing mode confusion via model checking*. In Dams, D., Gerth, R., Leue, S., and Massink, M., editors, "SPIN' 99", vol. 1680 of "LNCS", pp. 120–135. Springer (1999).

[MaCo00]   Mampaey, M. and Couturier, A. *Using TINA concepts for IN evolution*. IEEE Commun. Mag. **38**(6), 94–99 (June 2000).

[Mar03]   Martin, R. C. *Agile Software Development - Principles, Patterns, and Practices*. Prentice-Hall (2003).

[Mey88]   Meyer, B. *Object-oriented software construction*. Prentice-Hall (1988).

[Mey01]   Meyer, O. *Structural Decomposition of Timed-CSP and its Application in Real-Time Testing*. PhD thesis, University of Bremen, Germany (Dec. 2001).

[MGB⁺04]   Mittelbach, F., Goossens, M., Braams, J., Carlisle, D., and Rowley, C. *The LATEX Companion*. Addison-Wesley, 2nd ed. (Apr. 2004).

[MiHo97]   Miller, S. P. and Hoech, K. F. *Specifying the mode logic of a flight guidance system in CoRE*. Technical Report WP97-2011, Rockwell Collins, Inc., Avionics & Communications, Cedar Rapids, IA 52498 USA (Nov. 1997).

[Mil98]   Miller, S. P. *Specifying the mode logic of a flight guidance system in CoRE and SCR*. In "Second Workshop on Formal Methods in Software Practice", Clearwater Beach, Florida, USA (4–5 Mar. 1998).

[MoSk90]   Modarressi, A. R. and Skoog, R. A. *Signalling System No. 7: A tutorial*. IEEE Commun. Mag. **28**(7), 19–35 (July 1990).

[MSRP98]   Margaria, T., Steffen, B., Rückert, R., and Posegga, J., editors. *Services And Visualization: Towards User-Friendly Design – Selected Papers ACoS'98, VISUAL'98, AIN'97*, vol. 1385 of "LNCS". Springer (1998).

[Nor83]   Norman, D. A. *Some observations on mental models*. In Gentner, D. and Stevens, A. L., editors, "Mental Models", pp. 7–14. Lawrence Erlbaum Associates Inc., Hillsdale, NJ, USA (1983).

[Nor88]   Norman, D. A. *The Psychology of Everyday Things*. Basic Books, New York (1988).

[NPW02]   Nipkow, T., Paulson, L. C., and Wenzel, M. *Isabelle/HOL – A Proof Assistant for Higher-Order Logic*, vol. 2283 of "LNCS". Springer (2002).

[OMG03]   Object Management Group. *OMG Unified Modeling Language Specification – Version 1.5* (Mar. 2003). www.omg.org/cgi-bin/doc?formal/03-03-01.

[Oua01]   Oualline, S. *Vi IMproved, Vim*. New Riders (Apr. 2001).

[Pai94]   Paige, R. *Viewing a program transformation system at work*. In "Proc. Joint 6th Int. Conf. on Programming Language Implementation and Logic Programming (PLICLP) and 4th Int. Conf. on Agebraic and Logic Programming (ALP)", vol. 844 of "LNCS". Springer (Sept. 1994).

[Pal95]   Palmer, E. *"Oops, it didn't arm."* – *A case study of two automation surprises*. In "Proc. of the 8th Int'l Symp. on Aviation Psychology" (1995).

[PaLi92]   Palmer, J. D. and Liang, Y. *Indexing and clustering of software requirements specifications*. Information and Decision Technologies **18**(4), 283–299 (1992).

[PaMa95]   Parnas, D. L. and Madey, J. *Functional documents for computer systems*. Sci. Comput. Programming **25**(1), 41–61 (Oct. 1995).

[Par69]   Parnas, D. L. *On the use of transition diagrams in the design of a user interface for an interactive computer system*. In "Proc. 24th National ACM Conf.", pp. 379–385 (1969).

[Par72]   Parnas, D. L. *On the criteria to be used in decomposing systems into modules*. Commun. ACM **15**(12), 1053–1058 (1972). Reprinted in [HoWe01].

[Par76]   Parnas, D. L. *On the design and development of program families*. IEEE Trans. Softw. Eng. **2**(1), 1–9 (Mar. 1976). Reprinted in [HoWe01].

[Par79]   Parnas, D. L. *Designing software for ease of extension and contraction*. IEEE Trans. Softw. Eng. **SE-5**(2), 128–138 (Mar. 1979). Reprinted in [HoWe01].

[PCW85]   Parnas, D. L., Clements, P. C., and Weiss, D. M. *The modular structure of complex systems*. IEEE Trans. Softw. Eng. **11**(3), 259–266 (Mar. 1985). Reprinted in [HoWe01].

[Pel96]   Peleska, J. *Formal Methods and the Development of Dependable Systems*. Habilitation thesis, Report No. 9612, Christian-Albrechts-Universität Kiel, Germany, and UniForM project, Technical Report 9601, University of Bremen, Germany (Dec. 1996).

[Pet00]   Peters, D. K. *Deriving Real-Time Monitors from System Requirements Documentation*. PhD thesis, McMaster Univ., Hamilton, Canada (Jan. 2000).

[Pin03]   Pinard, D. *Reducing the feature interaction problem using an agent-based architecture*. In Amyot and Logrippo [AmLo03], pp. 13–22.

[PJ88]   Page-Jones, M. *The Practical Guide to Structured Systems Design*. Computing Series. Yourdon Press, Englewood Cliff, NJ, 2nd ed. (1988).

[RBSP02]   Riebisch, M., Böllert, K., Streitferdt, D., and Philippow, I. *Extending feature diagrams with UML multiplicities*. In IDPT'02 [IDP02].

[RCP99]   Rushby, J., Crow, J., and Palmer, E. *An automated method to detect potential mode confusions.* In "Proc. of the 18th Digital Avionics Systems Conf.", St. Louis, Montana, USA (1999). IEEE.

[Rea90]   Reason, J. *Human error.* Cambridge University Press (1990).

[Red97]   Redmiles, D. F. *Applying design critics to software requirements engineering.* Final report 1997–98 for MICRO project 97-148, Dept. of Information and Comp. Sce., Univ. of California, Irvine, Calif., USA (1997). Industrial sponsor: Rockwell International.

[Rie03]   Riebisch, M. *Towards a more precise definition of feature models.* In Riebisch, M., Coplien, J. O., and Streitferdt, D., editors, "Modelling Variability for Object-Oriented Product Lines", pp. 64–76, Norderstedt, Germany (2003). BookOnDemand Publ. Co.

[RJB98]   Rumbaugh, J., Jacobson, I., and Booch, G. *The Unified Modeling Language Reference Manual.* Addison-Wesley (1998).

[RLC01]   3rd Generation Partnership Project, 3GPP TS 25.322 V4.0.0. *RLC protocol specification* (Mar. 2001).

[RM04]   Reiff-Marganiec, S. *Policies: Giving users control over calls.* In Ryan, M. D., Meyer, J.-J. C., and Ehrich, H.-D., editors, "Objects, Agents, and Features", vol. 2975 of "LNCS", pp. 189–208. Springer (2004).

[Roc75]   Rochkind, M. J. *The source code control system.* IEEE Trans. Softw. Eng. **1**(4), 364–370 (Dec. 1975).

[RöLa00]   Röfer, T. and Lankenau, A. *Architecture and applications of the Bremen Autonomous Wheelchair.* Information Sciences **126**(1-4), 1–20 (July 2000).

[Ros94]   Roscoe, A. W. *Model-checking CSP.* In Roscoe, A. W., editor, "A Classical Mind, Essays in Honour of C.A.R. Hoare", pp. 353–378. Prentice-Hall (1994).

[Ros97]   Roscoe, A. W. *The Theory and Practice of Concurrency.* Prentice-Hall (1997).

[Rus01a]   Rushby, J. *Analyzing cockpit interfaces using formal methods.* In Bowman, H., editor, "Proc. of FM-Elsewhere", vol. 43 of "Electronic Notes in Theoretical Computer Science", invited paper presented at Pisa, Italy, in Oct. 2000 (2001). Elsevier.

[Rus01b]   Rushby, J. *Modeling the human in human factors.* In Voges, U., editor, "Computer Safety, Reliability and Security – 20th Int'l Conf., SafeComp 2001, Proc.", vol. 2187 of "LNCS", pp. 86–91, Budapest, Hungary (Sept. 2001). Springer.

[Rus02]   Rushby, J. *Using model checking to help discover mode confusions and other automation surprises.* Reliability Engineering & System Safety **75**(2), 167–177 (Feb. 2002).

[RZK+00]   Rodriguez, M., Zimmermann, M., Katahira, M., de Villepin, M., Ingram, B., and Leveson, N. *Identifying mode confusion potential in software design.* In "Proc. of the 19th Digital Avionics Systems Conf." [IEE00].

[SaJo02]   Sage, M. and Johnson, C. W. *Formally verified, rapid prototyping for air traffic control.* Reliability Engineering & System Safety **75**(2), 121–132 (Feb. 2002).

[SaKu01]   Savolainen, J. and Kuusela, J. *Consistency management of product line requirements.* In IEEE [IEE01], pp. 40–47.

[SaWo95]   Sarter, N. B. and Woods, D. D. *How in the world did we ever get into that mode? Mode error and awareness in supervisory control.* Human Factors **37**(1), 5–19 (Mar. 1995).

[Sch95]   Schneider, S. *An operational semantics for timed CSP.* Information and Computation **116**, 193–213 (Feb. 1995).

[Sch00]   Schneider, S. *Concurrent and Real-time Systems: the CSP approach.* Royal Holloway, University of London (2000).

[Shn97]   Shneiderman, B. *Designing the User Interface: Strategies for Effective Human-Computer Interaction.* Addison-Wesley, 3rd ed. (1997).

[Smi00]   Smith, G. *The Object-Z Specification Language.* Kluwer Academic Publishers (2000).

[Smi04]   Smith, G. *Object-Z Home Page.* Univ. of Queensland, Dept. of Comp. Sce., Australia (2004). www.itee.uq.edu.au/~smith/objectz.html.

[SORSC01]   Shankar, N., Owre, S., Rushby, J. M., and Stringer-Calvert, D. W. J. *PVS Prover Guide, Version 2.4.* Computer Science Lab., SRI International, Menlo Park, CA, USA (Nov. 2001).

[Spi95]   Spivey, J. M. *The Z notation: a reference manual.* Series in Computer Science. Prentice-Hall, New York, 2nd ed. (1995).

[SRP03]   Streitferdt, D., Riebisch, M., and Philippow, I. *Details of formalized relations in feature models using OCL.* In "Proc. of the 10th IEEE Symp. and Workshops on Engineering of Computer-Based Systems (ECBS)", pp. 297–304, Huntsville Alabama, USA (2003).

[SRP05]   Sochos, P., Riebisch, M., and Philippow, I. *Featuregesteuerte Architekturgestaltung zwecks Wartbarkeit und Evolution von Produktlinien.* In

Liggesmeyer, P., Pohl, K., and Goedicke, M., editors, "Software Engineering 2005. Proc. of the Conf. Software Engineering 2005", pp. 29–42, Essen, Germany (8–11 Mar. 2005). Gesellschaft für Informatik.

[Süh02]   Sühl, C. *An Integration of Z and Timed CSP for Specifying Real-Time Embedded Systems*. PhD thesis, Technische Universität Berlin, Germany (Dec. 2002).

[THE00]   Thompson, J. M., Heimdahl, M. P., and Erickson, D. M. *Structuring formal control systems specifications for reuse: Surviving hardware changes*. In Holloway, C. M., editor, "Proc. of 5th NASA Langley Formal Methods Workshop (LFM'2000)", pp. 117–128, Hampton, VA, USA (13–15 June 2000). NASA Conference Publication NASA/CP-2000-210100.

[ThHe02]   Thompson, J. M. and Heimdahl, M. P. E. *Structuring product family requirements for n-dimensional and hierarchical product lines*. Requirements Engineering Journal **8**(1), 42–54 (Jan. 2002).

[Thi82]   Thimbleby, H. *Character level ambiguity: consequences for user interface design*. Int'l. Jour. of Man-Machine Studies **16**(2), 211–225 (Feb. 1982).

[Thi90]   Thimbleby, H. *User Interface Design*. ACM Press, New York, USA (1990).

[Tic82]   Tichy, W. F. *A data model for programming support environments*. In "Proc. of the IFIP WG 8.1 Working Conf. on Automated Tools for Information System Design and Development", pp. 31–48, New Orleans, USA (Jan. 1982). North-Holland.

[Tic85]   Tichy, W. F. *RCS – a system for version control*. Software—Practice and Experience **15**(7), 637–654 (July 1985).

[To+02]   Toyn, I. et al.. *CADiZ reference manual*. University of York, Heslington, York, England (2002).

[Tri95]   Trigila, S., editor. *Open Services Architectural Framework for Integrated Service Engineering*, Deliverable R2049/FUB/SAR/DS/P/023/b1, Version 4, RACE Project 2049 (Cassiopeia) (24 Mar. 1995).

[VaHa02]   Vakil, S. S. and Hansman, Jr., R. J. *Approaches to mitigating complexity-driven issues in commercial autoflight systems*. Reliability Engineering & System Safety **75**(2), 133–145 (Feb. 2002).

[vdL94]   van der Linden, R. *Using an architecture to help beat feature interaction*. In Bouma and Velthuijsen [BoVe94], pp. 24–35.

[Vel95]   Velthuijsen, H. *Issues of non-monotonicity in feature-interaction detection*. In Cheng and Ohta [ChOh95], pp. 31–42.

[Ver]   *Verified Systems International GmbH*. www.verified.de.

[Ver04]   Verified Systems International GmbH, Bremen, Germany. *RT-Tester 6.0 User Manual Issue 1.0* (2004). www.verified.de.

[vG99]   von Garrel, J. *Parsing, Typechecking und Transformation von CSP-OZ nach Jass*. Masters thesis, University of Oldenburg, Germany, Dept. of Comp. Sci. (July 1999).

[Wei01]   Weiss, D. M. *Introduction to [Par72]*. In Hoffman and Weiss [HoWe01], pp. 143–144.

[WeLa99]   Weiss, D. M. and Lai, C. T. R. *Software Product Line Engineering – a Family-Based Software Development Process*. Addison Wesley Longman (1999).

[Wer05]   Werner, M. *uDraw(Graph) V3.1 Online Documentation*. University of Bremen (Feb. 2005). www.informatik.uni-bremen.de/uDrawGraph/en/service/uDG31_doc/.

[WFH94]   Wright, P., Fields, B., and Harrison, M. *Deriving human-error tolerance requirements from tasks*. In "Proc. of ICRE'94 – IEEE Int'l. Conf. on Requirements Engineering", Colorado, USA (1994).

[WKHM04]   Wolter, K., Krebs, T., Hotz, L., and Meijler, T. D. *Knowledge-based product derivation process*. In Mercier-Laurent, E. and Debenham, J., editors, "Proc. Symp. on Professional Practice in AI (1st Int'l. Conf. on Artificial Intelligence Applications and Innovations – AIAI-2004)", Toulouse, France (22–27 Aug. 2004). IFIP 18th World Computer Congress, IFIP Press.

[WLR98]   Wind, B. C. F., Lucidi, F., and Reynolds, P. *Open Service Architecture for Mobile and Fixed Environments (OSAM), Final Release*. DOLMEN Consortium, DOLMEN/AS-DEL04 (26 Aug. 1998).

[Z02]   *Information Technology – Z Formal specification notation – Syntax, type system and semantics*. ISO/IEC 13568:2002(E) (July 2002).

[Zav97]   Zave, P. *'Calls considered harmful' and other observations: A tutorial on telephony*. In Margaria, T., editor, "2nd International Workshop on Advanced Intelligent Networks '97 – AIN'97, Proceedings", Tech. Rep. MIP-9710, pp. 1–20. University of Passau, Germany (4–5 July 1997). Also in [MSRP98].

[Zel96]   Zeller, A. *Smooth operations with square operators – the version set model in ICE*. In Sommerville, I., editor, "Software Configuration Management: ICSE'96 SCM-6 Workshop", vol. 1167 of "LNCS", Berlin (Mar. 1996). Springer.

[ZeSn95]   Zeller, A. and Snelting, G. *Handling version sets through feature logic.*
            In Schäfer, W. and Botella, P., editors, "Proc. of the 5th European
            Software Engineering Conf. (ESEC '95)", vol. 989 of "LNCS", pp.
            191–204, Barcelona, Spain (Sept. 1995). Springer.

[ZGS04]   Zave, P., Goguen, H. H., and Smith, T. M. *Component coordination: a
            telecommunication case study.* Comp. Networks **45**(5), 645–664 (Aug.
            2004).

[ZRI+00]   Zimmermann, M., Rodriguez, M., Ingram, B., Katahira, M.,
            de Villepin, M., and Leveson, N. *Making formal methods practical.*
            In "Proc. of the 19th Digital Avionics Systems Conf." [IEE00].

[ZWO+96]   Zibman, I., Woolf, C., O'Reilly, P., Strickland, L., Willis, D., and
            Visser, J. *An architectural approach to minimizing feature interactions
            in telecommunications.* IEEE/ACM Trans. on Networking **4**(4), 582–
            596 (Aug. 1996).

Monographs of the Bremen Institute of Safe Systems

1   Buth, Bettina / Berghammer, Rudolf / Peleska, Jan (eds.): *Tools for System Development and Verification*. Workshop, Proceedings, Bremen, Germany, July 1996. ISBN 3-8265-3806-4. Aachen: Shaker Verlag, 1998.

2   Mossakowski, Till: *Representations, Hierarchies and Graphs of Institutions*. Dissertation, Universität Bremen, 1996. Revised version: ISBN 3-89722-831-9. Berlin: Logos Verlag, 2001.

3   Cerioli, Maura / Gogolla, Martin / Kirchner, Hélène / Krieg-Brückner, Bernd / Qian, Zhenyu / Wolf, Markus (eds.): *Algebraic System Specification and Development: Survey and Annotated Bibliography*. 2nd edition, 1997. ISBN 3-8265-4067-0. Aachen: Shaker Verlag, 1998.

4   Wolff, Burkhart: *A Generic Calculus of Transformation*. Dissertation, Universität Bremen, 1997. Revised version: ISBN 3-8265-3654-1. Aachen: Shaker Verlag, 1999.

5   Kolyang: *HOL-Z, An Integrated Formal Support Environment for Z in Isabelle/HOL*. Dissertation, Universität Bremen, 1997. ISBN 3-8265-4068-9. Aachen: Shaker Verlag, 1998.

6   Fröhlich, Michael: *Inkrementelles Graphlayout im Visualisierungssystem daVinci*. Dissertation, Universität Bremen, 1997. ISBN 3-8265-4069-7. Aachen: Shaker Verlag, 1998.

7   Röfer, Thomas: *Panoramic Image Processing and Route Navigation. Dissertation, Universität Bremen,* 1998. ISBN 3-8265-4070-0. Aachen: Shaker Verlag, 1998.

8   Schrönen, Michael: *Methodology for the Development of Microprocessor-Based Safety-Critical Systems*. Dissertation, Universität Bremen, 1998. ISBN 3-8265-3655-X. Aachen: Shaker Verlag, 1998.

9   Krieg-Brückner, Bernd / Peleska, Jan / Olderog, Ernst-Rüdiger / Balzer, Dietrich / Baer, Alexander: *UniForM Workbench, Universelle Entwicklungsumgebung für Formale Methoden; Schlußbericht*. ISBN 3-8265-3656-8. Aachen: Shaker Verlag, 1999.

10 Gärtner, Heino: *Schematransformationen in objektorientierten Informationssystemen*. Dissertation, Universität Bremen, 1999. ISBN 3-8265-6542-8. Aachen: Shaker Verlag, 1999.

11 Huge, Anne-Kathrin: *Ein Ansatz zur Formalisierung objektorientierter Datenbanken auf der Grundlage von ODMG*. Dissertation, Universität Bremen, 1999. ISBN 3-8265-6543-6. Aachen: Shaker Verlag, 2000.

12 Karlsen, Einar: *Tool Integration in a Functional Programming Language*. Dissertation, Universität Bremen, 1998. Revised version. Universität Bremen, 1999.

13   Amthor, Peter: *Structural Decomposition of Hybrid Systems.* Dissertation, Universität Bremen, 2000.

14   Richters, Mark: *A Precise Approach to Validating UML Models and OCL Constraints.* Dissertation, Universität Bremen, 2001. ISBN 3–89722-842-4. Berlin: Logos Verlag, 2002.

15   Buth, Bettina: *Formal and Semi-Formal Methods for the Analysis of Industrial Control Systems.* Habilitationsschrift, Universität Bremen, 2001. Berlin: Logos Verlag, 2002.

16   Meyer, Oliver: *Structural Decomposition of Timed CSP and its Application in Real-Time Testing.* Dissertation, Universität Bremen, 2001. Berlin: Logos Verlag, 2002.

17   Kollmann, Ralf: *Design Recovery Techniques for Object-Oriented Software Systems.* Dissertation, Universität Bremen, 2002. ISBN 3–8325-0141-X. Berlin: Logos Verlag, 2002.

18   Lankenau, Axel: *The Bremen Autonomous Wheelchair "Rolland": Self-Localization and Shared Control.* Dissertation, Universität Bremen, 2002. ISBN 3–8325-0306-4. Berlin: Logos Verlag, 2003.

19   Tej, Haykal: *HOL-CSP: Mechanised Formal Development of Concurrent Processes.* Dissertation, Universität Bremen, 2003. ISBN 3–8325-0287-4. Berlin: Logos Verlag, 2003.

20   Krieg-Brückner, Bernd / Mahnke, Achim: *MultiMedia Instruction in Safe and Secure Systems – Summary and Reference Manual.* Universität Bremen, 2004. (to appear)

21   Meyer, Thomas: *A Framework for Formal Representation and Transformational Optimisation of Executable Specifications.* Dissertation, Universität Bremen, 2005. ISBN Nr. 978-3-8325-1562-1. Berlin: Logos Verlag, 2007.

22   Radfelder, Oliver: *Dreidimensionale, interaktive und animierte Softwarevisualisierung zur Unterstützung im Softwareentwicklungsprozess.* Dissertation, Universität Bremen. ISBN Nr. 3-8325-1302-7. Berlin: Logos Verlag, 2006.

23   Ziemann, Paul: *An Integrated Operational Semantics for a UML Core Based on Graph Transformation.* Dissertation, Universität Bremen, 2005. ISBN 3-8325-1071-0. Berlin: Logos Verlag, 2006.

24   Hübner, Kai: *Symmetriesignaturen für bildbasierte Anwendungen in der Robotik.* Dissertation, Universität Bremen, 2006. ISBN 978-3-8325-1455-6. Berlin: Logos Verlag, 2007.

25   Bredereke, Jan: *Maintaining Families of Rigorous Requirements for Embedded Software Systems.* Habilitationsschrift, Universität Bremen, 2005. Revised version. ISBN 978-3-8325-1521-8. Berlin: Logos Verlag, 2007.